MEMOIRS
— *from a* —
STORMY PASSAGE

Mandy Innis

BALBOA
PRESS

A DIVISION OF HAY HOUSE

Balboa Press books may be ordered through booksellers or by contacting:

Balboa Press
A Division of Hay House
1663 Liberty Drive
Bloomington, IN 47403
www.balboapress.com.au
1-(877) 407-4847

ISBN: 978-1-4525-0948-8 (sc)
ISBN: 978-1-4525-0947-1 (e)

Because of the dynamic nature of the Internet, any web addresses or links contained in this book may have changed since publication and may no longer be valid. The views expressed in this work are solely those of the author and do not necessarily reflect the views of the publisher, and the publisher hereby disclaims any responsibility for them.

The author of this book does not dispense medical advice or prescribe the use of any technique as a form of treatment for physical, emotional, or medical problems without the advice of a physician, either directly or indirectly. The intent of the author is only to offer information of a general nature to help you in your quest for emotional and spiritual well-being. In the event you use any of the information in this book for yourself, which is your constitutional right, the author and the publisher assume no responsibility for your actions.

Any people depicted in stock imagery provided by Thinkstock are models, and such images are being used for illustrative purposes only.
Certain stock imagery © Thinkstock.

Printed in the United States of America

Balboa Press rev. date: 07/16/2013

Foreword

This is my story about a boy, Storm. It is a passage of life that has filled our hearts with great pain but also great moments that will supply me with endless memories and sustain me for the rest of my life. Storm showed me, and all who knew him, what really is important in life.

We are told as mothers that our disabled children are special, to me it is a word used to soften the blow of the difficulties we and our children will endure.

Special is not a word I would have used to describe Storm. I would say unique, strong, loving. To me as his mother, he was unique, not just because he was my long-awaited child, but more because of the way he lived his life—day to day, in the moment. It is what so many of us spend our lives trying to get to, living in the moment.

Storm took pleasure in his surroundings, the people in his life, he wanted for nothing, he had enough, he didn't live in fear because he knew what he needed in life would show up when he needed it. And because he believed it would show up, it always did.

This story is more like a diary of our life, and I hope it shows that even though it was quite difficult at times, it was truly a guided life. A gift.

Prologue

I was born Leigh Amanda Innis, the vertically challenged third child of tall parents who called me "Wee Lee" until just before I started school. At that time they decided Wee Lee was not an appropriate name at school and so I became, and remain, Mandy. My older brother and sister, Rodney and Toni, are twins.

I was born in New Zealand, but in 1966 we came to Australia on a working holiday and ended up living here. After about two years of working for farmers, my parents bought a farm of their own in the remote town of Perenjori, a four-hour drive north of Perth, Western Australia, wheat-farming land, dry dusty land so different from the rolling green hills of New Zealand.

My father's brother had married my mother's sister (yes, two brothers married two sisters), and they moved from New Zealand with their four children, two girls and two boys, to join us on the farm. The only accommodation was a two-bedroom bachelor house, converted from horse stables. The adults got the two bedrooms and all seven children lived and slept in the lounge-room until Dad and Uncle John built on an extra bedroom and the boys moved into that.

The townsfolk had trouble discerning which child belonged to which couple. Seven children in one house, but somehow we all got along. Even then I felt different, set apart. I was the youngest and was told I was too young to play with them, so I often ended up playing alone. That didn't really matter because I didn't always want to play their games. I think I was a very serious child—apparently my humour didn't turn up until I was in my 20s. I realise now that Toni and Rod may also have felt different but never voiced it—when you're a child it's all about yourself and your little world.

We didn't have a bathroom to start with—there was a rainwater tank on a stand, out from the house. The stand had been enclosed and a shower put up under the tank and that was where we washed, in cold water summer and winter. The toilet was an outdoor thunderbox (a big hole in the ground with a toilet sitting on the top of it) situated between the house and the machinery shed. When Uncle John and his family moved to a house they rented on another farm, Rod got a room of his own and Toni and I shared a room. We also eventually got a bathroom.

In winter the floor would flood if we had a lot of rain and in summer the snakes would wander through the house. It was a life so different from New Zealand especially for Mum, who loved gardening and in Perenjori that was challenging, if not impossible.

With Uncle John working the farm along with our parents, we survived years of drought and then had a few good years in a row. Uncle and Aunt ended up buying a farm of their own. My parents kept the original farm, and when I was about 14 they built a new house on it. That was really living.

My sister Toni had moved to Perth to work when she was 16. I think my parents were worried that all there was for Toni and me in a very small country town was to marry a farmer and they wanted more for us. Were they in for a surprise!

When I was 16 I too went from a sheltered life on the farm to life in the "big city". I still remember my first few days in Perth. My parents drove me down to a hostel for country girls, where Toni also had lived until moving out to a flat with friends.

My room was down in the basement with a couple of other rooms, cold and sterile. I sat on the bed and the biggest cockroach I had ever seen scuttled across the floor—I bet it had drunkenly wandered over from the Emu Brewery across the road. I wanted to scream, but I sucked it in. I deposited my luggage and then Mum and Dad took me to the cinema. They couldn't have picked a scarier movie for little farm-mouse Mandy—it was Sigourney Weaver in *Alien.* In the end Mum and I walked out and left Dad to watch the end.

Then they dropped me back at the hostel and headed back to the farm, where there was always work waiting to be done. I was left to spend my first night in the big city, alone and terrified, and I cried for three days.

I was, and at times still am, a very shy person, not confident. I didn't know how to interact with the other girls in the hostel. I didn't see how I was going to survive in this new world. But the strength that has always lingered in me rose up and after those days of crying I fronted up to the unemployment office, enrolled for the dole and began looking for work. Some of the girls in the hostel took an interest in me, and helped me to adjust. Eventually I got work at a stockbroker's agency, collecting cheques from different businesses. Sometimes I had to catch taxis, other times I walked, so I learnt my way around Perth and at the end of the day I would bank the cheques. The job didn't last long, but it gave me the confidence I needed to move about in the city.

I rarely saw my big sister, mainly only when I went back to the farm on the weekends that I could afford the bus fare home. Toni loved the city but I never felt comfortable in it, I missed the space of the farm, the green paddocks in winter, the quietness, the slower pace of life, and I went back there whenever I could. I lived in Perth for almost six years and never really had a long-lasting relationship—a few dates, but I didn't feel I had anything in common with the men in the city.

Then, on a weekend back in Perenjori for my brother's wedding, I met the man I was to marry. He had been invited to the wedding and from that day we were dating.

His family were station owners and he had a plane. He would fly down to Perth for the weekends, hire a car and we would go places and talk endlessly. He sent me beautiful roses at work. This was the man for me, and after my 21st birthday we decided to get married.

I was heading back to the country, leaving my life in the city completely behind. We bought a rundown house in Morawa, a town not too far from Perenjori, went overseas for a honeymoon and came back in time for mustering on the station. I remember arriving back at Morawa, to a house I hadn't chosen, our wedding presents piled up in the lounge room and our only piece of furniture, a bed I had bought, in the bedroom.

The next day my husband flew up to the station to start mustering. The honeymoon was well and truly over. But because of my husband I had made friends in the small town.

Three years into our marriage, we decided we would like to have children. I was about 25, and we just assumed I would fall pregnant within a couple of months of going off contraception. But months went by and after a year we ended up in Perth having tests. The specialist suggested we consider an IVF program, and it was decided that GIFT (Gamete Intrafallopian Transfer) would be our best option. That involved me having a lot of hormone injections (mmm, yummy) to produce a lot of eggs which were then harvested and mixed with my husband's sperm before being put back in me.

We tried three times, without success. It was a sad time—endless injections filling me with hormones, changing my personality, so much hope tied up in this procedure and then hope lost, three times. After the third failure I decided I obviously wasn't meant to have children, no matter how desperately I wanted it. I would have to accept that it wasn't to be, and do something different with my life. I wasn't sure what, only that it wasn't going to be farming. And while I was thinking about what I would like to do, I fell pregnant. After five years of trying and then giving up, I was pregnant! Whoo-hoo! Everything went fine until 10 weeks before I was due.

I was outside cleaning the house walls when I began getting bad cramps; I put it down to Braxston Hicks contractions, but it went on for quite a while so I thought I'd better see the doctor. It turned out I was in labour. The doctor put me on drugs to stop the labour and we had to drive to Perth to see the specialist who would be delivering the baby.

It was a nerve-racking time. After checking me over she said the baby was very small, and sent me off for tests. The ultrasound scans showed the baby had a small head; they thought it could be Down syndrome.

Oh my god, I thought, this can't be real. The world was crashing down around us and our hearts were breaking. Then amniocentesis showed the baby didn't have Down syndrome, that even though it was small all seemed fine. Joyous relief, after two weeks in Perth waiting for test results.

A few days later I went into the hospital for a check-up, and next thing I knew they were going to deliver the baby NOW, by caesarean. My husband had gone to get something to eat and had to be contacted to get his butt back—he wanted to be in the room when they delivered the baby, and I was having the epidural put in my spine when he arrived.

Then I was in the theatre, surrounded by about eight people, introducing themselves to me, a doctor telling me I wouldn't get to hold my baby because they expected his lungs to be underdeveloped and he would be whisked away for treatment. I was so goddamn petrified I just nodded my head.

Well, a perfect little boy was delivered. His lungs were perfect, he wasn't whisked away and I got to hold him. He was so tiny, just 4lb 6oz, but except for an unexplained dent in the left side of his head he was perfect, everything a mother's heart desires.

We had four months of happiness, and then it was whisked away. Then Storm was a boy with disabilities.

Chapter One

The Lessons Begin

The paediatrician who was standing by my head when my baby was delivered asked me what was I going to name him and out of my mouth came "Storm". We hadn't really discussed in depth names that we liked, but on the way to Perth we'd looked through a baby-naming book. I saw the name Storm and liked it, but didn't give it more thought until that moment after his birth. We tried other names, but Storm stuck.

Storm was a day old when he was taken off for X-rays on his head. Explanations for how he got the dent were vague, but the verdict based on the X-rays was that all was well. He spent the next two weeks in the preemie ward. Because we were from the country I stayed in the maternity ward and every four hours I would go down in the lift to feed him. After two weeks, my husband came back from the farm and picked us up. We were going home.

Before we left the hospital, the nurse issued us with strict instructions, which left me a very nervous mum. Storm was so little; he seemed too fragile. We had to come back in six weeks to see a specialist about the dent in his head—the doctors were positive he would have to have an operation to fix it. Either they would drill a little hole in the middle of the dent and use an instrument to flick it out, or they would cut the skull around the dent and flip it over. It sounds gruesome either way and I wasn't looking forward to it—what an awful thing to contemplate being done to my tiny baby.

Well, before the six weeks were up the dent miraculously popped out and we didn't even notice it happening. So when we did visit the specialist he was amazed at its disappearance; clearly he had not expected that.

Storm and I settled into farm life. My routine was different now; my life was focused on my baby. He was four months old when I took him to the clinic in Morawa for a regular check-up. The nurse noticed that his eyes weren't tracking when she moved toys in front of him, so she recommended I take him to the doctor, which I did, nervously, that same day. The doctor also was concerned, so he organised an appointment with an eye specialist in Perth. As we left his surgery I felt physically ill with worry: I had believed the worst was behind us now that Storm had arrived safely, but the thought of what could be ahead scared me.

We made the 400km trip to Perth. The eye specialist wasn't concerned; he explained that a baby's eyesight can take up to seven months to come on, so we were to come back in three months if there wasn't any improvement.

For the next couple of months I watched Storm like a hawk. I would constantly pass toys in front of his eyes to see if he would track, without any luck. My husband seemed to be confident that his eyesight would come good and all would be well, but I didn't feel good about it. I tried to act like everything was and would be okay, but I felt sick to the stomach with worry.

Storm, meanwhile, was unconcerned, happy, content and still tiny. I mean TINY. When I took him grocery shopping at the local store, I would put him in his capsule at the front of the shop and the cashiers would keep an eye on him while I toured the shelves (it also wasn't a large shop so he wasn't far from view). On one occasion I had got to the checkout and was putting the groceries through when I checked on Storm and couldn't see him in the capsule. At first I thought someone must have picked him up to give him a cuddle, but I pulled the blanket back and there he was; he had slid down and disappeared under the wide strap that was usually around his middle.

When he was seven months old, we took him back to the specialist in Perth. It appeared he still wasn't seeing, so more involved tests were organised for a couple of weeks' time. We were doing an awful lot of travelling now. After those tests, back came the news that Storm had Cortical Blindness. Basically, that meant his eyes were fine but his brain was unable to understand the messages that the eyes were sending.

I was devastated. The pain and heartache I felt was indescribable. We were ushered off to a social worker in the same building—to fill out forms to get a disability allowance for Storm.

Wow! Bonus! Makes it all worthwhile, an extra $70 or so a fortnight. Do you think money will heal my heart, broken after receiving this terrible *news about our precious son who will never know what we look like? Never will we ever be the same again.*

But here is the social worker passing us sheets of paper with poems telling us how we are special parents, how I am a special mother. I look at her and wonder if she has lost her brain. Maybe if I search around the room I will find it and give it back to her and then maybe she will tell me something that will ease this pain screaming inside me. I look around the room, under the desk, I glance in the rubbish bin and there it is, her brain, but it's stuck to one of those bloody poems about special mothers. All hope is lost so I give up and leave her to talk her social talk until we can leave.

We drove back to the farm in a state of shock. I can't remember what we talked about on the way home, and we were going to have to go back to Perth in a couple of weeks for more tests. How are you supposed to function physically when your head, your mind, just won't shut up? I didn't understand why this was happening to us, after waiting five long years for a baby and now this. Was God punishing us, didn't He like us, am I a bad person, is that why this has happened, is it something I did or something I didn't do? I carried a lot of guilt for years and then one day I gave it up. Maybe that dent in his head at birth had something to do with it; we will never know.

The only thing that kept me going was Storm. He needed me to keep it together and be strong for him; who would be there for him if I fell apart? So we went on with life as best as we could.

Then he became ill with a virus that made him projectile vomit. I took him to the local doctor, who told me it should pass. It didn't. I went back to the doctor, who told us to take Storm to hospital in Perth. So once again we did the four-hour drive to Perth and took him into emergency. When we finally got to see a doctor, and explained how sick Storm had been and where we had driven from, after examining him they sent us home to the farm saying it was a virus that would pass. We drove back to the farm with Storm vomiting in the car. The next day I rang our local doctor again, saying that Storm was still ill.

This had been going on for weeks. The doctor sent us back to the children's hospital in Perth, four hours driving again. This time we were admitted and more tests were run. Finally, after more than a month, Storm's virus was diagnosed and cured.

While we were in hospital the doctor ordered different tests done on Storm for reasons that weren't explained to us. This was a thing that happened a lot in Storm's life—doctors doing tests but not giving reasons why. It was all very odd.

When the doctor visited Storm and me, no husband in sight, she told me that, based on the tests she had ordered, Storm had epilepsy. Storm had begun rolling his eyes when he got ill with the virus, but the doctor told me it was an epileptic fit. She said also she believed he had cerebral palsy and she had organised for us to take him to hospital in Geraldton (much closer than Perth) once a week for physio.

She threw these words at me, then walked away; just dumped it on me, didn't even have the commonsense to wait until my husband was there.

There was no "I'm sorry to tell you I've got some bad news" and "if you have any questions I'm always available". No, she just left. Is it any wonder that eventually I hated the hospital with a passion?

It was all too much to take in, Storm wasn't even a year old, and we only had four precious months with a so-called normal life until it all fell apart. We never had enough time to digest each new diagnosis before another one was thrown at us. Our life had become a train ride of endless tests, trips back and forth from the farm to Perth; I wanted to get off this terrible train.

I had to give Storm phenobarb twice a day for his epilepsy. He cried every time I gave it to him and sometimes he vomited it back up. My stomach ached constantly with emotional pain; it was too much to bear.

At the time I still believed everything that the doctors told us about Storm's health. So far he had been diagnosed with cortical blindness, epilepsy and cerebral palsy.

Only three things wrong with him? I'm sure there's room for another condition. Sarcasm rules my mind and I'm also angry at the doctors' thoughtlessness and lack of compassion of the doctor.

And then one day I thought to myself: "Just wait a bloody minute, something is not right here." This moment was a new beginning for me, and I started to pay attention to my gut feelings, my mother's instinct (the thing I found many doctors rejected—one day they will learn to listen to us). This rolling of his eyes being a sign of epilepsy sounded like a load of . . . ! He only started rolling his eyes when he got the virus, and his ability to hold his head up had deteriorated when he started taking those god-awful drugs for epilepsy.

I myself had been diagnosed with epilepsy as a teenager, and had taken drugs for the condition for years, so I rang my specialist and told him about Storm. He didn't see babies, but he recommended another specialist who I phoned that day for an appointment. Another four-hour trip to Perth. The specialist checked Storm out, asked us a few questions and because his rooms were so close to where Storm had had his tests at the hospital he walked over and got the test results. When he came back, he looked over the results, then told us Storm didn't have epilepsy—the rolling of his eyes was most probably a consequence of the virus that he had had for months—and we should take him off the drugs! I was so grateful to this man, finally someone making sense. And good old mother's instinct!

Well! Only two things wrong with Storm, one eliminated. My husband and I were ecstatic, though a little ticked off—it seemed just too easy for the previous doctor to put Storm on to drugs in the first place after just one lot of tests. But we were willing to let it slide; we were so happy that Storm wouldn't have to be taking the drugs any more.

So the next thing on our list of things to do was to go to Geraldton to see the physiotherapist at the hospital about Storm's supposed cerebral palsy. I didn't believe that diagnosis, either; he had no stiffness in his limbs, or floppiness. Only a two and a half hour drive, and Storm was no trouble at all, just happy to be driven all over the countryside.

The physiotherapist was great. She took Storm through a series of exercises, to which he had no objections, then told us she didn't feel he had cerebral palsy although she couldn't officially say so. Another happy moment, and another diagnosis eliminated. It meant that Storm had at that moment only one thing wrong with him—he was blind.

We visited the physiotherapist a couple more times and then they didn't want to see us any more. I have seen many cerebral palsy children on many visits to the hospital in Perth, and Storm never had any of the physical appearances of that condition, except for the stiffness in his legs that became very noticeable in 1999, seven years after his birth.

Meanwhile, through all the tests and trips to Perth, I felt Storm needed a lot more help. We had been given a couple of exercises by the early intervention service at the hospital in Perth, but it didn't seem enough. I believed that the more input Storm had while he was little, the better. This was my new mission in life, but I didn't know how to get it, or even who to approach. The good thing about living in a small country town, though isolated from my family, was that I got a lot of support from the local people, especially the older ladies.

On one of my trips to town to do the grocery shopping I went to the local garden centre to see whether any new plants had arrived, as I am a great lover of gardening and was always looking for more plants. I got talking with the owner of the shop, and she asked me about Storm. She told me that years earlier, when she worked for a doctor, they had had a child with problems and had put him through a program of physio that had helped him immensely. Apparently it was a program outside the medical profession. I was immediately interested, and she said she would make inquiries and see what she could find out for me. How was that? I was looking for something or some way to help Storm and it seemed something might have turned up. Was this a coincidence? I think not. I went home elated and hopeful.

A couple of days later I got a call from the garden centre lady and she had a phone number for the centre from where assessments for the program were made. So appointments were made and another trip to Perth organised—of course, all things happen in Perth.

Ian Hunter, the man who did the assessments and set up the program, lived in the eastern states and came to Perth only every couple of months. His fees depended on how many people he would be seeing when he came over, as we all paid towards his flight to Perth and back. It actually turned out to be very expensive, but to me cost was irrelevant—if the program helped Storm, no price was too high.

The day of our appointment finally came and we had another long drive to Perth. By now Storm was a seasoned traveller. Ian asked us a lot of questions about Storm's condition and what he could and could not do, then took him through some exercises to assess him and talked to us about what he thought would help. He was positive about the chances of improving Storm's development. Being told anything positive concerning Storm was very rare in the medical world, so I latched on to that hope and was eager to do the program.

Through all the appointments and travelling, Storm bore all the poking and prodding with patience, humour and trust that we had his best interests at heart. He showed at a very early age he had faith that the universe would provide for him.

Ian wrote up a program and we were able to take exercise equipment from his organisation at no cost. We had been told to bring a car trailer, and the equipment only just fitted in. The only drawback to the program was that we were going to need a lot of volunteers to help. All of the exercises needed at least two people and one set needed a third person. I could not imagine how we were going to get people to help—first they would have to travel a fair way to get to our house on the farm and a lot of wives worked with their husbands on their own farms. It also meant that I would have to put myself out there in public and approach people for help, which I found very daunting. I'm not a social person and the thought of having to approach people to volunteer their time to help Storm scared the hell out of me.

In the end I didn't have to go to great lengths; it all fell into place quietly and with no fuss. On one of my regular trips to town to shop, I got talking with Shirley, a neighbouring farmer's wife. She asked how Storm was doing, so I told her I was looking for volunteers to help with his new physio program. Shirley instantly offered her time, saying she would love to help. She was my first volunteer.

Shirley also found the rest of the volunteers for me, more than 70 people in all, and even organised all the times and did up rosters. It was the most amazing experience. I was and am so very grateful to all the volunteers who gave their time to help Storm.

There I was getting all stressed out about finding volunteers, and within weeks Shirley had it all organised. When you give up trying to control your life, and trust in the universe providing, everything you need turns up. But it also shows the great spirit of country people and the greatness that is Shirley and all the volunteers. It is a wonderful feeling, knowing that so many people were so willing to do this thing for my son.

But before we could start the physio program we had to move from the house we were living in to the main house, the centre of the farm where my husband was born and raised and where his parents had lived all their married lives.

My father-in-law had carted the 16-inch granite blocks with which the stonemasons had built the house. It took two years to build. A large house, with jarrah flooring and cedar windows, it also had large gardens and fruit trees of every kind (which was totally lost on me, because I am strictly non-vegetarian and don't eat fruit of any kind). Now my husband's parents moved to a house on another farm they had recently acquired, and we moved into the main house, which had a room at the back that could be used for Storm's physio program. The equipment fitted in smoothly.

I painted rooms, we had ducted airconditioning installed and we had the windows tinted in the physio room because it got a lot of summer sun and I didn't want my volunteers overheating. We started the physio program a week or so after moving in. The first session started at nine in the morning. I would get up early, make lunches if my husband was going to be working away, clean the house, make the beds and have it all tidy before the first lot of angels arrived. In the beginning I was there with the ladies showing them the exercises I had been taught or filling in when someone couldn't make it.

Storm was amazing; so willing to do all the exercises. I don't think he actually thought of them as exercises, he thought two ladies had come to fuss over him so he enjoyed it. To him they wouldn't, couldn't possibly want to hurt him. So once we got into the swing of it and everyone felt confident about what they were doing, I would go off and work on the garden. The list of things to do was endless. I would be called back to help with exercises that needed a third person, then off I would go again—and, trust me, I didn't go make myself a coffee and sit down to watch television. The house and garden took a lot of time to keep up to scratch and maintain. There were more than 50 fruit trees and a large vegetable garden. Rose garden, lawns and flowering garden. I love gardening, and was totally in my element. Also, I would cook cakes and biscuits so that when they stopped halfway through the exercises they always had something nice for morning tea—my very small way of showing my appreciation for their time and effort to help me and my son.

The morning and afternoon tea breaks helped me to socialise, too. The volunteers gave me a lot of support at a time when I felt very lonely, isolated and out of my depth. I needed positive input, to know what we were doing was right for Storm.

Each session took two hours. When the morning session finished and the morning angels had left, Storm would have his lunch and go down for a nap before he started the afternoon session. While he slept I organised dinner. The next pair of volunteers would arrive at two o'clock and again they would call me when they needed me for the exercise that required three people. We would stop halfway through the session and I would give them afternoon tea.

So it went on, two sessions a day, six days a week (we had Sunday off). In all it was a very intense program—a lot for a one-year-old to endure, but Storm did it without any fuss. I know he slept well at night.

In the midst of it all, I had to find time to go to town at least once a week to do the shopping. Usually I would do it after the morning session, which meant Storm would have to have his nap in the car on the way to town or on the way home. I would feed him his lunch, then we would drive to town, which was about half an hour away. I would have an hour to race around doing the shopping, paying bills and collecting the mail, then we would have to get back home to be there in time for the next session of exercises.

One day when my husband was away, as he often was, the workman who was living with us at the time was working down in the shed and offered to look after Storm while I went into town. So I fed Storm, put him in the pram with his favourite toy and took him over to the shed, then raced off to town. When I got home I went over to the shed to get Storm, and as I was getting nearer I could hear the musical toy playing. As soon as I arrived the workman said he didn't mind looking after Storm, but next time could I please put a different toy in the pram—apparently Storm had driven him almost to distraction by playing the same song over and over and over. The toy actually played quite a few different tunes, but Storm would keep pressing the button until it went around to the same song again and again. I thought it was hilarious, but the workman was not amused. Storm liked music at a very young age.

The physio was showing signs that it was working—at 15 months Storm was finally sitting independently. He was quite behind in his milestones, but I had been told that being blind would delay him to some extent.

My husband had a way of making you believe you could do anything if you set just your mind to it. Whatever he decided to try, he would succeed at. He could get on a new piece of machinery for the first time and drive it as if he had been doing it for years. He flew his plane like it was a car. It was he who gave me the confidence to drive the harvester and basically anything else.

But I really came into my own when Storm was born; he brought out a side to me that I didn't know existed. When the heartbreak, pain and realisation of his disabilities hit home, I didn't think I would cope. I really thought it would be the end of me. Instead it was the making of me. I found an inner strength, confidence and determination—that no matter what obstacle we would have to overcome I would do everything in my power to help him develop in any way possible. There was also a feeling that Storm wasn't a tragedy but a gift, a delightful and inspiring soul.

That is what Storm showed me over the years. The beginning was something completely different. It was a tragedy to me, I grieved for a long time for the child he never was and the life he would never have. For the first year of his life I had a cry every day. It took me a long time to come to terms with his disability. I grieved, bargained with God, cursed Him and then eventually accepted it. In the midst of this journey from grief to acceptance my husband was changing. I take full responsibility that I didn't really reach out to help him. I focused on Storm. I became the stronger of the two of us; the roles had been reversed.

Before Storm was born I believed everything that happened in life happened for a reason, that there was a guiding force. But when his disabilities were diagnosed it shook me to the core. I couldn't see how God could be so cruel to us. How could this be how my life was divinely meant to be?

But as the years passed and the treatments and people I needed for Storm just turned up, my belief and faith returned. I learnt that you have to let the universe know what you need, then believe it will turn up in its time. And it did, not always exactly the way I thought it would, but it did.

I can't remember who told me about the cranial osteopath, or how I found her. It was another of those divine occurrences; I wanted help for Storm and she turned up. I didn't need to know how, just to be grateful that she had. She had actually originated from Morawa; her parents had farmed there years ago. She felt Storm's skull was too far forward and his scalp was very tight—you couldn't move the skin around on his head. Before he started going to her for therapy the back of his head was very flat, like the top of a table, but after a few weeks of manipulation his skull at the back was more rounded. His forehead also was a different shape, it certainly made a difference.

For our first appointment with her in Perth, I had my husband drive us because I didn't care to drive in the city and suburbs. But it became clear this was to be a weekly thing, and I realised he could not take us every Sunday so I had to learn how to drive there and back on my own. So on the way home I got my husband to name the streets, and when I got home I wrote down on a piece of paper which streets to turn left or right on, all the way there and back. I taped it to the console for my first trip to Perth on my own. It was nerve-racking, but I got more confident each week until I felt good enough to drive to other parts of Perth, such as the Wanneroo markets which were on the way home.

It turned out to be a bit of fun for both Storm and me. And we were due some fun. Even though it was a long day, an eight-hour round trip, and we couldn't linger for long because we had to get back to the farm for his next lot of exercises on Monday morning, it was still fun. Now my whole week was full, not one day off. I was amazed at the energy that kept me going.

I must confess I was a bit obsessed with trying anything new that I read about, or was told about, that would help Storm in any way. I didn't knock anything until I had tried it. My mother-in-law recommended a naturopath in Perth, so we took Storm along to him. I can't be certain he made a big difference, because Storm was already doing a few different therapies (physio, cranial therapy), but he was developing in small ways and it could have been down to a combination of all his treatments. But really it didn't matter; the improvements were the important things. He was getting really good at sitting independently and if he fell over he could get himself back up. He was also learning to feed himself biscuits and sandwiches. He did the cutest thing, when you put a biscuit or sandwich into his hands he always had his pinkie finger out to the side, he looked so POSH!

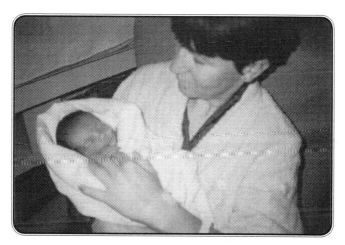

1992 Storm two days old

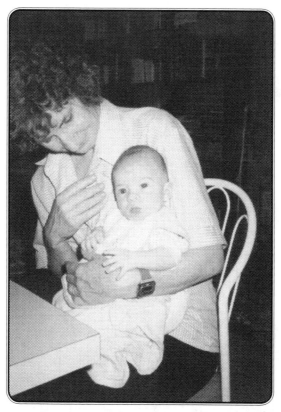

four months old at christmas time in Dunsborough

1993 Storm 8 months old

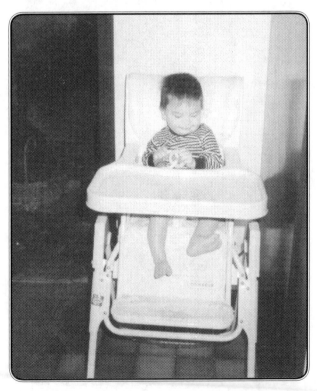

18 months old playing in his highchair

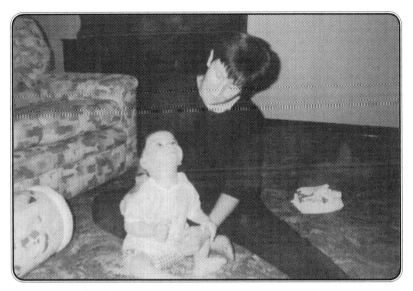

19 months getting really good at sitting independantly

1994 20 months with his favourite musical toy

We had been doing the physio for Storm for almost six months when my husband decided to go away on a farming tour in America with a group of farmers. He had been gone only a day or two when his father became ill, which left me with the responsibility of looking after the sheep and buffalo on our end of the farm.

So when the ladies had finished the afternoon exercises and left, I would put Storm in the car and go and check on the sheep, making sure the troughs were clean and full of water, then go and check the buffalo, which were always out. I would have to put them back in the paddock and pray that they wouldn't get out during the night, then come home, feed Storm and put him to bed. I was a tad tired after all that, and followed not long after. It was a busy and stressful life normally, but with my husband away I had even more to do. He rang a couple of times from America to tell me what a great time he was having.

Just before he went away on his holiday I had started a morning ritual that was a stress release for me. It was odd, I admit, but whatever works. I had a .22 rifle that had once belonged to my father. We had all learnt to shoot with it when we were children, and I had bought it off him to shoot the rabbits that were chewing their way through the garden. I kept the rifle under my side of the bed (this was long before the current strict rules came into place) and every morning I would get up, sneak out into the garden with it before anyone got up, and shoot those cheeky rabbits. I always felt better after that, it was like I was shooting off my stress and tension.

My husband was still away when Storm had his second birthday, September 19. I decided to have a party in the morning to celebrate. I invited the ladies who helped with Storm's physio, and a few other friends, and I think Storm quite enjoyed it. After everyone left, Storm and I went to a friend's barbecue in the bush—it was a great day.

Finally, my husband's holiday was over and reality beckoned for him. I had to go to Perth to pick him up from the airport. His mother looked after Storm and helped with his exercises while I drove to Toni's house in Perth and she drove me out to the airport. I don't think he was happy to be back, the husband who had gone to America was not the husband who came back—he looked the same, but somehow it wasn't him. As we drove back to the farm, he talked a little about his holiday, but not much. And, as the days passed, I start to notice changes in him. We used to discuss the ins and outs of the farm, he would tell me what he would be up to that day, and now he didn't. The first I knew we were buying a new harvester was when I saw it coming up our driveway. My husband had become secretive; it made me feel like an outsider.

Alarm bells were going off in my head. Eventually my body told me something was wrong, and I had better start listening to those bells. Because he always worked late I would be asleep when he came to bed, but I would wake up as soon as he got in the bed and I would feel sick in the stomach. In the end I would get up and sleep on the couch and then the sick feeling would go away. This became a regular occurrence. I felt so hurt by his behaviour towards Storm and now me, but I struggled on. I had to think of Storm.

Christmas 1994 was the worst Christmas of my life. For some reason we were spending our first Christmas Day alone, without extended family, and it was a disaster. No matter how I tried to be happy it wouldn't work. Storm was miserable; he cried most of the day and couldn't be consoled. I had chicken pox for the second time in my life, so it wasn't very pleasant, and my husband just wanted to be anywhere else but with Storm and me. I was glad when the day was over.

That was the last day Storm cried and shed tears. This was a huge thing, something quite serious obviously happened, and no one cared. They brushed it aside. It blew me away that no one in the medical profession had concerns that a child who cried when he was hungry and upset, who shed tears when he cried, just suddenly stopped, the day after Christmas Day, and was never able to cry again. I have asked doctors and no one can give me an answer. One asked why would I want to know, because it wouldn't change anything. Like hell it wouldn't. To this day I can't grasp that no doctor even wanted to do tests. I personally believe something happened to the part of Storm's brain that triggers the ability to cry. I guess I will never know.

I also realised that whatever happened to stop Storm's ability to cry and shed tears meant something was going on in his brain that could possibly kill him—there was nothing to say that what took away his ability to cry wasn't still growing. It was a feeling that would not go away.

It was so much easier when Storm could cry and shed tears; you knew he was unhappy. Now he had to learn to show his emotions in another way that I could understand, and Storm being Storm he found a way. Or rather, we found a way. We were so connected spiritually, it was like he spoke to my mind. I knew, for example, when he wanted a drink. When he was going to school and I was making his lunch in the morning to take with him, I might have made Vegemite sandwiches the day before and then, for no apparent reason, I would make peanut butter sandwiches. I'd find out later from his aides that he hadn't been enjoying the Vegemite but loved the peanut butter sandwiches I had made that day.

My beautiful Storm never got to walk independently, he couldn't see and he only ever learnt to say a few words. But he learnt how to copy the sound of a beat on drums if you let him hear it; he knew what he liked and what he didn't. He knew how to hug and how to give you the sweetest kisses. He felt his way through life, he felt movement and he felt sincerity and he always responded to love. He had you sussed in your first "hello". If it was a loving and caring hello, you would receive a tiny smile; if it was a judging confused hello he would ignore you and sometimes turn his head away from you. Although he was what most people would call severely disabled, he was so able in the areas that matter—matters of the heart. People would say that after meeting Storm, you left questioning who really was the disabled one—him, or us.

We carried on, Storm and I, with his physio sessions. My husband managed to get work with his bulldozer on a mine that was starting up out our way, so he was gone for weeks at a time, though he would ring now and then to see how we were going. Of course, while he was away I had the pleasant job of getting the buffalo in every time they got out, which was nearly every day. And nearly every day I would have to get bales of hay with the tractor to feed them.

On one of these occasions when the buffalo had got out and into a neighbour's paddock and were eating their crop, I managed to round them up with the farm Landcruiser and our trusted sheepdog, Bud. I had got them into a group and was moving them off the paddock and hopefully on to the road when the Landcruiser simply died, in the middle of the paddock. It wouldn't start again and the buffalo wandered off in all directions, feeding again. There was no way I was going to get out of the Landcruiser and walk past the buffalo. I decided to send Bud off in one direction so I could run off safely in the opposite direction, to the main road.

Off went Bud and the buffalo started chasing him, as I knew they would—they didn't like him at all. I bolted to the main road and started the 10km walk to the neighbours who were looking after Storm. I hadn't been walking long when Bud turned up, minus the buffalo. I could have sworn he was grinning, he knew why I had sent him off in that direction. He truly was an amazing dog.

On the walk to the neighbours we passed a truck in one of our paddocks. I tried to get it started so that we wouldn't have to walk the whole way, but the battery was flat. It was getting dark by the time we reached the house, thankfully there was still some light, because I can't see a thing at night unless there is a full moon. The neighbours lent me a ute to drive until my husband came home and got the Landcruiser and brought it home to fix it.

My husband had to come home from the mine to go with us to Perth for one of Storm's appointments at the hospital's early intervention clinic. On the drive down we stopped at a country town for fuel. I was watching him fill the tank when it suddenly dawned on me that he had had his hair cut. He was supposed to be busy working on a mine! When he had finished filling the car, I quietly asked him where he had had his hair cut; he said he had gone to Geraldton for a day and had it cut there. You know the saying "the straw that broke the camel's back". Well, a tonne of straw fell on this little camel's back, and I snapped, I got out of the passenger side of the car, got in the driver's side and told him to get in, and I drove us back to the farm. I had been doing physio twice a day, six days a week, and driving to Perth every Sunday so Storm could see an osteopath. There had been no time for me, I would have loved a day in Geraldton, I didn't go to America on a holiday, a heart can go on for only so long without being loved before it breaks, mine had finally broken and I needed to leave this loveless marriage. I was so hurt.

He wanted us to keep Storm's appointment in Perth and then discuss our problems when we got home; I wanted out then and there, to be as far away as possible from him and his deceit. I drove home, hitched the trailer to the car, loaded Storm's physio equipment on to the trailer, then filled the car with suitcases and plastic bags full of clothes—along with my rifle. I rang Mum and told her what had happened. She agreed I should leave (some part of me needed my parents' permission to go, and now I had it I was off). I took off my wedding and engagement rings and left them on the kitchen bench. Then I put Storm in the car and we left.

You might think that with all the shouting, arguing and tension in the air Storm would have been upset, but he was calm.

I drove to the first town and went to a pay phone to call my friends and let them know I was going. Then I rang my brother, Rod, for instructions on how to get to his house, and drove off. I cried, I ranted in anger, and Storm sat quietly in the back of the car listening to me. I stopped a few times to feed him.

Chapter Two

I don't have any recollection of getting to Rod's house, I don't even know whether I stayed overnight. I do remember that my cousin drove Storm and I in my car to my parents' home in Dunsborough—a good thing since I wasn't in a fit state of mind and my concentration wouldn't have been the best.

Storm took time to adapt to our new situation. He was so used to his daily routine and now it was gone. Sometimes he woke in the night, screaming fearfully. I would rush into the room, pick him up and he would wrap his arms around my neck, holding me so tight, his eyes filled with fear. It was terrible and so hard not to cry. Eventually, thank God, he settled down.

It was nice to be with my parents, but I had no idea what to do next. I met up with my husband at a coffee shop in Perth, and the meeting made it clear to me that we were done. I hadn't left him hoping he would want us back and run after us—I left because Storm and I deserved so much more. Now we had no home, no stability, the car was on its last legs and I couldn't see how I was going to be able to work with Storm's needs. It would have been impossible without my parents' support.

I ended up staying with them for about seven weeks, then moved to Augusta on the south coast, to a house owned by my aunt and uncle. Their daughter Diedre was renting it from them, she was divorced with two girls, so moving in would help her with the rent. It was a two-storey house with views of the ocean, delicious. Storm and I had the room upstairs. We had our own ensuite, and I bought two single beds.

Diedre was a great support and was wonderful with Storm. There were times when she would look after him so I could go for long restorative walks along the beach, and Storm thoroughly enjoyed the fuss she made of him.

For most of the years of my marriage I had been isolated from my family—my parents sold their farm and moved to Dunsborough not long after we married and my brother and sister had moved to Perth so I rarely saw them—but now I had family close by. It was hard not to worry about our future and eventually I had to make some decisions about what I was going to do. But of course things just seem to fall into place.

The more I try to control my life and worry about where it is going, the more it spirals out of control. The hard bit is having faith that if you let go and trust that all will work out the way it is intended, it will. But it is a hard lesson for a control freak, like me, to learn.

I had spent a lot of time analysing my marriage and what went wrong, but now I had to move on to the next stage so I approached Legal Aid for a lawyer to negotiate a property settlement. Nobody had suggested that, the idea was purely mine. And even though I didn't feel I had much of a fighting chance, I felt driven to pursue it. If I had left without a child I wouldn't have bothered going to court. But I had Storm's needs to think of; we had lost our home, our friends and a way of life that we enjoyed.

While I waited to hear from Legal Aid I focused on our immediate needs. Storm's physio sessions and appointments with the cranial osteopath had stopped, and I felt a lot of guilt about that. Storm was not well. I had taken him to my parents' doctor while I was staying with them and it turned out his iron levels were so low that in a so-called normal child it would retard development. So I let his exercises slide and concentrated on getting his iron levels up.

After a couple of months I wrote to my husband about furniture and other items I wanted from the farm. I asked him not to be there when we arrived for pick-up, and he agreed to all conditions. I arranged to hire a truck that my brother would drive for me, and on the day before I was meant to go to the farm I drove up from Augusta in the morning, dropped Storm off at my parents' place and then continued on to my sister's house in Perth—a 500km drive.

That night I couldn't sleep, I was so nervous about going back to the farm and hoping it would go all right without any dramas. I don't think Toni slept, either. Rod picked us up about 5am and when we arrived at the farm my husband went down to the shed while we packed the truck. I took a few items of furniture, including an old desk that belonged to our grandfather's brother. I took half the linen, a few kitchen items and other knick-knacky things. It took us at most two hours to load the truck, literally throwing stuff in the back in the rush to be gone from the place.

It was four months since I had left and the house had already changed, it was dark and dingy, part of the verandah had fallen down and the swimming pool was black and had things floating in it. I walked into our bedroom and my cat was asleep on the bed; he woke up, saw me and took to his scrapers—it was a bit creepy. At least our dog, Bud, was happy to see me; he was so excited I thought his tail was going to fall off. It was hard to leave him behind.

My husband came back to the house as we were finishing and offered us a coffee but we were eager to be gone. We talked briefly, and then we left. I was so glad Rod and Toni were there and I didn't have to do it on my own.

When we got back to Perth we unloaded some furniture at Toni's house and the rest went to Rod's. The next morning I packed the car with a few things I'd brought from the farm and headed for Dunsborough.

When I got to my parents' house Storm was in his stroller on the lawn. Mum was watering the plants on the patio nearby and didn't hear me so I walked up to Storm and said hello. There was no doubting he knew my voice; he started babbling excitedly.

The next day we headed back to Augusta, but by the time we got there Storm was getting quite grizzly. I thought he was probably getting a cold, but by the next morning he was breathing so fast it frightened me. I took him to the local hospital where they admitted him straight away and put him on oxygen. He had developed pneumonia. We ended up staying the night, but he recovered fairly quickly and we were allowed to go home the next day. While he was in hospital they weighed him—he was two and a half years old and weighed just 8.2kg.

Soon after that he developed a cough that would keep him awake at night. Eventually I took him to my parents' doctor in Dunsborough. It seemed he had bronchitis, so the doctor put him on Painstop, which stopped the coughing and he finally came good.

In July that year I went back to Morawa to visit my best friend, Roma. We stayed with her for a couple of days and in that time I bravely rang my husband to see if he wanted to have Storm for a couple of hours. To my surprise, he did. He came to Roma's, picked Storm up and disappeared back to the farm, bringing him back in a couple of hours along with a garbage bag full of stuff. After he left I went through the things in the bag, amongst them photos. I don't think he kept one photo of Storm, how sad.

I finally got an appointment with someone from Legal Aid. Mum looked after Stormy while I drove to Busselton for the interview, where I had to answer a lot of questions about my marriage and how the farm was run—it was rather nerve-racking as I didn't want to stuff it up, I needed their help. I obviously didn't stuff it up, and they agreed to take the case. I was allocated a lawyer in Margaret River, to whom I had already given $4000, all the money I had, to get the ball rolling.

Eventually I had to apply for more funding from Legal Aid and luckily they agreed on the condition that I used their lawyers in Perth. I agreed, of course, even though it meant endless hours driving the 500km from Augusta to Perth for meetings. Storm didn't mind the long-distance driving and I was becoming more confident behind the wheel.

Staying over with my sister on one of my many trips to Perth for meetings with the lawyer I met someone who was to become a vital part of Storm's, and my, life journey. Her name is Rae, and Toni had arranged for her to come to her house to give her a quote for a stained-glass window. While there, Rae asked me some questions about Storm, who was sitting quietly on my lap, and asked if I played dolphin tapes for him to listen to. It was strange she would ask me that—a couple of months earlier I had been to a person who did "channelling" and had suggested, among other things, that I should play tapes of whale or dolphin sounds for Storm when he went to bed at night.

After Rae left I didn't think much more of it, but Rae told me later she couldn't get Storm out of her mind. She ended up going to a shop where they sold crystals, incense, spiritual things etc, and asking about tapes of dolphin music. The proprietor, Lynn, played a few tapes for her and she ended up buying one, along with some crystals. In the process Rae told Lynn about Storm, and the next thing was, Lynn wanted to meet him, too. My son, the pied piper.

I was still at Toni's house a few days later when Rae returned with her stained-glass window sketches; I had planned to leave a day or so before, but had ended up staying on. Rae gave me the dolphin tape and crystals for Storm. The crystals were to be put under his pillow. She had only met Storm once and here she was giving him gifts. Gorgeous.

That was when she told me the lady from the shop wanted to meet Storm. This was bizarre; two total strangers drawn to Storm for reasons I couldn't understand. I'm his mother, I always thought he was gorgeous, but now I was seeing he has this effect on other people, so I agreed that next time I was in Perth we would all meet up. I think Storm should have been nicknamed Mystical Storm.

Rae has been in our lives now for more than 16 years and I am so grateful that divine intervention, God, whatever, brought her into our lives. She is the most amazing intuitive, spiritual, loving and giving person—it is actually a privilege that she regards me as a friend. Our journey would have been extremely bumpy without her guidance and support. God bless you, Rae.

Toni was working at the Argyle diamond mine in the north of WA, two weeks on at Kununurra and two weeks off in Perth. When she decided to spend her weeks off in Broome for a couple of months, she asked me if I wanted to stay in her house in Perth while she was away and I jumped at the chance. It was an opportunity for me to check out some other alternative therapies for Storm. Also, I would save a lot of money by not having to travel from Augusta to Perth all the time. So we moved temporarily into Toni's house. Sheer luxury, we had a room each. Whoo-hoo!!

Now we were in Perth I arranged for Rae and Lynn to come to the house to meet Storm. They came in the morning for coffee. Storm knew all

*the attention was on him and he lapped it up. Lynn seemed a very nice person
also deeply into spirituality.*

My brother was working at the same mine as Toni, and since I was
in Perth for a while his wife asked me if I would look after their children
while he was away as she had got a job. It meant a bit of extra money for
me, so I was happy to do it. Chevy was only a couple of months older than
Storm and Kyra was going to primary school. Luckily they didn't live far
from Toni's house. I would get to their house in the morning and take Kyra
to school, then Chevy was with Storm and me for the rest of the day. If I
had appointments for Storm, Chevy would have to tag along.

One of the first of the new therapies I tried was with a registered
chiropractor, Lucie. I can't remember how I found out about her—another
one of those things that just turned up at the appropriate time for us.
Her approach to Storm was Bowen therapy a prescribed set of moves
which immediately leads the body into a relaxed state, allowing oxygen
to circulate more thoroughly throughout the system, releasing toxins and
eliminating dysfunctional fluids. On one of our weekly visits Lucie picked
up that Storm had stress around his head and neck, which could affect the
muscles around his eyes; I had told her he had been rolling his eyes now and
then. Since that visit he had started smiling again, which he hadn't done
for quite some time, and he had even started laughing for the first time.
Almost three years old and he was just beginning to laugh—and what a
precious laugh, it made me laugh with him.

But his ability to sit up had nose-dived. Every time I sat him up he would fall over again and he wouldn't try to sit up again as he had done before. He had also been very quiet and had begun hitting his head with his hand. Even though the therapies helped immensely and these setbacks passed, I know without a doubt they had something to do with the day he stopped crying. I also know that without these alternative therapies he wouldn't have done so well. And he never gave up fighting.

After the next Bowen session his neck was a lot better than before and Lucie said there wasn't so much stress around his head. When we got home I fed him and then decided to do a little gardening, so I put him on his stomach with some toys in the lounge room and pulled the curtains back so I could check on him from the garden. I was out gardening for about 10 minutes when I checked on him and there he was, sitting up, playing with his toys.

Whatever Lucie did that day created instant changes in Storm; it was amazing. I decided I would have a few sessions with her myself and I have to admit I cried during every treatment. I hate crying, it feels like an act of weakness, but I suppose it was good for me, releasing all that pent-up emotion. I would also sleep really well the night after I had the treatment.

I was taking Storm to a kinesiologist, too. Kinesiology is a form of chiropractic, a diagnostic method through muscle testing and a therapy in which the practitioner applies light fingertip massage to pressure points on the body to stimulate or relax key muscles. Because Storm didn't talk we didn't know how he was really feeling, but with muscle testing the kinesiologist could get answers from Storm's body and it was helping him. I also had a few treatments.

We were also still visiting the naturopath we had been seeing while living on the farm, and during one visit he remarked on how open and focused Storm's eyes were. (When Storm was a baby, he was like those toy dolls that when you sit them up there eyes open but if you lay them down they close. It eventually stopped happening, but it was a bit odd. Also, even though Storm was blind, he didn't look blind, sometimes I had difficulty persuading people he was, he had the most beautiful bluey-grey eyes.) I told the naturopath I had taken him for Bowen therapy and kinesiology. He was impressed and asked for the practitioners' names and addresses.

Expressing concern about Storm's lack of muscle development, the naturopath told me that tests on the oil in mullet fish had shown it was very good for building muscles and had shown amazing results in patients with muscular dystrophy. I was to steam the fish, then mix it into his evening meal. On the drive back home I was wondering where on earth I was going to find some mullet; it didn't sound very appetising so I thought it would be difficult to find. But later that day, grocery shopping at my usual haunt, I went into the fish section and there on special was Baby Red Mullet. Well, there you go. Storm had mullet for dinner amongst his vegetables and actually loved it.

The naturopath also gave me some drops for Storm's immune system and blood. He was great for my morale; his positive attitude lifted me up and I needed all the lifting up I could get. It was always an expensive visit but worth every cent.

All the therapies where costing me a lot of money, in fact, and I had to go without a lot of things for Storm to be able to do it. Thank God we live in a country where we can get a pension.

Now that I wasn't staying in Augusta for weeks on end, Diedre decided to rent out the room we had been using—which I understood because the rent would help her—so I drove back to Augusta to pack up our things and store them at my parents' house. I was a bit worried as to where we were going to live when Toni came back from Broome, because most of my money was spent on Storm's therapies and because of my lack of furniture I would have to rent a furnished apartment. It was all a bit too stressful to think about, so I decided to leave it up to God to fix.

I decided also that I really needed to look at my belief system—I didn't want to carry with me for the rest of my life the beliefs I had brought away from my failed marriage. So I started to read a lot, books about what your thoughts create and how to change your thought patterns. The power of positive thinking, how your longstanding thought patterns can actually create physical ailments, blah, blah, blah. I also had a few psychic and tarot readings, some far-fetched and others spot on. I read so many self-help books I'm so over it, for now, though I'm sure I will return to it if and when I need to.

What I really needed to do was watch how Storm simply brought into his life the people and treatments he needed, his complete trust in the universe always providing for him.

I never looked for psychic readings to tell me of a shining future; I wanted to know whether I was on the right track with my life or whether I had veered off the bitumen on to the gravel and if so what did I need to do to get back on to the bitumen.

The one thing almost every psychic told me was that Storm was not going to be on this earth for a long time. I wasn't at all shocked the first time I heard that; I'd already felt it. When Storm cried all Christmas Day in 1994 and then was never able to cry or shed tears again, I knew something bad had happened, that there was every possibility that whatever had happened would affect his life in the future and every chance he would not live a long life. A mother's knowing.

When my husband asked for access time with Storm, part of me rebelled at the idea. How would I know if he was looked after properly? My husband had rarely looked after him, and never for long periods, so I agreed he could have Storm for four hours. The first time it happened I just paced the house for the whole four hours, incapable of focusing on anything and so glad when I got Storm home again. To think many mothers have to do this on a regular basis—I take my hat off to them. It turned out not to be a big deal, as he asked for access only once a year and it stopped immediately the property settlement was finalised.

I was back on the hunt for another type of therapy, leaving no stone unturned. Lynn had read a newspaper article about a woman from overseas who had set up private Conductive Education sessions at her house in Perth. I found her name in the newspaper, looked her up in the telephone directory and rang for an appointment. When we arrived, a session had just finished. There were three children with their mothers. It was the first time I had been in a room with other disabled children, usually Storm was the only one. At first I felt sad, but then I realised there were no sad faces; they were happy children in the room with parents chatting away. They came up and introduced themselves and asked Storm his name, we said hello, then they all left.

After they left, Ildiko introduced herself and asked me a few questions about Storm, then put him through a few exercises to see what he could do. Sadly, it wasn't much. Unfortunately, Ildiko was fully booked at the time but she said she knew she could help Storm and would ring as soon as a vacancy came up. She showed me a few exercises I could do with him in the meantime. My experience with raising a disabled child is that formal medical professionals give you little positive feedback, perhaps for fear of raising false hopes, but those providing the other treatments I have tried have given so much positive support. Ildiko was another of those people.

Now that Rod's wife's job had finished I was no longer needed to babysit, which gave me more time to myself. The year was coming to a close, and what a year it had been. I think that because it had been such a full year I hadn't felt the full emotional brunt of the separation, I didn't get a lot of time to wallow in it, which at the time was not such a bad thing. Mind you, I still had my "poor me" days, I'm not a perfect person and I felt down at times, the responsibility I felt for Storm was huge. But I don't think Storm had any "poor me" moments and it was his life that was affected the most. That kid was showing me up. *Who does he think he is—the Dalai Lama?*

Since Storm was seven months old and his blindness was first diagnosed, life had been an emotional roller-coaster—appointments with doctors that brought more bad news, endless trips to Perth searching for people who could help in any way, therapy sessions six days a week and another trip to Perth every Sunday, trying to come to terms with a child we had dreamed of, a future planned for destroyed, then having to walk away from a marriage, a lifestyle and friends and as if all that wasn't enough, having to fight in court for something with which to rebuild a life. It was painful and I had more pain to go through. It has taken me years to heal emotionally, but in the end you do or you play the victim for the rest of your life.

So Storm and I came to our first Christmas without my husband and his family, which actually wasn't bad, it was good. We ended up spending Christmas Day at my parents' home. Toni had to work, but Rod and his family spent it with us and it turned out really nice. Of course, it didn't take much to beat the last horrendous Christmas, with my husband.

Chapter Three

1996

A new year, a year full of possibilities. Finally a vacancy for Storm with Ildiko (Conductive Education). He would be starting in February, and I was so excited. Now that Toni was no longer spending her time off in Broome, she was again home in Perth for two weeks and then at work for two weeks. So for the two weeks she was away at work, I stayed in her house and then when she came back to Perth for two weeks I went and stayed with our parents in Dunsborough. Toni worked hard during those two weeks up north, the hours were long and it was very noisy, so the last thing she needed was to come home to a child who was quite noisy.

It actually worked out well for me, during the two weeks she was away Storm could go to Ildiko for Conductive Therapy four or five days a week and then when I stayed with Mum and Dad I was able to save up the money for the sessions which cost at that time $45 a day. They were not funded in any way, but when something works you find the money. So far I hadn't had to go to court for any hearings, only appointments with lawyers, so I still had time for Storm's treatments.

February arrived and Storm had his first day at Ildiko's. There were three other children and their mothers there. The session started about 9am and, boy, did Storm perform. Usually he was quite placid but on this day he shouted at me when I started putting him through the exercises, he was not at all impressed. The other children were very well-behaved compared with Storm, and I was a little embarrassed. We stopped for morning tea and then started again, finishing just before lunchtime, and by that time Storm was trying to bite me. He really objected to the exercises—the trouble being that he had had a year off from the Ian Hunter program so he had become a bit complacent. Mind you, he was only three and a half years old. Ildiko had told me that the earlier I started the more progress I would get out of Storm. I believed her but, boy, he was angry with me.

It was also the first time I had spent time with other women who had disabled children and were pushing them to be the best they could. It was a revelation, and made me feel less alone, less isolated. They believed, as I do, in developing their children to their fullest capabilities, just as you do with so-called normal children, though with disabled children it takes a lot more effort and perseverance.

Having a child with differences really can be isolating. People treat you differently. In later years, when Storm was in school, one of the mothers would not stand next to me when she became pregnant and even though her child liked playing with Storm, she was encouraged not to. Putting Storm in a "normal" school made us both very noticeable. I found it very hard, but Storm didn't give a toss—as far as he was concerned he was like every other child and I was the one with the problem.

When Storm is ill, it is brushed aside like he is unimportant. I wonder
if it's because they can't figure out what is wrong with him and don't want to
admit they just don't know. Symptoms are dismissed as "part of his condition",
whatever that means. What condition? All I know at this time is he is blind
and developmentally delayed.

I remember a mother telling me how her child had been having
headaches for a couple of days so she had taken the child to the doctor
and he had ordered an MRI scan to make sure all was well. Apparently
a headache was a lot more serious than losing the ability to cry or
shed tears.

See how it would have been easy for me to become bitter. But even
when I felt we were subjected to terrible injustices, after a few moments of
ranting and raving and "poor me" I would look at Storm going about his
day, living in the moment. He was OK with his situation, naturally he was
unhappy when he was ill but as soon as the illness passed he was happy
again. If he could get past it, I could, too. So through watching my son I
learnt a very valuable lesson of acceptance—that there are things in life
you just can't change. But what I could change, I would, and alternative
treatments were what I could do.

Ildiko also was a great support and gave guidance that I needed,
especially when it came to Storm's needs and knowing what was the best
schooling for him. She told me once that if he could see, there would be
nothing holding him back. I believed her. It was great having someone
else who could also see past his physical disabilities. I looked forward to

his sessions with Ildiko, he was making great progress and I had met some

great mothers.

While I was busy working with Storm and travelling to and from

Dunsborough in between therapies, the one thing that I thought would

never again happen to me, happened. I had been sure that so much of my

time was spent with Storm and his needs that sharing my life with someone

else would be impossible. Then I met Joe.

I put off introducing him to Storm, as I couldn't cope with the

possibility of Storm being rejected again. But finally I bit the bullet and

brought them together. Well, I don't know what I was so worried about.

Storm took to Joe and though I think it took Joe a while to warm to Storm,

when he did it was the best thing. Storm idolised him. When I couldn't

get him to sleep at night, Joe would sit and cuddle him and in about five

minutes he would be sound asleep. Joe was the male influence that had

been missing from Storm's life, and Storm loved him.

March arrived, and my husband came for his yearly access day

with Storm. I said as little as possible to him, only what needed to be said.

I didn't want him to have Storm; I didn't understand why he asked for the

four-hour access once a year; I didn't want to think about Storm being

with someone who was practically a stranger to him. Would he know what

Storm wanted, when he needed to be fed or given a drink? It was all too

hard, so the sooner he left with Storm the sooner he would be back again,

only to visit again next year.

The divorce hearing has come and gone, and now he is my ex-husband.

The mistake I made with the lawyer in Margaret River was that I never took Storm to any of the meetings. Storm was the sole reason I wanted a property settlement—I didn't like taking my ex-husband to court, it seemed tacky to me, but it was something I needed to do to provide for Storm. Now, every time we had a meeting with a new lawyer I would take Storm with me so they knew it was Storm's needs they were fighting for, and it worked.

Storm drew people to him. It was just something he did. I wouldn't mind a bit of what he had, and he certainly didn't get it from me, or my ex-husband. I didn't notice it on the farm but I should have—so many people volunteered their time for his physio sessions, he was the Pied Piper. People would come up to me in the shop and tell me how gorgeous he was. He had his hair cut with the clippers because it just grew straight up, and people loved to run their hands over his head. When I got my hair cut the other hairdressers would want to hold him. When he was ill and we visited the hospital, the nurses would remember him and come and talk to him. At three years old his disabilities were not noticeable, people wouldn't believe me when I told them he was blind and I would have to convince them that he was.

During the two weeks out of four when we stayed in Toni's house I pottered in her garden whenever I could. Toni said I could do up the front garden the way I wanted and I had a great time. There are so many more plants that can be grown in Perth than we could grow on the farm, so we would spend time hunting for plants at garden centres. Storm also enjoyed being out in the garden.

As much as I liked staying at Toni's so that Storm could go to Ildiko's and the other therapies I took him to, I felt it would be better if we weren't moving every two weeks, so I began looking around for somewhere to rent. I didn't have much furniture, so it would have be furnished, and in the end the only thing I found that I could afford was a semi-furnished two-bedroom park home in a caravan park. Rod and his wife lent me a spare sofa and Rod steam-cleaned the carpet and walls for me. The home was fairly dark and dingy, with a separate bathroom-cum-laundry. No bath for Storm, so I bathed him in the laundry tub, and if it rained we would get wet going to the bathroom. But it was all I could afford at the time, and it wasn't that cheap.

There was a storm our first night there. The wind rocked the home, the rain on the roof was deafening and there was no heating so it was freezing cold. All this to create some stability in Storm's life. "I must be mad," I thought. "Obviously I am."

Now we were in Perth permanently we were going to Ildiko every week, so with the cost of physio, rent, fuel and groceries finances were incredible tight. The park home was so cold in the mornings that I would light the oven and leave the oven door open to warm it up before getting Storm up for his breakfast. In the end it was too miserable a life to lead all in the name of stability, and we moved out after six weeks. I have no problem admitting I made a mistake.

We moved back to Toni's house and went back to alternating two weeks in Perth with two weeks in Dunsborough. It was so much nicer, and a hell of a lot warmer.

We were able to get occupational therapies, speech therapy and physiotherapy through Disability Services when we were in Perth. They even came out to Toni's house to see Storm and of course he charmed everyone. Actually it was a relief to go off to Dunsborough two weeks out of four because the fortnights in Perth were so busy with lawyer meetings, court hearings, Conductive Education sessions with Ildiko, Bowen therapy, kinesiology sessions and now the therapies from Disability Services. I think being so busy really was a good thing because it stopped me from falling into all the pain I felt.

I don't believe the pain I feel about Storm will ever completely disappear, though it may become duller. It hurts to love someone so much, to watch him struggle through his life, to be so different from everyone else. I wanted to protect him from every slight in his life, worried so much about the future he would have. I never could have dreamed I would be leading this life, I had to find strength and courage in myself to do and be what Storm needed me to be. I adjusted over time and I travelled through the obstacles that confronted us a lot better, less traumatically and with more humour, and I know I'm a better person for it.

Luckily I was given the opportunity to befriend a great person, Rae, who appeared just at the right time in my life. She has supported and encouraged me, been honest with me, led me down the path to healing and I am grateful to her for helping me to let go of the destructive patterns I had developed.

When I first met Rae she was doing stained glass for people's homes, tarot readings, healings, bringing colour into people's lives with her presence. She loves people, loves to help them find peace within themselves. Her workshops were loving, honest without being hurtful, that led us to lightbulb moments when we got to what was holding us back. When I felt like giving up, when it seemed to me the property settlement process was too hard and nasty, Rae encouraged me to fight on. Rae never gives up on you.

Because Storm was going to Conductive Ed with children who had siblings his age, I was advised it was time to find a kindergarten for next year. It was a daunting thought. If he was to go to kindergarten we would have to be living in Perth permanently. Should I put him in the normal school or, considering his disabilities, in a special school for the disabled? What would be best for him?, "Bugger," I thought, "I don't want to do this."

Ildiko advised me to enrol him in a regular kindergarten. She didn't say why, but I was confident she knew what would be best for him. One of the other mothers gave me the name of a private kindy that she had taken her children to, that wasn't far from Toni's home. So I rang up and made an appointment to see the teacher. I explained over the phone that

Storm was disabled, and what his disabilities were. It didn't seem to worry them. Still, I was very nervous about the meeting; my fear of Storm being rejected was ever-present.

Of course, my fears were groundless. Storm was on his best behaviour, all charm. I said I knew that legally they couldn't reject him on the basis of his disabilities, but if they really didn't want him I would rather they told me. I didn't want him to be somewhere he wasn't wanted, because I knew he would feel it. They didn't see that there would be any problem. The teacher said they would organise an aide for Storm and the meeting was over. It was that simple.

It was hard to comprehend that he was old enough to be going to kindy. It was coming up to two years since we had left the farm and he was just two when we left. Where had the years gone?

Chapter Four

1997

A quiet start to the new year. No Conductive Ed until school was due to start, but Ildiko had given me some exercises to do with Storm each day so he didn't become too complacent. The beginning of the year seemed to be more of a socialising time, with dinner and barbecues with Joe and his friends. Storm was becoming quite the social butterfly, which he gets from his father. As I have mentioned previously I am not much for socialising, I like to keep to myself; if Storm hadn't come into my life I would have become a reclusive person.

After a chat with Toni it was decided we would stay in Perth permanently, even when she was down for her two weeks in Perth. That was going to take some adjusting, for all of us. I was worried that Storm would be too noisy; he had a way of taking over the place and he seemed to be especially noisy in Perth. I think he disliked all the traffic noises.

School started and as Storm went off for his first day at kindy you could tell by his posture he was like "bring it on". But I worried about how the other children would react to him. I knew it would take a while for the school aide to get to know him, so I stayed for the whole first day, answering any questions she had about him. I was nervous the whole time.

Storm seemed quite comfortable with the aide, he had a great time painting and playing in the sandpit. It was his first experience of a sandpit and he loved running his hands through the sand. He got into the play dough and even attempted to eat it, I think all kids do that. I noticed children inching closer and closer to him as the day progressed and at the end of the day some of the other mothers came up and introduced themselves.

As much as it turned out to be a great day for Storm, there are parts of this new life I will never get used to. It hurts so much that he is blind, that he has no idea what I look like, that he can't see the things I take for granted, that he can't run or walk. It hurts that his physical disabilities make it impossible for him to be just another child in a classroom full of children. I don't like it that we park in a "disabled parking" bay to make it easier to get to class. I want to know what it is like to walk your child to school. Time has helped me grow accustomed to the pain, but I have learnt also that pain is a part of everyone's life and we have a choice whether to let it consume us or just acknowledge it but don't dwell on it. I don't want Storm's life to be only about pain, differences, struggles. That is not who he is. He is gentleness, humour, a great heart, laughter and total enjoyment, and at his best is totally in the moment.

The car with the heart murmur finally had a heart attack and died. Luckily I had been saving up for the inevitable. I hadn't actually managed to save enough to buy a decent replacement, however, so my parents lent me some money to make up the difference. Also luckily, Joe was an ex-mechanic, so he helped me choose the car. It took some hunting around, but eventually I bought a little silver car and we loved it.

With school starting so did the sessions with Ildiko, so unless I had court hearings or appointments with lawyers, Storm would have Conductive Ed three days a week. On those days I would pick him up from kindy and drive to Ildiko's place in Bullcreek. When we got there I would feed him his lunch while the first session was finishing and then we would start the afternoon session which finished around 3pm or a little after, with a pause halfway through for afternoon tea. They were fairly hectic days for Storm and usually he would go to sleep quite early that night. It was a lot for a four-and-a-half-year-old to be expected to do and he did it extremely well with minimal grumbling.

If I was pushing Storm constantly outside his comfort zone to improve physically, I was also pushing myself in my continual search for help in improving his quality of life. Sending him to a normal school was the best choice I had made. He wasn't allowed to get away with anything that any other child in the school wasn't allowed to do, and I liked that he was learning acceptable social behaviour.

Now that there was going to be someone in her house all the time Toni could get a pet, so along came Zorro. And what started out as a cute kitten grew up to be a psychotic cat. Except for Toni and Storm, everyone was nervous around Zorro. He was a complete nut, you never knew what mood he was in, he might pounce on you when you walked past him, and at other times he might let you pat him only to turn around and attack you. At night when I was watching television he would come and sit on the couch next to me and just stare at me with his piercing gold-coloured eyes, so unnerving, then he would start flicking his tail and next thing he would just leap and attack me. I would untangle myself from him and he might go off for a while then come back and do it all over again. Zorro was one scary cat. But with Storm he was a completely different animal. When Storm was in the lounge room playing with his toys, Zorro would just lie nearby sleeping. Sometimes he got within Storm's range and Storm would pull his tail or grab his face and pull it, and not once did Zorro scratch or bite him. Storm could do whatever he liked to Zorro and Zorro never retaliated.

March arrived, again, and my now ex-husband asked for his annual access day with Storm, again. Again I roamed the house for the four hours until Storm arrived safely back home. We are done for another year, phew!

Back to our new life. Storm was doing well with his Conductive Ed sessions and loved kindergarten. Disability Services had come up with a walking frame and he was learning to walk with it, he was quite proud of himself, even trying to push the frame forward by himself although he had no idea to what he was pushing it. As always, my heart ached for him.

He got his first invitation to a birthday party, from one of the boys at kindy. It was at McDonald's, another first for us. Because they didn't have backs to the chairs I had to sit with Storm and all the kids while the other mothers moved to another section where they could chat. Though inviting

Storm was a lovely gesture it served as another reminder of how different his life and mine were, a reminder of the basic things children of his age could do that he couldn't. Storm was happy, though; he came home with balloons, which he just loved to pop.

Toni had decided to move out of her house and into an apartment with our cousin in a more upbeat suburb (the house was in a family suburb, not exactly a single person's place). I was able to get rent assistance and rented the house off her. She didn't need to take much furniture so I only needed to buy a couch, which I did, and we had the whole place to ourselves, what luxury—I was able to move into the master bedroom and have my own ensuite. I had also introduced myself to the next-door neighbours, a couple with two children. I got invited over for coffees and now and then the wife would look after Storm if I couldn't get anyone else to do it when I had court hearings.

Joe had finished building his house and was now looking at blocks of land in Bindoon, a small town about 45 minutes north of Perth. I used to drive through it every time we came down from the farm to Perth for appointments. In winter it looks like New Zealand, with beautiful rolling hills that are green for far longer than on the farm. Joe's continued interest in moving there meant many weekend trips to look at blocks. Storm and I enjoyed getting back to the countryside.

Another opportunity showed up for me and Storm when my sister-in-law told me about a home respite service—qualified people came to your house and looked after your child for a couple of hours so you could do some shopping, take in a movie, or whatever. I phoned the co-ordinator and they came out a week or so later to assess Storm's needs and to see if they could provide a service. Turned out they would be able to provide respite for four hours a week on Wednesdays—luckily not a day when Storm had his sessions in Bullcreek and in the afternoon after school had finished. Wow, time to myself, to do whatever the heart desired, unimaginable, time and space to myself. Awesome, and it was assisted by the government so it wasn't going to cost me anything, wow.

I would make Storm's dinner before I left to go shopping or visiting friends, so when I came back after four hours he had already had his bath and dinner and was ready for bed after a little quality play time. Bliss. And Storm loved all the attention from the lady who came and looked after him.

About the same time, the Association for the Blind provided me with a piece of equipment called the Little Room. Devised especially for multi-handicapped blind children, it is a simple three-sided perspex-topped box placed over a child lying on a "resonance board". Objects that are fun and tactile to touch hang from the top of the box, always in the same place, providing a stable environment that allows the child to experience the same feedback from movement over and over again. Storm learned quickly where his favourite objects were in the box and would reach for them as soon as I placed him in it. It was working well for him and while he was playing in the box I whizzed around the house cleaning and tidying up.

Also at this time I was having more meetings with lawyers, seemingly without getting any closer to a settlement, so it took some juggling with school and therapy sessions and luckily I had friends and family willing to help with Storm. I was actually beginning to understand lawyers' lingo, which previously had gone quite over my head.

Halfway through another year, Storm was settled into school, interacting really well with the other children, and progressing slowly with his sessions in Bullcreek. We were still taking weekend trips to Bindoon but now we were looking at display homes because Joe was determined to build. It was fun in the beginning but after a while it was fun no more.

I also came across another natural therapy that I hadn't tried, so of course I had to try it. Iridology isn't a new kind of therapy; it has been around for centuries, and it allows trained people to see into the body through the eyes. The pharmacist at my local shopping centre had advertised that you could make an appointment to see the iridologist for free on certain days, so I went in and made an appointment for myself but ended up asking the iridologist if he could look at Storm's eyes instead. I thought that because Storm was blind he wouldn't be able to make a diagnosis, but after looking into Storm's eyes he told me that he had a weak heart, that he had allergies, that he had night sweats because his body was worn out, that his sinuses were blocked and that he had an itchy throat. He also picked up that Storm was having headaches and that his back was out of alignment—all that, just from looking into his eyes.

Because Storm could not speak to tell me what he was feeling, maybe this was another way of him being able to communicate. I didn't know his back was out, or that he was having headaches, and the iridologist was right about the night sweats. I was willing to accept what he said, so I got the herbal tablets he recommended—once again I had nothing to lose in giving it a try, and so much to gain if it worked.

MUM'S THE WORD

Storm had become a lot happier now, perhaps because his world was settled and had a routine. I cherished his laughter, something that had taken years for him to learn. Still the only one word I had heard him say was "mum" and of course of all the words I would have chosen him to say if he could have only one, that was it. Since then I heard him say "home" a few times in his life, and it was always in an appropriate situation.

For his fifth birthday, at his teacher's suggestion I baked biscuits with lolly faces on them for recess. They put five candles in a biscuit and all the kids sang happy birthday to him. I stayed so that I could take some photos. It had become a tradition since his second birthday that he had a chocolate birthday cake with freckles on it, so when he got home from school there was a chocolate cake waiting for him. He loved chocolate cake.

Joe brought him a soft Elmo toy that sang *You Are My Sunshine* when you pressed its stomach. Storm loved it, played in bed with it every night and was still taking it to bed with him five years on. It no longer sang

You Are My Sunshine and had had reconstructive surgery many times, but it was his prized possession.

Storm was going along fine with only a few illnesses now and then, nothing major. His iron levels were up and down, though, and my iron levels had also become low. We had an appointment together with a blood specialist and I had to have a iron infusion that took an hour, so while I has having it they took Storm off for blood tests. It turned out his iron levels were fine but his white cell count was low, so he had to have blood tests every week for three weeks to see if it improved. Of course he had all the women coming up and talking to him, telling him how handsome he was. He just lapped it up, making all the appropriate sounds and smiles. Nothing came of the blood tests—he had an irregular white cell count and it could go quite low then go up again but still be considered low. Storm was always a bit of an enigma, why should this have been any different?

The only definite diagnosis made at this particular time was that he had "cortical blindness", lacking the corpus colostrum which connects the two sides of the brain, passing messages from one side of the brain to the other. But the doctors couldn't explain to me why he could put a toy in one hand and pass it to his other hand when really he shouldn't have been able to do that. Also he shouldn't have been able to walk, because that takes left-brain/right-brain action. I commented on that during a visit to Storm's paediatrician; he admitted there was a lot about the brain that they didn't know.

One night when I went in to check on Storm, as I usually did, there he was standing beside the bed, using his hands on the bed to keep his balance. I was chuffed. My little enigma.

It was time to book Storm in for his next year of school and the dilemma was the same as last year. I always found it hard to make the decisions, who knew what the next year would bring? Luckily, one of the mothers that I saw during the Conductive Ed sessions lived in the same suburb as us and her boy was going to the local pre-primary school next year, so I made an appointment and took Storm along to meet the principal and class teacher. Again I asked did they want to have Storm and if they didn't could they tell me to my face because I didn't want him to pick up that he wasn't wanted. Again they didn't have a problem, so this would be his new school. And it was actually only walking distance from Toni's house.

Christmas time came round again. Another year had passed and Toni moved back in. She and Rod flew in from work on Christmas Day so I picked them up from the airport. We spent the day with Rod and his family, then on Boxing Day we drove to Dunsborough to spend it with our parents.

Joe had put his house in Perth on the market and bought a block of land at Bindoon. I was still waiting, not always patiently, for the property settlement to reach an end. Because it was school holidays, Storm didn't have physio in Bullcreek, but we still had Disability Services coming to the house. I enjoyed the school holidays because we had more time at home.

Chapter Five

1998

This year turned out to be the best in a long time, but still as busy as the previous couple of years. My ex-husband made an offer of settlement that was so small it was instantly rejected and a counter-offer made. At least they made an offer, this was something new. In January Storm's father asked for his annual access time. It was a little easier this time because it was only a couple of hours and it was only once a year. In fact, it turned out to be the last time he ever asked to see Storm, and the last time we saw him. Storm was so besotted with Joe that he didn't notice his father wasn't in his life.

Storm wouldn't be going to natural therapies as much as he did last year; they had done all they could at that time and he was quite healthy. But we were still going to do another year of Conductive Ed at Bullcreek. Some weeks we went two days and other weeks we only went once. It still wasn't recognised by the government so we couldn't get any subsidies or even claim it on my health benefits policy. It didn't really make any difference because it worked and I would always find the money for it. We did have to slow down for a while when he contracted a lung infection and had trouble breathing. But he recovered. As kids do.

Though the new year meant a new school, we were able to get Storm's aide from last year to look after him again. It made the transition into a new school, with a new teacher and new environment, so much easier. When he got through the first day without a hiccup, and with obvious enjoyment, I sighed with relief. I know I was always being over-protective, and unnecessarily so. It didn't matter who was his aide, they all took great care of him and he loved them all.

Both of us really looked forward to the four hours a week of respite from Catholic Care; Storm loved the fuss and I enjoyed the freedom.

With Joe buying the block we were still driving all over the countryside looking at different types of houses and building styles. I had decided that if and when I finally got a settlement I would consider moving to Bindoon, but of course before making any final commitment I would have to approach the school there to see if they would take Storm.

In March Storm began having strange little turns. Quite out of the blue, he would suddenly go red in the face and pull himself into a foetal position as if he had a tummy-ache. It only lasted seconds and when it was over he would relax and go quite floppy. Sometimes he would be tired and sleepy afterwards, and at other times it had no effect. He hadn't been ill, and there seemed to be no real reason why they started.

The first one he had that was noticed was at school. I was at home when the office rang to say he wasn't well. I raced to the school where his aide told me what had happened. After he relaxed they had laid him down on a mat and he went to sleep. When he woke up he seemed fine, but an hour later he had another turn. This time he wasn't tired afterwards and didn't want to rest. That was when they rang me. I took him home and fed him his lunch. He seemed fine.

Five days later he had another one. I had picked him up from school, brought him home and given him his lunch. He seemed a bit tired so I cuddled him on the couch and sat and watched television while he slept in my arms. Then all of a sudden he woke up with a shout and went into a foetal position for about 30 seconds, then went limp. After a while he went back to sleep.

I sat there with him in my arms, trying not to cry. What was wrong with him? He looked so scared when it happened, and my heart was racing. Eventually he seemed to be in a deep sleep so I put him in his bed, then rang and made an appointment with the doctor for the next day. I was so scared for Storm; I suspected he was having seizures of some kind, but I tried not to assume anything, better to wait until we had seen the doctor. To calm down, I made myself a coffee. Whisky would have been preferable.

We saw the doctor the next afternoon. He didn't think Storm was having fits, but gave me a referral to see a neurologist. Of course, it takes time to get an appointment with specialists so we had to wait a couple of weeks; fingers crossed that he wouldn't have any more attacks until then.

At the same time as all this was happening my ex-husband had put a settlement offer to my lawyer. It came right out of the blue and was actually reasonable, so I had to go into town to see the lawyer, all the time worrying about Storm and fearing that he might have had another turn. The meeting came to an end with the decision being made that I would accept the offer, all a bit of an anticlimax. It would have being more enjoyable if I hadn't been so worried about Storm. Also I was a bit sceptical about it, I would believe it when I had the cheque in the bank and it hadn't bounced—until then I would reserve my excitement.

We still had to wait to hear back from my ex-husband's lawyer, as I had terms added to the offer. It took a couple of weeks.

In the meantime, Storm had his appointment with the neurologist and it was decided he would need an EEG as soon as the hospital could fit him in. The doctor thought Storm was having epileptic seizures; I thought it odd that he didn't want to do a CAT scan or an MRI scan, but I'm not a doctor, just a mother with instincts. When I had my one seizure as a child I had to have an MRI scan and an EEG, but then I must have been classed as a normal child—a different ballgame, I guess.

This was the second time it was suggested Storm was epileptic. The first time it was disproved by a review of the old EEG results and he had only been briefly rolling his eyes; this time something really was happening and even I was aware that something was wrong. He definitely was having some kind of turn. I felt sick. I didn't want to have to cope with any more, and I didn't want anything more to happen to Storm. I know how I felt taking epilepsy drugs for years—they made me feel so tired, everything was a struggle, I didn't want Storm to have to experience the same.

And I bet this new thing has something to do with his inability to cry.

Storm got an appointment for April 30; so until then we had to sit tight, hope he didn't have any more seizures, and continue the therapy in Bullcreek.

On April 23 my lawyer rang to say my ex-husband had accepted my terms and I should be able to pick up the cheque in a couple of weeks. It was enough to buy a small house, furniture and a new car, debt free. It was all I desired and wanted for Storm and me, and we got it. I didn't want a large house—I have never felt safe in large houses. I ended up buying a small cedar house, it is very cottagey and I love it.

At the time, though, we didn't yet have the cheque and anyway my mind was more on Storm. On April 30 we went to the hospital for his EEG tests and he had to be sedated halfway through. I always found it hard to go to the hospital as it was always for tests and results that had always been bad news.

That same day I got a phone call from the lawyer saying the cheque had arrived for me to pick up. Strange how something that was so important to me, and had taken so many years to achieve, was not that exciting, even though it meant we could move on from the past.

The next day, May 1, I caught the train into town after dropping Storm off at school. I went to the lawyer's office and picked up the cheque, a piece of paper with numbers on it that would bring some freedom for Storm and me. I got the shakes and became tearful. Picking up the cheque was the moment it all sank in: I didn't have to fight any more for what I knew I deserved; the cheque was in my hand and our past life was finished with, done. I was a nervous wreck when I walked out of the lawyer's office, cheque in handbag, handbag clutched tightly under arm. I walked to the closest bank and deposited the cheque into my account. The teller asked me if I had won the lottery. I explained that no, this was better than Lotto, this cheque proved I believed in my worth. She would have thought I was just plain strange, but I didn't care.

Now I seriously had to decide where we were going to live. Should we stay in Perth, or should we go to Bindoon, 75km away? My heart screamed for the country, but I had to consider Storm and his needs—they were the most important issues to consider even though I knew he loved the country also.

I had to be sure the Bindoon school had facilities for him, so I made an appointment to see the principal. It transpired that the school already had a disabled child in one of its classes and there was an Education Support Unit already in place. The principal didn't see any problem with Storm attending next year and would go ahead and make the appropriate applications for an aide for him.

The inquiries I had made in Perth indicated that because Storm was considered to have multiple disabilities it would be hard to find a place for him in a standard school and he would end up attending a special school fulltime. That didn't sit right with my gut feeling of what was the best for him. So it seemed it would be possible for us to move to the country after all. The decision had been made and I needed to approach a real-estate agent to start looking for a home.

It wasn't until Storm actually started going to Bindoon Primary that I found out he wouldn't get all the help he needed, and it would take a few years to get it all. But in the meantime it was back to the usual things, school, physio—life goes on, stopping for nothing and no-one.

We had been back to the doctor for the EEG results, which showed abnormalities on the left side of Storm's brain. The doctor decided it was epilepsy and put him on anti-seizure drugs. I wanted more tests done, not just one, I wanted Storm to have a CAT or MRI scan but the doctor couldn't see any point. I wanted to know why this had happened all of a sudden. Weren't they even curious? Silly me.

In my heart of hearts, I know this has something to do with the loss of his ability to cry, and just maybe the stiffening of the muscles in his legs is also connected with the sudden onset of seizures.

So now we had to go through the process of introducing the anti-seizure drug into his system and having blood tests to make sure they got the levels right. I didn't want him taking a really strong dose because it would make him tired so life became more unenjoyable.

I don't want to do this, but I do want his seizures to stop.

Meanwhile, I was looking for a home. I didn't want to spend all the money on the house; I needed furniture and I needed another car. This one was starting to break down, it would get stuck in gear and you couldn't get it out again. One day I reversed into a driveway so I could turn around and it stuck in reverse. Nothing I did could get it out. I had to go and knock on the owners' door, explain what had happened and ask if I could use their phone to ring for a tow truck to come and pick it up. They were very obliging—even invited me in for a coffee and a chat while I waited for the tow truck. The car had to go, it was embarrassing me.

Now when we went to Bindoon I would be looking at houses. But I couldn't find any in my price range and those I did look at weren't even nice houses, some weren't even finished off. I'm not a miracle-maker—I had intended to do up whatever house I eventually bought, but reconstruction was not on my agenda. Because of the prices I made inquiries about borrowing some money, but being on the pension meant I couldn't borrow much. It was a bit disheartening and I was beginning to think maybe we weren't meant to move to Bindoon after all.

My psychic friend Lynn told me she could "see" a house with a tin roof with different angles and there were "criss-crosses" at the front of the house. We couldn't figure out what criss-crosses at the front meant. I didn't really think much about it and then a couple of weekends later Joe told me the real-estate agent that sold him his block had told him of a house for sale nearby, so he arranged for me to look at it. I could hardly believe it when we drove up to the house—it had a multi-angled tin roof and criss-cross railing between the veranda posts. It was rented at the time but the people didn't mind us looking it over.

The house was small and the walls were covered with wallpaper and heavy curtains, it needed a lot of work and the patio out the back needed replacing. But I loved it. Joe and I talked it over and the next weekend I got my brother and sister to have a look at it, to see what they thought. We all agreed it would be a fairly good buy if I could get it at a reasonable price. It was six weeks since I had picked up the settlement cheque.

On Monday June 15 I drove to Bindoon to see the real-estate agent. I offered $25,000 less than the advertised price. I said the house would need a lot of work and it was a cash offer and also my first and final offer (the cheek of me, pure bluff). The agent said she would put the offer to the owners, but was quite sure they would reject it. Well, bugger me, that same day I got a phone call and they had accepted my offer. I was ecstatic, we were going to be owners of a house, mortgage-free and all ours. Lynn had been right, it was like the house was waiting for us.

I decided to continue renting it out until the end of the year, so I was also getting rent money also, not bad. Settlement went through in July. I was now a home-owner with a sense of security that I hadn't felt since we left the farm. At least now, whatever happened in our lives, Storm and I had the security of our home.

I couldn't do any work on the house until the end of the year, which was a bit of a bummer, but I did get a fence put up around three sides of about an acre of land surrounding the house and garden, linking up with the existing rail fence along the front of the house. I decided to leave the other four acres to the kangaroos and other wildlife. The man I hired to do the fencing turned out to be from Perenjori, where I grew up, and his parents had a farm not far from my parents' farm. It's a small world.

1996 Living with parents eating his breakfast by himself

1996 doing his physio at bullcreek

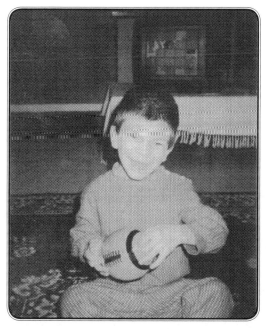

1997 a very happy chap

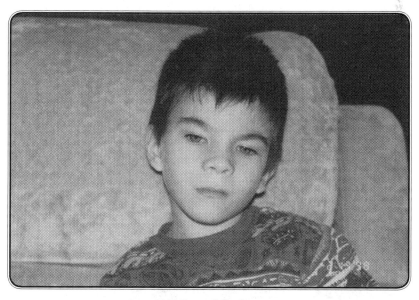

1998 Love this photo

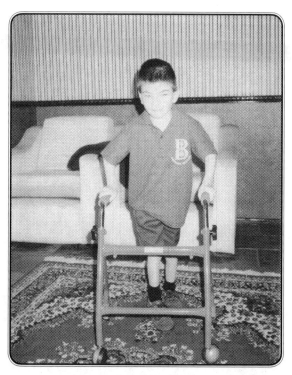

1999 First day at bindoon school

August 1999 with Temily

Christmas 1999

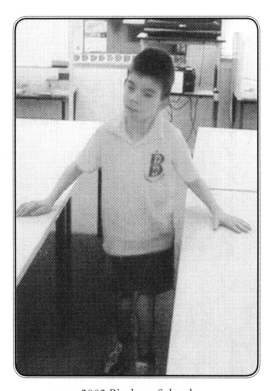

2002 Bindoon School

2003 at school playing with shaving cream

december 2004 at home with Jet

This should have been a happy time. The court case was over, I had bought a house and we would be settling into a stable life. But I felt battle-weary. It has taken three years, this battle for a bit of stability. Hurtful words had been uttered against me, against Storm, words that once said can't be forgotten. I had been putting aside the pain and battling on in my determination to make Storm's life as good as I could possibly make it. It had put me in places I didn't want to be, but it had made me strong and it was all worthwhile for all the love Storm returned.

I do not think, though, that this is the end of our battles.

The Bindoon principal had organised a meeting with all the parents of the children who would be in Storm's class, and I was to bring him along to the meeting, introduce him and talk to them about him. I had never heard of this being done before and I wasn't sure what it was supposed to achieve—you can bet none of the mothers of the "normal" children were having to do what I was doing. The unknown creates fear in people and Storm was an unknown factor to them. So Storm's aide at his school in Perth generously offered to come to the meeting and talk about him.

On the day of the meeting Storm and I met the aide at the General Store and we went to the school together. I was very nervous about standing up in front of a crowd of parents and speaking, but I did. I spoke about Storm's disability, then his aide got up and spoke about how she worked with him and how he interacted with other children. None of the parents had any questions to ask and thankfully Storm sat quietly on my lap all the way through the meeting, so at least they didn't think he was a disruptive child. One woman stood up and welcomed us to Bindoon. I have never forgotten that moment.

With the speeches done, I could breathe again—I had been practically holding my breath the whole time. I had images of parents not being keen for Storm to be in their child's class. What was I going to do if that happened? Again, these were my fears, not Storm's—I don't believe he ever thought he wouldn't be liked or loved.

It turned out he was only going to be at Bindoon Primary for two days a week. The principal said that was the only aide time she could get for him. I didn't understand that, since he had an aide with him for five half-days in Perth, but I thought it best not to rock the boat, at least not for his first year in Bindoon.

Because Storm and I were still living in Perth we were still getting visits from Disability Services' occupational therapist etcetera. I had spoken to them about our move, and it was then I found out the assistance we had been getting didn't extend as far as Bindoon. Not to worry, I thought, it would be the same as when we were on the farm—we would get the country assistance. I was wrong. Bindoon was beginning to look like a kind of No-Man's Land, not considered country and not considered city, so no assistance. Had a made a big mistake? But Storm loved the country. He was so much happier on our days in Bindoon with Joe, and I had to hold on to that.

One of his therapists suggested I try to get him into a special school in Perth on the days he wasn't at the Bindoon school, to get him the extra help he needed. She wasn't allowed to recommend a school, so she suggested a few to look at. I settled on one that had a multiple sensory room and a heated pool for hydrotherapy and a Disability Services office on site that could provide physio for Storm. I didn't mind that it meant a day in Perth each week, because I could make it my shopping day and catch up with friends.

I'm very good at worrying: Will the kids treat Storm alright or will they be mean to him? I do this every year and every year Storm is fine, more than fine, the kids play with him and he is liked. But I have to worry because I'm his mum and I can.

My car had broken down, again, the gearbox, again. Joe had spent time on it to get it going, again, but it was time for it to be retired. Eventually I bought a new car and it served us well.

Life was OK. Storm hadn't had a seizure for quite a while, and was loving school. I'd bought a house, and a car, and now my sister had asked me if I would like to go to Bali for a week with her and two other ladies and I didn't have to pay the airfare, just the cost of the hotel in Bali. Fantastic—the last time I had travelled was the year before Storm was born. Someone pinch me quick, this was sooo good.

Mum and Dad were more than happy to look after Storm, so two days before we flew out I drove to Dunsborough and dropped him off, then drove back to Perth the next day. This would be the longest I had been away from Storm, ever.

We flew to Bali the next day. I think Toni could quite easily have pushed me out the emergency door. I wouldn't have blamed her. I don't like flying at the best of times and being so far away from Storm, phew, not good! Once we arrived I was fine and we had a nice holiday, but it was good to get home again.

The day after we got back I drove to Dunsborough to fetch Storm. No-one heard me arrive, and I found Storm in his stroller out near the patio where Mum was watering some plants. I walked up to him quietly and said: "Hello, Stormy." Well, he got that excited. I picked him up and he started babbling. That was when Mum turned around to see what he was so excited about. Storm cuddled and chatted away; his awareness of what was going on around him was growing and growing.

I have always treated Storm as a "normal" child, never let his disabilities be an excuse for bad behaviour and never let him get away with bad behaviour because he is considered disabled—to me he is my normal son.

Not long after we got back to Perth another incident occurred to show me there are people who could see past the differences in Storm. Rae and I had decided to have lunch at the local pub. Storm came with us and we chose bench seats so he could sit next to me without falling off a chair. He sat there quietly through lunch, now and then banging his hand on the table, and we had finished eating and were just chatting when a waiter came up out of nowhere with an ice-cream-sundae-with-the-works for Storm.

It was a reminder for me that Storm was not always seen for his disability, that people see what is on the inside.

The September school holidays arrived, and so no physio in Bullcreek. We spent quite a lot of time in Bindoon. Rae's sister Marteena had moved to Bindoon with her husband and kids, they had opened a video store there, so I visited her whenever I was up. It was good to know that when we moved to Bindoon next year there would be someone else there who I knew.

Storm really took to Marteena—and her magic hands. No one, and I mean no one, gives massages like Marteena, they are the best. At the start of a massage Storm would be like a twisted-up old sandshoe and by the time she had finished he was stretched out and relaxed. He had also learnt on his own to kiss people, not just anyone—he was not free and easy with his kisses—but he would now and then reach out and kiss Marteena. You knew he really liked you if you got a kiss—and a kiss on the lips, well, you were just plain special.

Storm came down with colds and a phlegmy chest. I put phone books under his bed legs to raise it so he wouldn't cough all night, it helped a bit. But as the holidays progressed his illness worsened. The doctor prescribed stronger antibiotics. Storm finished those but didn't seem to be any better and I was getting really concerned, so back we went again to the doctor. The verdict was that we should continue with more antibiotics. The doctor believed Storm had an infection somewhere in his body but he didn't know where, so he organised blood and urine tests. The next step would be to start X-raying to pinpoint the infection, but the last lot of antibiotics did the trick and he finally got better. Maybe the threat of X-rays sent the infection packing after two weeks. Then he developed and fought off a kidney infection. At least he hadn't had any more seizures.

The lady who came to the house and looked after Storm for the four-hours-a-week respite was a blessing throughout his illness. She would sit with him and spoil him, and of course I got to have a much-needed break—looking after sick children can suck the life out of you no matter how much you adore them.

Storm needed time to build up his strength and he always perked up when we went to Bindoon for the weekends. Joe was keen on old pubs, so if he wasn't working on his house we would drive all over the countryside checking them out. Storm would sit up at the bar on my lap, nibbling on chips and taking in the atmosphere. By the end of October he was a lot better and back at school, so I could go shopping for furniture for the house. To start with we needed a kitchen table and chairs, fridge and washing machine.

Christmas came around again and we spent it with my parents in Dunsborough, then drove back to Perth. The tenants had moved out of the Bindoon house before Christmas and I was eager to work on it, so the day after we got back from Dunsborough we went to Bindoon and while Storm played in the kitchen I pulled the wallpaper off the laundry walls. I really wanted to be outside working on the garden, but I had to concentrate on the laundry because I wanted to get it painted before the washing machine was put in. At least the garden was all on reticulation so I didn't have to worry about watering it.

Storm, Joe and I spent New Year's Eve at a friend of Joe's on the coast, a nice and relaxing way to ring in the New Year.

Chapter Six

1999

S ix days into the new year, still living in Perth, I was feeding Storm his breakfast when I noticed an unusual rash on his arm, so I rang a doctor nearby and got in within an hour. The doctor took one look at the rash, made an immediate phone call and then told me I must take Storm straight to the hospital, that they would be waiting for us. Then it clicked, so I asked the doctor if they thought it was the meningitis rash, he said they were concerned that it could be and weren't taking any chances.

So I put Storm in the car and raced to the hospital. I carried him into emergency and we were taken straight through to a bed in the emergency ward. The rash was examined, then a drip was put in his hand and strong antibiotics were put into the drip. It was all done with no fuss, everyone was very calm, just moving briskly, so though I had noticed the rash had grown I didn't panic; they had taken blood samples but they hadn't waited for the results and Storm was already on strong antibiotics.

I was told I would need strong antibiotics myself, just in case, and so would anyone else who had been in close contact with Storm recently, which was Joe and my sister, Toni. Getting antibiotics to Joe was not a problem, but getting them to Toni might be because she had just flown back to work on the mine.

Storm was moved up to a room of his own in the children's ward and I had started taking the antibiotics. In the end Toni and Joe didn't need any antibiotics because the rash turned out not to be meningococcal but another type of virus. Whew!! Talk about drama. Storm got better, the rash disappeared and he was free to go home a day or so later. What a humdinger way to start the year.

Two days after getting home from hospital, Storm had a really bad attack. It was eight o'clock at night, he had been in bed asleep for at least an hour, I was watching television and when a commercial came on I went to check on him and found him tossing and turning. I picked him up and he went limp in my arms. I raced him next door to my neighbour, who was a nurse, but she wasn't home so I laid him in the back of the car and raced him to the hospital. The triage nurse looked him over and then he was given a bed in emergency. But of course by then he was coming to and seemed fine; they couldn't find anything wrong with him so we eventually went home. Obviously he had had an epileptic seizure, though it was different from any of this other attacks and a lot worse. I had a restless night, checking on him frequently to make sure he hadn't had another attack, and next day he was fine, just as if nothing had happened.

We were due to move to Bindoon in four days, and I was so busy getting organised I didn't have time to dwell too much on this new development, and the reality was there was nothing I could do about it.

The removalist arrived at 7am on Moving Day and I already had Storm fed and changed. It took just half an hour to load the truck and by the time we had driven to Bindoon and unloaded it was still only 10 o'clock. The moving men carried everything in for me, all I had to do was show them were to put it, well worth the cost. I spent the rest of the day unpacking and settling in, and by nightfall it was all done. We had made the big move without a hitch; now was the beginning of a new chapter in our lives and I walked around the house and garden that evening picturing all the changes I was going to make.

While out the back I saw my neighbour, Jan, out in the summer heat, digging trenches. I assumed they were for the foundations for her house. Jan was also raising her two children on her own, plus taking on the task of building there house herself, and at that time they were living in a caravan parked next to the shed. I'd gone over and introduced myself before we moved in; it turned out she had grown up and lived in the country town not far from where I had lived while I was married. Small world.

The morning after Moving Day, while Storm was still sleeping, I did a bit of pottering around the garden. Joe and I had pulled down the old back patio and Joe was going to build a new one. The area was a bit of a mess, so I cleaned it up a bit. Then after getting Storm fed and organised we went and visited Marteena and her new baby daughter, Temily. While we were there Storm had another attack so I took him home and put him on the couch where he went to sleep. He woke after an hour and seemed to be all right so later on we went out to visit Joe's friends. There he had another attack so we came home again but this time he didn't want to sleep and just played in the lounge room with his toys. Joe turned up in the afternoon to work on the patio and as he was leaving, a couple of hours later, Storm had another attack. I laid him on the couch and sat with him until he went to sleep. It was the greatest number of attacks I had ever seen him have in one day and I was very concerned. Had I made a terrible mistake moving to Bindoon? He was getting worse, and now we were a lot further from the hospital; it would take at least an hour to get there.

There was no explanation as to why he suddenly started having seizures. Scar tissue on the brain, they say. Well, how did it get there, and why now?

It was a turning point in Storm's life, a decline in his life physically. Watching him having his seizures, seeing him so scared and not being able to do anything but hold him until they were over, seeing his physical abilities dissipate instead of improving was just so bloody awful and made my fears for his future so much more real.

We had an appointment with a paediatrician the next day, so perhaps we would get some answers. That night Storm didn't sleep until 2am, and I couldn't sleep if he was awake, I was so in tune with him. It was a struggle to get to the doctor's appointment in Perth on time. The paediatrician wasn't sure what was going on, so he organised for Storm to have another EEG. By the next day Storm had had three more attacks and was looking quite drained. He had had six attacks in two days and not a lot of sleep. But his next appointment was 11 days away, so we would have to play the waiting game.

In the meantime Joe and I worked on the patio. One morning Joe was measuring the patio roof to work out how much tin we would need and got a nasty electric shock from the gutter. We switched off the main power and I rang a local electrician who turned up quickly and found there definitely was electricity running through the gutter but he couldn't see how or why. He thought we might have to take part of the roof off the house so that he could have a look at the wiring. All I could see was dollar signs with wings, so while Joe and the electrician were talking I snuck inside the house and said, quietly: "Please, God, tell me where the problem is." Instantly I heard in my head, "security lights", so feeling quite silly I went outside and asked the electrician if he could test the security lights at the front of the house to humour me. And bugger me that was what was causing the gutter to be alive. The sparky fixed the problem and left, and I snuck back into the house and said: "Thank you, God." The truth is, when I asked I didn't really think I would get an answer.

Storm was having more attacks every couple of days, and finally the day arrived for his EEG tests at the hospital in Perth. He was very good about having a whole lot of wires attached to his head, and I had to try to keep him as still as possible while they ran the tests. Then the lady running the tests came in told him to close his eyes and go to sleep. Yeah, right. I couldn't help laughing: as if that was going to happen. Eventually they realised he wasn't just going to go to sleep because they told him to, and they gave him a sedative. The look on his face when the sedative started to take effect! Like "I know you have done something to me, but

I don't know what." Eventually he went to sleep and they ran the rest of the tests. I wouldn't get any results until we had our appointment with the paediatrician.

February 4 was Storm's first day at the special school in Perth and we had to get up early to be there on time. I spent the day with him so they could ask me any questions about him. He had a great day and especially enjoyed the multiple sensory room, a dark room with many different switches that operated all sorts of lights and sounds. After school we drove to Bullcreek for three hours of physio and then we drove home. He was asleep fairly early that night and so was I; it had been a very long day.

The next day Joe and I ended our relationship, 20 days after moving to Bindoon. It was a bit of a bugger that he hadn't finished the paving or the patio, but I had watched him doing the paving and reckoned I could finish it myself, and I finished the shade house with help from my neighbour. One thing I am good at is recognising when a relationship is over, and I'm very good at moving on. I like things cut and dried. No lingering, that just hurts each other. Storm was really going to miss Joe because they really had a strong bond going. But it really was for the best, Storm really needed all my attention even more now. And he still got to see Joe now and then.

February 8, Storm's first day at Bindoon Primary School. Again I spent the day with him so his new aide could ask me questions about him. Amazingly, I knew her. Her name was Judy Capor, she had lived in the same town as I did when I was married and had looked after Storm when he went to daycare sometimes while I went shopping. She and her husband had sold up and moved to Bindoon before us and I didn't know. I couldn't have been happier.

The Bindoon school had an Ed Support Unit for children who needed extra help, so Storm would be spending half the time in the ESU and the other half in the normal class. For a week or two it would be only half a day at a time, but after that it would be whole days.

On the first day the ESU teacher brought in six 10-week-old white rabbits, arranged the children in a circle and then put the rabbits in the middle. The children got to hold them, and they gave one to Storm. That rabbit got the short straw; Storm was a bit rough with it, he gave its ears a really good feel, bending them this way and that, and roughed up its fur. It couldn't get away from him fast enough. When he let it go and it moved back into the circle with the rest of the rabbits I could still pick it out from the bunch; its fur was facing every which way. It was a big day for that rabbit. It was also a big day for Storm, and he loved it.

The next day Storm went off to school I spent the day pacing around unable to concentrate on anything—and it wasn't like it was his very first day in school; it was his third year. I did get better as time went on, I distracted myself visiting people and pottering in the garden, but it was going to take some adjusting when he would be going off for the whole day, the last two years of school had only been half days.

He had settled well into both new schools. On the day he went to the special school in Perth we would drive to Bullcreek afterwards for his usual physio, then drive back to Bindoon. We were both pooped at the end of those days and in bed early that night. At weekends I would put him in his stroller with some toys and we would go outside. He would sit there listening to the wind in the trees and the birds singing, and now and then he would laugh for no other reason than he was happy.

In the end I knew that settling in Bindoon had been the right move. The only downside was that in this small town Storm was the only disabled child so I was conscious of people looking at us. I'm a behind-the-scenes person, I like to blend in. Storm didn't care; he was so sure of himself and happy with who he was and eventually everyone was so used to us we were just another mum with her child.

Toni told me about another iridologist who had impressed her, so I made an appointment for both Storm and me. He said the whole left side of Storm's brain was damaged (that's where the dent had been) and the damage was affecting his immune system and weakening his heart. He also said I needed to be strong because Storm didn't have a long life to live. Then he looked into my eyes and told me I had a hormonal problem. He also said I didn't eat enough (*I'm living on a pension and paying for all Storm's treatments, of course I don't eat much*), and prescribed some tablets for both of us.

Less than two weeks later we had the results from Storm's EEG. The paediatrician told me they showed a lot of abnormalities in the brain, especially on the left side (exactly what the iridologist had said), and there was a high risk of him having seizures. He fobbed off my urging for a CAT or MRI scan to see if anything else would show up, but for some reason decided that Storm should have a sweat test for cystic fibrosis. I told him I didn't want Storm medicated too heavily, because I knew it would make him very lethargic and I didn't want that for him, he had to be able to enjoy his life and we would deal with the seizures.

A year or two after Storm and I left the farm I went back to attend a neighbour's funeral. The man had led a healthy life, never drank or smoked, but out of the blue started having epileptic seizures. After many tests they found an inoperable tumour that ended up killing him. They found the problem because they did the tests, which they wouldn't do for Storm. Would tests have revealed that Storm had the same problem? We will never know. When I nagged doctors about why they wouldn't do more tests, some replies were why would I want know, what difference would it make? Um, doesn't it make a difference when a cancer patient finds out they have cancer? Change the things you can and accept the things you can't.

Back into school life, and I decided I wouldn't keep pushing Storm so much. The seizures were really affecting him and he was having a lot more of them. I felt that if I pushed him too much he would get really ill again, so I cancelled physio in Bullcreek—he was supposed to be getting physio at the special school once a week anyway. The tests for cystic fibrosis came back negative. He had tests also for muscular dystrophy, because he had trouble absorbing fat, and those results proved negative, too. So he actually did have some tests, just none on his head other than the EEG and CAT scan. A couple of days later he had four attacks in one day. They were coming in cycles. About every seven weeks he would have two or more a day for a couple of days, then they would stop for weeks, then start again. I had been told they weren't painful, but he certainly looked like he was in pain. Sometimes he would go bright red and break out in a sweat.

When he had the days of attacks I would put a mattress in the lounge room and sit with him for the duration. I would hold him until they were over, then watch over him while he slept. It took a while to adjust to sitting in one room for days at a time, especially when I was itching to get outside and work in the garden or pull wallpaper off the walls. I couldn't take the seizures away but I could at least sit with Storm while he slept so he never felt alone.

It took him a couple of days to regain his strength after each cycle, but then he was back at school and it was like it never happened—until the next time.

Seizures aside, we were really beginning to love living in Bindoon. Storm loved being outside, listening to all the birds and the wind in the trees, being in his swing while I worked close by in the garden. Even though he did have his noisy days, he was a lot quieter and calmer than when we were in Perth.

Summer in Bindoon is hot, but thankfully the house was airconditioned. Often it was too hot to work in the garden during the day, so we spent the day indoors and in the evenings when Storm had gone to bed I would work in the garden until it got dark or I was chased inside by the mosquitoes. At times the airconditioner would run for days non-stop.

Storm was not so good with really cold nights, so I would have to organise some form of heating for winter, because the house had none.

When the April school holidays arrived, Storm and I drove down to my parents' place in Dunsborough—and what a smooth drive it was in the new car, no more breaking down on the side of the road. I raided Mum's garden, taking cuttings and digging up plants that I wanted to try in Bindoon. Halfway through our stay my brother's children arrived for a couple of days with their grandparents. They kept us entertained.

Storm and I were settling into our quiet life in Bindoon, going to Perth only once a week for his day at the special school. I also made that my shopping day, and catch up with my sister if she was down from work and Rae if she wasn't busy. No more rushing around unless I chose to, no more court hearings or meetings with lawyers. Six hours a day to myself when Storm was at school in Bindoon. Sometimes I would get so much done; at other times I spent the whole time relaxing, reading a book.

Storm was a lot happier since I put him on the tablets from the iridologist. He was going to sleep a lot earlier, and though it hadn't stopped him from having his attacks I guess you can't have everything. I was a lot happier, too. I had made friends in Bindoon and Storm really loved it there.

May arrived and we were heading for our first winter in Bindoon. I love winter, so I was busy outside raking up and burning all the gum leaves that had fallen in the summer and harboured kangaroo ticks. Ghastly things, I hated them. In all the years I have on the farm as a child and then as a wife I never saw a kangaroo tick, but Bindoon was loaded with them. Joe and I found some on Storm's legs not long after we moved there. We didn't know how to kill them. We hit them with fly spray but that didn't work. Someone said they breathe through their bums, so we tried putting Vaseline on them. That killed them, all right, but you still had to pull them out, they must leave poison in the skin as the bite got so itchy and it was hard to get Storm to stop scratching his bites. The first time I got one on me I freaked. I went over to my neighbour, Jan, to get her to remove it. Her daughter Emily was hand-rearing a chicken; she showed the chicken the tick and it just pecked it off. Revolting things, I rake my yard every year and every year I get fewer of them, thank God.

Storm's cycle of attacks was continuing, and because of that I realised I would never be able to get a fulltime job. No matter, I would just have to make do with the pension, which we were lucky to get. So when Storm wasn't ill I worked on the house and gardens. I borrowed Jan's electric sander, took off the internal doors, sanded off the glossy blue paint off and varnished them to match the doorframes. It was a big job, but luckily it's a small house, so not so many doors.

I finished renovating the inside of the house at the end of 2003. I will never finish working on the garden, though; if I did it would be time to leave.

We had another encounter with the iridologist. Storm had got ill again, he was grizzly and couldn't sleep at night. At first I thought it was just a cold but he didn't get better so I ended up taking him to our GP in Perth. After checking Storm out he said he had a viral infection, prescribed penicillin and suggested maybe we should stay in Perth for a couple of hours to make sure he didn't get any worse. So I thought of seeing the iridologist, and managed to get in.

The iridologist doesn't like you to tell him anything, he tells you how you are feeling and what is wrong. He looked in Storm's eyes and said Storm had a viral infection situated right between his eyes—how's that? Then he gave me some herbal drops for Storm and we drove home. On the way I wondered whether to give Storm the drops or the penicillin that the doctor had prescribed. He had taken so many antibiotics in his short life I was worried he would be come immune to them. In the end I decided to give him the drops and if he didn't improve within a day I would start on the penicillin. After a couple of days of taking the drops he was well, back to sleeping and back at school.

In June my parents came to visit for a day and see the house for the first time. They liked the house and Mum and I wandered around the garden planning what I would transplant and what I would put where. Meanwhile, Dad installed a kitchen cabinet he had made for me. He had also made me a wooden chest to put in the lounge room for all Storm's toys. About a year earlier Dad had decided that since most of their gardens were finished he would turn his hand to making furniture. Despite having had no training in working with wood, he just decided to give it a go and he turned out to be seriously good at it. Toni, Rod and I all love having furniture he has made, a bit of him that will remain long after he has gone. There seems to be no limit to what he can make. Almost every room in my house has furniture by him, and it is better made and better quality than you buy in any furniture shop.

The seven weeks must have passed again, because Storm had more attacks—10 of them this time, over six days. I confess that when he first started having his attacks I was impatient, I felt that they restricted me from being able to do the things I was in a rush to do. But by now I was a seasoned sitter, no longer impatient to be anywhere else but with Storm, knowing there would be other days for me to do those other things. So for the days he had his attacks I sat in the lounge room with him and found things to do there, reading, crotcheting, but Storm always knowing I was close by. I decided to do a correspondence course in iridology, so when he had his attacks I would do my assignments.

The next couple of months were quite ordinary. I hadn't fully appreciated how wonderful ordinary life is, it's to be admired and cherished. Storm went to school, I worked on the house and gardens, visited friends, visited my parents in Dunsborough in the July school holidays, helped my neighbour with her house now and then, enjoyed the peacefulness, the birds flitting through the garden, the simple things in life that we surely take for granted.

Storm had become a lot quieter and preferred to spend as much time as possible outside, he smiled a lot more and he laughed like I had never heard him laugh. And I was getting kisses on the lips. I could never figure out how he knew where my lips were on my face; he never searched with his hands, just leaned over and kissed me on the lips.

I'm past trying to figure out how Storm does the things he does, I just love what he does and his kisses make me feel privileged, like I'm one of the chosen ones, the honoured.

Storm and I loved our new home. It's really a cottage with french doors off the lounge room. Rooms in bright colours. I have a child who can't see, but I can't live without colour, so I have it everywhere. I planted climbing wisteria along the front verandah and when they flower they are awesome. The house is made out of cedar, very country, very me. I had also got back into baking, cakes and biscuits, which I love to do. I would make them for Storm and me, for our neighbour and friends. Storm loves food, especially sweets, lemon meringues, apple pie etc.

Marteena's youngest daughter, Temily, was about nine months now. I looked after her a few times and on one occasion I wanted to work in the back garden so I put Storm, who was nearly six, and Temily in a play-pen on the back verandah with a whole heap of toys to play with. They sat together playing happily. Temily would babble away to Storm and Storm would laugh so Temily would also laugh; it was as if they had their own language going on. It was very entertaining, so I stopped what I was doing and just listened to them chatting back and forth.

Storm came home from school with something for me for Mothers Day. Through the years, I had avoided any kind of fuss on that day—when my first Mothers Day arrived we had just found out that Storm was blind and I was devastated. My husband had tried to make it better by spoiling me with presents, but it was still a sad day for me, and since then I had not been one for celebrating it. But now, all the other kids at school wanted to do something for their mothers, so this year Storm came home with a card for me. His aides always went to a lot of effort to make sure he had something to bring home for me. *They were the best, and I am truly grateful for their presence in my life.* It took me seven years to make the decision that I was going to enjoy Mothers Day. Though our lives hadn't turn out like I'd hoped, I was still a mother with a great son. I regret it took me all those years to realise how precious it is to be able to celebrate being a mother— and not just on a designated day chosen by someone I don't know.

Our first winter in Bindoon was a bloody cold one. If Toni hadn't given us an electric heater that she no longer used we would have frozen. The previous owner had removed the wood heater before putting the house on the market, so saving for a wood heater was going to be my first priority. It seemed the sensible choice as we had five acres of trees, including a few dead jarrah trees that would make great firewood, and I was not new to chopping wood—I did it on the farm. it was also a cheap way of heating the house, but unfortunately we would have to survive the first winter huddled near the electric heater. Storm could either feel or see the glow from the heater, as he would turn himself and lean over towards it. He never reached out to touch it when it was on. But I watched him like a hawk in case he did.

Days cruised along nicely until Storm's attacks started again. By the end of the econd day he had had three attacks and was exhausted even though he had slept after each one. The next day blood vessels in one eye burst. And on the fourth day he was squealing in pain and reached out to grab me when an attack hit. I was devastated, the doctors had told me the seizures did not hurt him. But it was clear he was hurting, and scared. In five days he had 11 attacks and was so worn out he couldn't sit up independently for days. He had his seventh birthday five days after the last attack and was still not able to sit up on his own. Physically he was broken, but emotionally he seemed calm. His body had failed him but that was not going to stop him from enjoying his birthday. He had his traditional chocolate birthday cake covered in freckle lollies. I prayed we still had a few more years together.

Three days after his birthday he was ill again. It was different this time. When I checked on him during the night he was soaked in sweat and hot with fever. I stripped the blankets off his bed and he didn't wake up when I moved him to change the sheets, but eventually his temperature went down. In the morning his eyes were swollen so I made an appointment with our doctor in Perth. When we went into the doctor's room Storm started shouting in pain. His ears turned out to be a little inflamed, so in the hope that was the reason for his pain and why his eyes were swollen, he was put on antibiotics and Panadol for 24 hours. His eyes were still swollen the next morning and he was still hurting, but finally the antibiotics kicked in and the next day he was much better. He certainly had had a rough week or two, and it was hell watching him in so much pain.

The rest of year passed much like the beginning. When Storm had attacks I was with him and when he was well enough he went back to school and I continued working on the house and gardens. We had got into a routine and there were chores I did when Storm was at school, such as vacuuming the house. For some reason Storm had decided he didn't like the sound of the vacuum cleaner, though it had never bothered him before. When he was home I put him in a portable cot out in the garden with me.

Storm needed so much of my attention I never did anything without having to stop to make sure he didn't want food or a drink or need changing (we had tried to toilet-train him but it never really happened). I did chores when he was asleep or at school—everything was always shipshape in case he got ill and I would have to stop and sit with him.

When Storm goes to bed and all my chores for the night are done, that is my chill-out time. Thankfully he is quite happy in his bed at night, he chats and plays until he goes to sleep and I check on him frequently when the commercials are on TV. He enjoys going to bed as much as I enjoy the time to myself; he must get very tired sitting in his wheelchair at school. Even though all his life I have had to feed him, bathe him, I have been doing it for so long that I don't even notice how long it takes me and I enjoy his company. But he does know how to press my buttons; he is not all that different from average children, he still plays up.

At that time the doctors had put Storm's intellectual and physical development at just six months. I had lost belief in most of what they told me, they could only measure his ability on how he presented himself to them, and they certainly weren't going to believe anything I said. Over the years I learnt without doubt that he had a great capacity for understanding, just an inability to express it in ways that people who didn't spend a lot of time with him could understand.

I have treated Storm as a child who understands everything. I'm not in denial, I know he has disabilities, he can't talk, or walk independently, he has limited fine motor skills, his physical disabilities restrict his ability to show that he understands, so he is considered mentally disabled by the medical profession, but I know differently and so do my friends and family along with the people who work closely with him. He has a very expressive face, that lets you know he understands.

Many years ago during one of my many conversations with God I told Him my one wish was that if there was only one word that Storm would ever be able to say, "mum" was the word I would like to hear from him. I can't remember the exact day he first said it—you would think I could, but I can't—but I loved it whenever he said it. Some days he would just repeat it over and over because he had been a bit of a bugger and he knew that word would soften his mother's heart. Some nights he would lie in bed saying mum, mum, mum over and over in a deep voice, then change and say it over and over in a high-pitched voice. I would sit in the lounge room giggling, what a card!

Storm also is a bit of a womaniser. He loves women, loves to give them hugs and kisses. Many of the therapists have said that it is inappropriate behaviour for him to be affectionate to his aides. Well, no offence, but stuff them. Storm is blind and touch is everything to him, what an awful world it would be without touch and affection in it. I am amazed that he doesn't often show he is frustrated—and he must get frustrated at times, especially when he is treated as a baby by people who don't know him.

An amazing year had come to an end; a happier year even though Storm had had quite a few seizures.

Chapter Seven

2000

A week or so into Y2K we had an appointment with a doctor from Disability Services. What a total waste of time. Even though this doctor worked with the disabled, our treatment was the same as from some other doctors—my concerns for Storm were duly noted, then ignored. It was incredibly frustrating and I feel I failed Storm because I couldn't get anyone to listen to me. When I asked doctors to do tests and they felt there was no reason you would think that the tests were going to cost them personally. God forbid that they listen to a mother who spends so much time with her child that she actually might know something.

Children like Storm know more about unconditional love than we will ever hope to, they live in the moment, they don't need more of anything to be happy, while we "normals" are always chasing the "thing" that will make us happy. I learnt more from Storm than from anyone or anything else about what is important in life. He had every reason to be a sad, unhappy child, a child judged, ignored and thought less important, but despite all this he chose to be happy, joyful and always loving.

We had acquired a small dog on loan from Marteena. Children (I'm assuming it was children) were prowling around the house now and then but this came to an end when Simba the dog came to visit. He barked his lungs out at people when they passed the house—mind you, he would be in his kennel barking, so not the bravest dog in the world, but he achieved the effect I was looking for and we had no more trouble while he was with us.

Simba was good with Storm. If Storm was outside in his stroller while I worked in the garden, Simba would sit by him the whole time and at other times when Storm was in the lounge room playing, Simba would sit outside the lounge room windows. I have never seen a dog so devoted to a child that he has not grown up with—Simba would let Storm be as rough as he liked with him. And Storm could get quite rough with animals— once he nearly squeezed the life out of a child's pet hamster. The hamster survived—just—and Storm was left with a large handful of fur.

My neighbour at the time had a rather large, elderly rottweiler, Shelby, another animal devoted to Storm. When Jan went off to Perth, you could guarantee that within a couple of minutes Shelby would wander over to our house. If we were inside, she would walk around the house until she had figured out which room Storm was in then she would sit there, along with Simba, until Jan came home. If anyone drove up to the house or past it, Shelby also would bark at them and if we went outside, she would be right there, wherever Storm was.

On some occasions I would go for a walk and Jan would look after Storm and sometimes I would take Simba with me. Jan's younger daughter,

Emily, once dug out a little hole in a pile of sand that had been brought in for the cement; she sat Storm in it and covered his lap in sand. Storm loved it and was running his hands through the sand. When we got back from our walk, Simba saw Storm in the sand and he raced over and was trying to dig him out and he barked at Emily—he must have thought Storm was in trouble and needed digging out. Storm didn't know what all the fuss was about, but Simba was devoted.

It was still school holidays, always good since Storm and I got to sleep in. Sometimes, when I really wanted to sleep in, I would put him into bed with me with some toys to play with. I would make a coffee and jump back into bed, and while I was enjoying my coffee, I would watch Storm move his leg under the sheets, "looking" for me. It always made me laugh.

I wasn't pushing him to develop physically as much as before, and I had cut back on his physiotherapies in Perth. The seizures really exhausted him so I wasn't keen to make him do lots of exercises. It was more important that he was happy and as healthy as possible. It didn't mean I stopped expecting him to make progress, I just wasn't so pushy about it. He was still learning to walk independently with his frame, and I was supposed to make him walk to the car, etc. But I carried him around the house. He never got too heavy for me to carry him, and that was when I got to hug him and feel close to him.

I still took him to the iridologist and other alternative therapies to help improve his health. I never gave up trying to help him, but always knowing that it really was out of my hands. It was so hard—loving him like I have loved no other, while knowing he was very slowly deteriorating.

I know I can't change the outcome, I have tried everything I can, left no rock unturned, so now all I can do is accept that this is it, there is no more to be done—just to love him and enjoy every moment with him and continue on with the therapies that are helping him.

We had mild weather that summer, even rain on a couple of days. It was very pleasant and meant we have had more days outside. I asked Marteena to cut Storm's hair with her clippers—usually I took him to a hairdresser but she said she could do it. It was always a bit of a wrestle because Storm loved anything that vibrated and tried to grab hold of the clippers. He looked gorgeous with his hair cut really short—most likely it annoyed him because we always ran our hands through it when it was short; it was so irresistibly prickly we couldn't help ourselves, even the kids at school did it.

Not long after coming home with his new haircut, Storm's head started hurting so I gave him some Painstop. Then he had a seizure in the bath. I yanked him out of the bath, dried him, then lay him on the couch. As usual I sat with him until he fell asleep. I felt awful that having his hair cut had caused him pain and a seizure. The next day I watched and waited for another seizure but he seemed fine. He was tired for a few days and went to bed fairly early at night—and then the seizures started up again.

He ended up having nine attacks over four days and I sat with him for the whole time. It never got easier to deal with—the seizures frightened Storm and they really frightened me. What if he had an attack when I wasn't there?

School holidays were coming to an end, and Marteena looked after Storm a couple of times so I could go to Perth to shop for school stuff. He loved school and I didn't think I gave him enough stimulation, so he would be glad to get back there. He was a people person, a lot more sociable than I, and he knew he was totally accepted there.

Chapter Eight

F *irst day back at school in Bindoon. Ann Graham, his Education Support teacher from last year, will be his Ed Support teacher again as well as teaching him when he goes to "normal" class after lunch. He adores Ann and is going to love this. We have a new principal this year, a younger man.*

This year, Storm was going to the Bindoon school on Monday and Tuesday, having Wednesday off and then going to Burbridge Special School in Perth on Thursday and Friday. It seemed Bindoon really was some kind of "no-man's land"—it wasn't considered a country town, nor was it considered part of Perth. There were no therapies available from the country disability sector (not like when I lived on the farm), and none available from Perth (not like when I lived in Perth). All I could do for now was send Storm to the special school in Perth which provided physiotherapy, speech and occupational therapy—all therapies that he needed. It wasn't until the end of the year that the new principal at Bindoon told me I could have had him in the Bindoon school for four days a week and an aide would have been provided. This raised questions about what the previous principal had told me, but I'm not going to dwell on it.

Storm was so revved up after his first day of school it took him a long time to go to sleep that night. The next day he didn't have school and it was my birthday. Toni surprised me by turning up with pressies and a cabinet that Dad had made for me—it was a good day and when Toni left, Jan came over and helped me fix the cabinet to the kitchen wall. Then we celebrated with drinks—a thoroughly enjoyable birthday!

The next day was Storm's first day at the special school in Perth and since it was for two days in a row I decided that if Toni was working away we would stay at her house. It also suited Toni to have someone in the house while she was away. Storm had a new teacher at the special school; she seemed nice so after saying goodbye to Storm I went off to have a post-birthday lunch with Rae and Marteena. Storm had been a little out of sorts, so I arranged an appointment with the iridologist for Saturday morning. It turned out he had an ear infection. We were given drops, which fixed the problem in a couple of days.

Back in Bindoon it was too hot too work outside in the garden, so I worked on the house—there was endless wallpaper to be stripped off the walls; you wouldn't believe how much!

Storm's head was still hurting. The earache had gone but the airconditioner was upsetting him again so it had to be turned off at night until he went to sleep and then turned on again. Panadol didn't always help. I worried about the amount of Panadol he had been taking for his headaches but felt there was no other option.

Jan offered to look after Storm for about an hour in the evenings
so I could go for a walk—a real stress reliever. I was really grateful, and I
know Storm loved the fussing he got from Jan and her family.

Storm picked up a cold, perhaps from school, and ended up on
antibiotics and Panadol. The school year had only just begun and already
he was having quite a few days off. Then the special school told me that
because Storm only came to the school two days a week they couldn't
provide therapy for him. They didn't tell me that the previous year, when he
was only going one day a week! The only reason we were going to the special
school was because we couldn't get help anywhere else and it was their job to
provide therapy (physiotherapy, occupational therapy, speech therapy) for
the children in the school. The system was letting him down again. Once
he hit school age, every therapy that he got through Disability Services
disappeared and there was nothing to replace it. The people at the Bindoon
school wanted to help him in any way they could, but kept hitting brick
walls trying to find a service that would provide the help he needed. And the
special school, which had a service in-house, would not provide it.

One day I was pulling weeds for the chooks when a bee stung me
on the leg. Because I am slightly allergic to them, I had to race inside and
take some antihistamine tablets, which helped straight away, but they made
me very tired so I dozed on the couch in the lounge room with Storm,
getting up to feed and change him. Jan came over in the afternoon to
check on us. I had taken up the couch so she sat on the floor next to Storm.

While we were chatting, he kept leaning over to her until she said to him: "Do you want me to pick you up?" She picked him up and put him on her lap and he reached up and kissed her smack on the lips. Once again I was stunned that he knew where her lips were without using his hands to find them. Smart little bugger.

Storm loved Jan and her two children, Greg and Emily. Emily would sit and play with him, and Greg would push him around in his three-wheeled stroller, tipping it on its side or backwards so he was upside down (he was always well strapped in). Storm loved it and would crack up laughing. Emily made him toys that made sounds and he loved every one of them, playing with them until he had wrecked. We were so fortunate to have this family as neighbours. Jan helped me heaps. Together we built the chookyard and finished the shade house at the end of the verandah. I wouldn't have been able to do any of it without her.

Jan and Marteena both looked after Storm at times for a couple of hours so I could have some time to myself, especially in the school holidays. Since moving to Bindoon I had lost the in-house respite with Catholic Care. Jan and Marteena turning up in our lives was a sign to me that we were always looked after.

I had been busy painting my bedroom; in the end it took five coats of paint because it was a dark colour. I would take Storm to school, then come home and get into the painting. One morning I got a phone call from the school saying Storm was not responding to anything, so I raced back there. He hadn't had a seizure but was very listless, so I brought him home. He couldn't sit up on his own so I propped him up on the couch to feed him, then laid him on the bed in the spare room and went back to painting. It was just over a year since he started having the seizures and other odd turns, but already it was a way of life that both of us had become quite used to.

Storm had eaten, bathed and was in bed after a day in Perth for school, and I was watching television, when I heard a gurgling sound and raced into his room. He had phlegm coming out of his mouth and his body was twitching. I picked him up and he was floppy in my arms and I couldn't get him to open his eyes. I kept saying his name over and over and eventually he did open them. I was so frightened I rang Jan and she came over and sat with me until I felt calmer. Storm eventually drifted off to sleep again. Probably it was an epileptic seizure, I don't know, but the reality, that he could have a seizure bad enough that he could stop breathing, hit me. The next morning he woke early with no after-effects from the night before, so we ended up going to Perth and he went to school as usual. When I picked him up at the end of the day, he was fine. No drama was going to stop him going to school and going swimming, especially swimming—his one great love.

A few days before the next school holidays he was irritable and off his food. Something was not right—not that I always knew what was wrong, and sometimes Panadol gave him no relief. He was happier when he was in the bath, it gave him some relief from I-had-no-idea-what and he would eat his dinner if I fed him while he was in the bath, which I did. He also seemed more relaxed when he was outside in his stroller with me. I hoped whatever was upsetting him would pass soon. But he didn't get any better so I started giving him Panadol every four hours. The next morning I noticed a rash on his arm—almost the same as the one he had last year that they thought was meningococcal. So I took him to the local doctor. He thought it was just a pressure mark but said that to be sure I must take him to Joondalup Health Campus, a little closer than the hospital in Perth, where they would be waiting for us in emergency. The doctor in the ED also thought it was a pressure mark but took blood for tests. He asked if we wanted to wait at the hospital for the results but I decided to go on to Toni's house in Perth where I could make Storm more comfortable while we waited. They had given me antibiotics to give him so I did that and kept giving him Panadol every four hours. I rang the doctor as requested at 4pm and it turned out he had a viral infection. At least something had shown up to explain his unhappiness. We drove home to Bindoon as soon as I got the results. His appetite returned within a couple of days but he still seemed very tired.

Toni and I decided to visit our parents in Dunsborough for a couple of days. Storm was still not totally well but certainly better, and it was school holiday time so we had five days in Dunsborough then returned home and by then he was a lot happier and sleeping well. The holidays gave him the time to rest and get well and I could enjoy not having to drive him to school in Perth. But on what should have been his second day back at school he had a longer-than-usual seizure while I was feeding him his breakfast. I laid him on the couch afterwards and he fell into an exhausted sleep. I tippee-toed around finishing the housework and then I sat with him until he woke up.

Our life seems wrapped up in Storm's seizures. What I do or don't get done depends on how he is travelling; everything comes to a halt now when he has a seizure. There is nothing we can do but move on through it, making the most of the good times, it does challenge us both, but more so Storm.

I was still studying iridology so I had something to do while he slept between seizures. Still, I got frustrated at times. I was trying to get all the doors in the house stripped and varnished and it was taking longer than I hoped because Storm had been ill quite a bit.

One day when Jan and I went off to get a load of horse manure for my garden, Storm sat in the car while we shovelled the stuff into the trailer. We hadn't been back long and were still at Jan's when he had another attack so I brought him home and settled him on the couch again. That attack occurred just after 4pm and he slept through dinnertime. In the end, I put him to bed without his dinner and he didn't wake up when I carried him to his bed. His breathing seemed fine so I decided not to wake him. The next day, Saturday, he had another seizure during breakfast, so I put him on the couch again and he went back to sleep. *When he has these runs of seizures, he nearly always has one the next morning during breakfast. I wonder whether getting him up in the morning and moving him about causes it. Who knows?*

He seemed fine when he woke, and he stayed on the couch while I fetched some of his favourite toys for him to play with. Then he had another seizure but this time he didn't want to sleep afterwards, just continued playing with his toys. Jan came over around lunchtime with a jubilee twist bun for us. Storm sat on her lap while she fed him slices of the twist and he was really enjoying it when he had another seizure. I felt so hurt for him—why couldn't he be allowed to enjoy eating his bun without having it spoiled by another seizure? I was so ticked off for him because he didn't deserve that.

The next morning I woke up to . . . silence. Usually Storm woke me with his chatter and I lay there with my heart racing, listening for any sounds from his room. I often worried that he would have a seizure in the night and not survive, so I was too scared to get up and check, until finally he made a noise. Relieved, I got up. He had no seizures that day, he was quiet but okay, so I hoped he had come to the end of another cycle.

Life returned to its usual routine, and then it was Mothers Day again. I'm not a great one for making a big deal about it; it's all so commercialised. But my wood heater was installed on this Mothers Day, so if I'm supposed to get a pressie, nothing could be better than having heating for winter. Jan and I got a trailer-load of wood, then Jan cut some up with her chainsaw and brought it over and I lit the fire. *Awesome! I am so lucky.* Storm and I wouldn't freeze our butts off this winter.

At school assembly at the Bindoon school the next day Storm got a certificate from his teacher "for spreading happiness to others". He was so proud and I was proud of him. Happiness is what Storm was all about. He loved school, his teacher, his aides and his classmates. If ever there was a child who lived in the moment, it was Storm.

Life plodded on. I spent as much time as possible in the garden. It was where both of us loved to be, with sunny days and blue wrens and robins flitting around the garden, chirping away, and the wind in the trees. Storm took in everything, even the sound the shovel made when I was turning the soil. With winter arriving we had fewer days in the garden, but on any sunny day you would find us outside enjoying the moment.

School holidays came around again and the rainy days also turned up. So now I was doing stuff in the house, pulling wallpaper off the bathroom walls while Storm was in the lounge room playing with his toys. I would check on him and talk to him from the bathroom, and he would chatter back, laughing sometimes. *What goes on in this boy's mind? I would love to know. He has the most gorgeous laugh, a belly laugh that is contagious.*

But by the end of the day Storm was lethargic and his pulse was racing. I wasn't sure what to do so I rang Jan and she had recently seen a commercial on television for a medical centre that you could ring for advice. She had written down the number so I rang them straight away. I spoke to a nurse and she asked me to take Storm's temperature, which was

38, and checked his pulse, which was 200. She then advised to take him straight away to hospital, an hour away. Jan couldn't come with me so I asked Marteena—I needed someone to watch Storm while I drove. We got to the hospital around 9pm and after the triage nurse checked Storm out we sat in emergency until midnight. Of course, by then Storm was better so we drove back to Bindoon with no idea what had happened to him. When we got home after dropping Marteena off I put Storm into bed with me and we both fell instantly asleep.

In the morning I phoned for an appointment with our doctor in Perth because Storm still had no energy. I didn't have much either, but worry drove me into action and we were on our way to Perth and at the doctor's by 10am. I explained what had happened the day before and the doctor felt sure Storm had a kidney infection. He gave me a prescription for antibiotics. Rae looked after Storm while I went to the chemist and she decided to do a healing on him while I was away. She didn't believe it was a kidney problem. There was no way of knowing if she was right, and there was certainly no way I would be going back to the doctor and telling him my friend did a healing on Storm and she doesn't think the problem is in his kidneys. He would think I was cracked, and it is bad enough having the stigma of a single mother. There seems to be a consensus that some single mothers just over-react, and the fact that there isn't a man in our lives makes us incapable of raising our children. That's rubbish; one thing I know is that I am great in a crisis and I would have to be to have raised Storm on my own.

Anyway, I decided to give Storm the antibiotics. At least if he had an infection somewhere, hopefully the drugs would help. We headed back to Bindoon and on the way I glanced in the rear-view mirror in time to see Storm having a seizure. We were almost home so I didn't stop, I just kept driving. I kept talking to him while I drove and when I got home I carried him inside and settled him on the couch. Then I made myself coffee and sat with him quietly so he would go off to sleep, which he did.

Watching him sleep I felt so helpless again, so overwhelmed and so terribly alone. Where was this all going? How bad was it going to get, and why can't I get anyone to listen to me? Epilepsy is not such a bad thing, but since Storm had been having seizures he was deteriorating physically, not at a rate that was hugely noticeable, but I had noticed that his walking was actually getting worse, his legs were getting stiffer and I didn't think epilepsy was causing any of it. But because no-one would listen, I just had to watch it happen.

The special school in Perth was staging an auction of paintings the kids had done on canvas, to raise money for the school, and I was going along to bid for Storm's. I had organised for him to stay the night with Jan and was a bit worried because he was still quite listless, but he enjoyed being with Jan and her family so I decided to risk it. It would be the first time he would be away from me for a night since I had gone to Bali more than two years earlier. I took $150 with me, expecting that I wouldn't need even half of that. Wrong!

I arrived about 6.30pm, expecting to see only the parents of the children, but there were all these people who had been invited from various organisations. They were even serving drinks—it was very much an upmarket evening and I was under-dressed! I found Storm's painting. It was amazing; the boy had talent. I loved it, but was a bit daunted by the interest being shown in it. While I was wandering around looking at other paintings before the auction started, Storm's art teacher—who was also the auctioneer—came up to me and we began talking. He also knew there had been a bit of interest in Storm's painting; When I told him I had only brought $150 with me he said he thought it would sell for a lot more than that. I desperately wanted Storm's painting and couldn't contemplate a stranger taking it home. When the bidding began, I moved in close to the art teacher/auctioneer. Quite a few paintings were auctioned, and then it was time for Storm's. Every time I bid, someone would counter with a higher bid, and we got closer and closer to my limit. When it reached $150, the auctioneer said "Sold", and handed the painting to me. Yay! I had the painting and I was so happy. I left, heading back to Bindoon, and as soon as I was home I put the painting up on the kitchen wall and that's where it has been ever since. I love that painting.

Storm must suffer a lot of frustration, being totally aware of his surroundings and yet unable to express himself except by shouting and pinching (he doesn't hit, but boy does he have a mean pinch) and the expressions on his face. I get a bit angry when people see his disabled body, the boy in the wheelchair, and instantly judge him, speaking down to him with baby talk as if he's someone who isn't capable of understanding. I have also had to hold back my laughter when he's raised his eyebrows at such people while they talked down to him, as if to say: "Whatever!" You have to spend time with Storm, to watch his face and divine what he is thinking, know him and know he understands. When he's not playing noisily with his toys he loves being outside with the sounds of the surrounding bush, the birds, the wind in the trees and me working in the garden nearby. You can tell by the look of concentration on his face that he is listening carefully to all the different sounds around him.

Storm recovered enough to go back to school but only for a few days before coming down with bronchitis. I decided we both needed a break so we headed for Dunsborough. It was a relaxing couple of days with Mum helping and spoiling Storm with his favourite foods. Then we headed back to Bindoon to get back on the treadmill.

The Bindoon school was gearing up for its sports carnival and for the first time Storm was going to be in a race or two. The other children had practised pushing him in his wheelchair and were as excited as he was about him participating. On the day of the carnival I got him up, fed him, dressed him in his team's colours—and just as I was carrying him to the car he had a seizure in my arms. I was so upset for him I could have cried. I carried him back inside, put him on the couch and then rang the school to let them know he wouldn't be coming to the carnival. It was so disappointing for him. He ended up having three attacks that day.

After a couple of days at home he was well enough to go back to school. After dropping him off I called in on Marteena for a coffee and some chat and she insisted on giving me a massage. You don't say no to Marteena's massages—they are the ultimate. So I had my fantastic massage and a glass of wine, after which I came home, set the alarm so I would wake in time to fetch Storm from school and then I went to bed and dozed. It was blissful. Thank you, God, for Marteena!

On Storm's birthday, September 19, I made pancakes for his breakfast with real maple syrup, our favourite. Toni rang and sang happy birthday to him over the phone, then Rae rang and did the same; he was all smiles. Mum phoned soon after and then we left for school with the patty cakes for his class that I had made the previous day. His classmates made him a banana smoothie for his birthday, he had a grand old day and was smiling when I picked him up. We hadn't been home long when Jan, Greg and Emily came over from next door to give him his presents. Storm got himself so excited he couldn't keep still, and the chocolate birthday cake he ate wouldn't have helped. Then Marteena and her girls turned up, so more cake and coffee was had. Storm was having the best day ever, and it warmed my heart to see him so happy. It took him so long to go to sleep that night that he didn't wake up the next day until 11am. When I went to check on him he was sleeping with a smile on his face, so I decided not to disturb him. I was so happy he had such a great birthday. The next day we took Rae a piece of his birthday cake on our way to school in Perth.

The school holidays had arrived again, the days were sunny and there wasn't anywhere we had to be. We went for walks, with me pushing Storm in the stroller of course, spent days in the garden enjoying the birds and the sun, just sitting back and chilling out together. What could be better?

Marteena brought Temily over for a play day with Storm. They sat in the lounge room playing together. Unused to a child who could walk, I locked the lounge room door in case Temily wandered out and I didn't notice. She and Storm were amazing together—she would chat to Storm in her baby language and Storm would make noises back and then they would laugh together. It was a bond that continued to grow as they got older. When Temily could talk she would tell me that Storm needed a drink or if he wanted to go home, even that he wanted his Elmo toy. And when I did what Temily said, it would be exactly what he wanted.

Towards the end of the holidays Toni and I decided to invite Rae and Marteena down to Mum and Dad's place for a girls' weekend. I picked up Marteena in Bindoon, drove to Perth, then picked up Rae and Toni and we all headed off to Dunsborough with Storm sitting between Toni and Rae in the back seat. The next morning we had a yummy cooked breakfast, compliments of Mum and Dad, and then we were driven to the pickup point for a wine tour while Mum looked after Storm. We tasted a lot of wines (some of them much too good not to swallow), then got back and had coffee with Mum and Dad before heading into town for dinner at a Thai restaurant. It was a great weekend but all too soon it was time to head back home. Reality beckoned and school started on Monday.

Storm was happy to be going back to school and when I dropped him off on the Monday he reached up and gave me a hug. I got all tearful; with Storm in my life I was moved by the simplest of moments. The next day when I was dressing him after his bath, I picked him up as I always did to give him a hug. He reached up to touch my face with his hands, then leaned over and kissed me on the lips and again I got tearful. *This kid is messing with my heart.*

The two weeks following were smooth sailing for Storm, he went to school and enjoyed himself, and I went for walks between working on the house and gardens. It was great to see Storm well and having fun. Then the poo hit the fan!

It was a Saturday and I'd got up fairly early while Storm was still asleep. Jan was away and I was looking after some eggs she was incubating. I raced over to her place and turned the eggs in her incubator then raced back home. When Storm woke up, I got him up, fed and changed then set him up in the lounge room with his toys. Then I raced around making beds, cleaning the house, etc. I went back into the lounge room to check on him and he had a seizure just as I walked into the room. *Damn!*

I picked him up and held him until it was over, then laid him on the couch; it was about 8.30am and eventually he went off to sleep. I stayed in the room, watching him. He woke 30 minutes later and had another attack, and this time HE STOPPED BREATHING! I freaked, I couldn't persuade him to take a breath, I didn't know what to do and I was still holding him in my arms when I picked up the phone and rang Marteena. I don't know what I thought she was going to do, and after telling her what had happened I phoned for an ambulance. While I was talking to the operator, Storm was limp in my arms and saliva was dripping out of his mouth. I thought I was being over-dramatic perhaps, ringing for an ambulance, but he still wasn't breathing! That made two of us. After I finished on the phone he did start breathing again, but it was very shallow. Marteena and the ambulance turned up at the same time. I was embarrassed that I had called for the ambulance; they were trying to persuade me to let them take Storm to the hospital and I was thinking: "He's breathing again, drama averted, moving on." Eventually I saw reason and let them load Storm into the ambulance. I got in the back and Marteena said she would follow in my car in case we ended up coming home that day. Our first trip in an ambulance! Storm had another attack on the way and after it subsided they gave him oxygen. He was exhausted and it seemed to take forever to get to the hospital.

We had to wait in emergency for a doctor to come and see us. When he did, Storm had another attack in front of him—the first time a doctor had witnessed one of his seizures. As it finished, he vomited, really vomited like he had never done before. Just something else to get freaked out about!

Perhaps because of the vomiting, the doctor decided to admit Storm for observation, so we had to wait for a bed to become available in a ward. I had heard of people dying from epileptic seizures and had put it to the back of my mind, believing it was a rare thing. But now it seemed so possible and it was scaring me. *Just breathe, Mandy, you will get through this, you always do, just hang on.*

Once Storm was settled in the ward, the nurses promised me they would watch him so Marteena and I went for coffee before she headed off back to Bindoon in my car and I settled myself in a chair beside Storm's bed. At 7pm he had another attack and stopped breathing again for a few seconds. It seemed forever but by the time I called the nurses and they had arrived in the room he was breathing again. They gave him oxygen, and some drugs to stop the seizures, hopefully.

A while later he vomited again, all over the bed, so while the nurses changed the sheets I cradled his exhausted body in my arms. Once the bed was made and he was settled, he went to sleep. The nurses made up a foldout bed for me alongside him. I couldn't sleep so I just sat watching him, and while I was watching he opened his eyes. He looked so frightened and then he had another seizure. I wrapped my arms around him and held him until it was over and his body had relaxed, then I called the nurses and told them he had had another seizure.

It was 1am and he had had seven attacks. The nurses decided to move his bed closer to the nursing station so they could keep a closer eye on him. When they moved him, there wasn't enough room next to his bed for mine so I lay on his bed next to him and it was comforting to hear him breathing. I cuddled up to him and drifted off to sleep, just grateful that he was breathing easily.

The nature of Storm's seizures has changed; he never stopped breathing before. There are always new twists and turns in his life that we have to get used to. I admit that when he stopped breathing I totally freaked. But I know I will cope with it, all we can do is adjust to the changes and keep moving on with our lives. It is what it is.

Marteena had phoned Rae early in the morning to tell her about Storm. She headed straight to the hospital and it was only 7am when she walked into our room. I was so glad to see her; her mere presence is calming. She stayed with us for as long as she could then she had to go to work, and she was not long gone when the doctor came in. He said Storm could go home. His epilim would be increased, and tests would be needed to ensure the correct dosage. Of course I was worried about increasing the epilim, because it could make him very tired, but the doctor assured me the dosage wasn't that high. Still, I was concerned—I didn't want Storm to be wanting to sleep all the time, too tired to enjoy playing.

Marteena picked us up in my car. I was too tired to drive so she drove us back to her house and I put Storm on her couch while we had coffee. Temily hovered around him while we sat outside with our coffee, and while we were talking she came up to the flyscreen door and said: "Storm, car." Marteena asked her if Storm wanted to go home and she nodded yes, Then she went over to Storm, kissed him on the cheek and said "Elmo"—all this from a little girl who wasn't quite two. Elmo was Storm's favourite of all favourite toys, he obviously wanted his toy so I packed him into the car and drove home. I put him on the couch in the lounge and fetched Elmo—he grabbed the toy off me and started playing with it, and I was already an emotional wreck so of course I cried. After that day, I always remembered to take Elmo with us if we had to go to hospital.

That night Storm slept with me because I had put him to bed and gone to check on him just in time to watch him have another attack. He was fine afterwards but I wasn't, so I put him in bed with me where I could hear him breathing. I knew I would get past this, but I was so much on edge at the moment.

School was forgotten; getting Storm strong again was the main priority. He took up residence in the lounge room with his toys all around and his mother hovering over him. The next day he had another attack. I felt overwhelmed, frightened at the possibility of losing him, and constantly expecting him to stop breathing. I rang Marteena and she came and sat with us for a while. His life seemed so fragile that it could slip away at any moment if I didn't watch him.

The ravings of a very tired, emotional mum. I can't go on like this; I'm going to have to get a grip. I keep telling myself that if he is meant to leave me, I can't stop it, I can't save him, just be there every moment. Let go, Mandy, you can't stop the inevitable and he is actually all right.

My parents were too far away to drop everything and run after me if I fell apart. Finally, with Marteena's support, I pulled myself together, regained my senses and resilience. During the next couple of days we got phone calls from family, friends and Storm's teacher asking how he was doing. Marteena gave him a massage a couple of days after he came out of hospital and he just loved it. He smiled the whole time and was so relaxed by the time she finished. When I brought him home he smiled every time I talked to him. Obviously he was feeling better and ready to go back to school, but I decided to start with half days to make sure it wasn't too much for him.

When Marteena had massaged him she had noticed how large his chest was getting, and his heart seemed larger. We didn't know what that meant, and it wasn't like I was going to waste my time telling any doctor. I suppose I sound bitter but I'm not, just realistic—no amount of shouting and stamping of my feet was going to get them to actually listen to me. I had given up on that.

My whole life was all about Storm. I enjoyed working on the house and the garden, but they were my only outlet. Rae had persuaded me I should do more for myself so, once a month, I started having facials when Storm was at school in Perth. Also, Rae and I started a six-week course of kickboxing. What a great way to vent some anger and frustration—I have a pathetic kick but a hell of a punch.

Storm was now in fine form; back at school and loving it. It had been 18 days since his last attack and things were looking good, the hospital incident all but forgotten. Summer was coming and the reticulation in the garden had to be checked so that all the plants—my precious plants—were watered, and more days were spent in the garden.

I also spent two days helping Jan put up the ceiling in her house. Storm sat on a rug and played, enjoying all the noises and activity surrounding him, besides being fussed over by everyone who was helping Jan. Joe had come to lend a hand; Storm loved the sound of Joe's voice and recognised it instantly as soon as Joe spoke to him.

Amazing how my happiness is so wrapped up in Storm's health and happiness. I know that it is quite likely dysfunctional for so much of my life to be about him, but sadly I know it's not going to be forever. Meanwhile, life is good.

Storm was so happy, no attack for 39 days. Then he had one while he was playing with his toys in the lounge room. I had just walked in to check on him (why is that so often the case, I wonder) and he looked truly scared. I picked him up and held him until it was over, then settled him on the couch and he went to sleep. I made myself a coffee and sat watching him. I was calm, I didn't freak out, he was okay, his breathing was fine. I can understand him being frightened after going so long without an attack, it must have taken him by surprise. But it was the weekend and we didn't need to be anywhere so I relaxed. He had another attack the next day during breakfast, slept afterwards and by the end of the day he was able to sit up independently and play with his toys.

I made pancakes for a treat, our favourite with loads of real maple syrup. Storm ate the whole lot. He had recovered so quickly he was able to go to school the next day. There is nothing I can buy to cheer him up, but food that he loves will do the trick.

It's December and we have had an appointment with Storm's specialist in Perth. He's decided he should change Storm's medication because it hasn't stopped the seizures. Silly man. I never believed it would, but I'd best humour him and try the new medication. It makes Storm tired and I am angry because

I told the doctor I didn't want him to be too tired to enjoy his life; he obviously wasn't listening. Well, if Storm doesn't adjust to this medication there will be some changes made, you can be sure of that!

The school year was ending, and the Christmas shopping needed to be done. On one of my days hunting for presents someone hit my lovely new car while it was parked and pushed in the front fender, and just drove off. Ho, ho, ho. Merry Christmas, Mandy! I managed to get all the Christmas pressies bought by Storm's last day of school and then it was holiday time, nowhere we had to be, all sleep-ins and time to chill out in the garden. Storm adjusted to his new medication and wasn't tired all the time, all was good. *Doctor forgiven.*

It was so hot the airconditioner was on continuously for days and we spent the evenings in the garden until the mosquitoes chased us back inside. Toni, Storm and I spent Christmas in Dunsborough; Rod and his family couldn't make it this year. It was a quiet and relaxing Christmas and then Storm and I headed home to spend New Year's Eve in Bindoon. Marteena persuaded me to go to a local restaurant for dinner. It was a quiet night and the end of Y2K; we had made it through another year.

Chapter Nine

2001

In the beginning, it was too hot to do anything outside until the late evenings. So, while Storm played, I stripped the wallpaper off another room, the office this time. It seemed I had been pulling wallpaper off walls for a very, very long time.

We had to make another trip to Perth because Storm needed blood tests to check the level of drugs in his system, then a week later we had to go back to get the results from the specialist. It turned out his new medication was affecting his white blood-cell count. *Aah . . . the mystery of the low white blood-cell count!* He was to go back to the drug regime he had been on before. Whatever. He hadn't had an attack since November and it was now the middle of January—so good.

Sadly for us, Marteena and her family were moving back to Perth, and they decided to take their dog, Simba, with them. I didn't mind too much, it would be good to be without the responsibility of a dog—so she got her dog back and I got her chooks, fair trade!

We went to Rockingham for a couple of days to catch up with my friend Roma from Morawa, then travelled on to see my parents in Dunsborough for a couple of days. We came home loaded up with plants from Mum's garden, stopped off at Toni's house for lunch, then headed to Bindoon. Storm had two attacks in the car on our way home and was exhausted by the time we arrived. The garden appeared a bit feral—it looked suspiciously like the chooks had got into it and Jan confirmed that they had. Never mind, it was good to be home. What with travelling and having attacks, Storm was exhausted, so he went to bed early and we slept in the next morning. It was still too hot to go outside so he and I lounged around the house for days. School would be starting again soon and I was determined to make the most of our freedom to do absolutely nothing before we got busy again. We had coffee with Jan and she looked after Storm in the evenings so I could go for my usual walks. The garden was wilting in the heat and the heat was making me tired and grumpy, but not Storm; he just got noisy and the noisier he got the grumpier I got.

I think it's time for Storm to go back to school. He is obviously not getting enough stimulation.

School would be different this year. Storm was going to the special school in Perth only on Mondays and for the rest of the week he would be at Bindoon. I had found out that he didn't like Fridays at the special school. That was "social interaction day", which meant a trip to a shopping complex, hardly thrilling for a blind child, just a lot of noise coming at him from all directions. On one of those Fridays, when I had picked Storm up from school, he was sitting in his wheelchair gripping the armrests tightly, and while I was pushing him out to the car he said in a loud voice: "Home." He was not happy. He said it clearly, just once, and never said it again, but I got the message—Fridays were not enjoyable for him.

I also didn't see the point in taking him for the two days because the physio and other therapies that the school said they were going to provide had stopped early in his first year there. They knew from the beginning he would be attending two days a week and at the time they said they could and would provide therapy. Still, he had got the hydrotherapy that he loved. The year had been extremely hard on him physically so I don't know whether he would have been up to any physio, anyway. And he had his healings with Rae and his delicious massages with Marteena, which always helped immensely.

Attempts to get any type of therapies for him in Bindoon had so far failed, not through lack of trying by the school. But he was encouraged to walk with his walking frame, and was doing fairly well considering the year he'd had.

We got a few cool days before school started so Storm and I spent them in the garden where we were both happy. We seemed to have more small birds coming into the garden, blue wrens and red robins. I kicked butt in the garden, weeding and pruning, while Stormy listened to all the sounds around him, laughing at the sounds I made.

School started again. His first day back was at the school in Perth, and he had a nice new young teacher. But when I picked him up he was very noisy—and not a happy noisy, a very agitated noisy. He calmed down when I got him into the car, but obviously it had not been a good day.

The next day he was back at school in Bindoon. He was very excited when I wheeled him into his class and he heard Leanne's voice (his aide). Storm has been blessed with the most amazing aides at Bindoon, they were the best people I could have asked for and they treated him like any other child in the class. Bad behaviour was not tolerated. As usual, the right people were turning up in our lives again.

Why can't the special school treat Storm like these aides do? There is less chance of behavioural problems if the child is given boundaries that can't be crossed. Children like Storm need boundaries just like any ordinary child. But at the special school the children are allowed to behave quite badly and are never pulled up for it. I don't like that.

On Friday morning Storm was quite ill so I rang the school to let them know he wouldn't be coming in. Jan offered to look after him so I could buy some groceries. I put him in his stroller and took him over to Jan's then headed to the shop, but when I got back he still looked ill. Jan said he had perked up when I left and as soon as I came back he looked ill again. Obviously something was on his mind. That was when Jan said to him he wouldn't have to go to the special school today (it being Friday, the day he normally went to Perth) like last year—and that he would have gone to the Bindoon school today. Instantly, his face changed and he smiled and clapped his hands. I just stood there with my mouth open—he knew it was Friday!

How frustrating it must be for him that he can't tell me how he feels. And how frustrating for me that I can't always know what he is thinking or feeling I know ho didn't like the special school on Fridays but I didn't know it made him so unhappy that he got ill. And I hadn't thought to tell him he wouldn't be going there on Fridays in the future.

So when we got back home I sat him on my lap and told him he would only be going to the special school on Mondays, which meant no more social interaction trips, and every other day he would be going to Bindoon. I also told him I was sorry I hadn't explained that to him before, and in future I would try to remember to tell him more of what we were doing. He seemed happy with that and proceeded to try to get to his toys. I had learned a valuable lesson; here I was trying to teach others not to underestimate him and I was guilty of doing just that.

March was so hot, too hot to do anything at all. Storm had another bout of seizures, nothing unusual about them except that for some reason this time I had moments when I was totally overwhelmed with fear—what lay ahead for my son? How bad was his life going to get? How was I going to look after him when he got too big for me to carry? I couldn't contemplate putting him in a home; the thought of not knowing how he would be looked after when he was not in my care was always my biggest worry. Even when he was at school I worried about his welfare, even though I had never been given any cause to think that he wasn't in excellent hands.

Eventually, the fear subsides after I have talked myself down, telling myself I've got this far and I can make it the rest of the way, remembering everything that Storm and I have ever needed in our life has shown up—it just takes a leap of faith.

Storm's specialist asked for urgent tests to monitor his white blood-cell count, which could be affected by his epilepsy drugs. So we had an appointment with haematology at the hospital in a couple of days (usually it took weeks to get an appointment). I had this wild idea that maybe they would really look into Storm's health now, since they were so concerned about the low white-cell count. Silly, delusional me! The tests showed his white-cell count was still considerably low and the outcome was they would "keep an eye on it", with tests every couple of months. His white-cell count never did come good.

We got an appointment with Catholic Care, the same people who used to come to the house in Perth when we lived there. They had a couple of houses in Perth suburbs, taking six children at a time for weekends and for a couple of days in the school holidays. I wasn't sure I could let Storm go to strangers for a weekend no matter how qualified they were, but I recognised that it wasn't healthy for my whole life to revolve around him.

My appointment was at the respite house and I expected it to look like an institution with high fences around the building, and it took me some time to find it because it actually looked like any other house in the street. In we went and there were children watching television, a lady in the kitchen cooking dinner and another looking after the children.

Storm and I were led into the office by the co-ordinator and by the end of the meeting Storm was booked in for a weekend in four weeks. I was nervous—giving him up for a weekend—what was I supposed to do with myself? He had stayed overnight with Jan and Rae and even a couple of nights with Toni many years ago. The last time I had been away from him was in 1998 when I went to Bali for a week. These people were total strangers, but I was going to have to trust that they would look after him well.

The next couple of weeks were a struggle. I felt exhausted, and couldn't understand why. After taking Storm to school in the mornings I would come home, clean the house then collapse on the couch until it was time to pick him up, and the day in Perth for his special school sucked the life out of me. I finally faced the fact that I needed to see my own doctor in Perth. It turned out that I was anaemic—thank God there was actually something wrong with me that could be fixed.

Then Storm had four days of seizures and serious vomiting. I had to dig really deep to find the energy to clean it all up every time. His weekend at Catholic Care arrived right at the end of those four days. I wasn't sure if he should go, even though I knew they had a nurse there all the time. In the end I dropped him off at the house on the Friday afternoon. We discussed his medications and their timing and I gave them his Elmo toy to take to bed and made sure they knew they must phone me if they were unsure about anything, anything at all. When I kissed him, he turned his face away from me and I felt awful—*he thinks I'm deserting him!* I wanted to pack up all his stuff and take him home but I didn't, in the end I just left.

Back in Bindoon, I went to the local restaurant that night for dinner and slept in the next morning, but of course the first thing I did when I got up was to phone to see how Storm was doing. He was fine. But I felt restless the whole time he was away and I was glad when it was time to pick him up on Sunday afternoon. I think he was totally fussed over for the two days he was there—he looked very pleased with himself—so it was decided he would go off to Catholic Care again in a few weeks. Hopefully I would get better at being by myself.

Another appointment with the specialist, and again he wasn't happy that Storm was still having quite a few seizures, so he wanted to increase his drugs. I wasn't convinced, but eventually I agreed after he reassured me the increased medications were not going to make Storm tired.

School holidays rolled around again, and it was great to be able to sleep in—if Storm let me. He woke me early one morning with his chatter so I called out that is was the school holidays and he laughed. I couldn't help laughing at his happiness, so I got up. A happy Storm made the world a perfect place for me. I even caught him trying to get up on his hands and knees—clever boy, he must have been feeling good. He was even going to sleep early and sleeping all night. The drug increase seemed not to have made him tired, and the seizures stopped. We made our usual visit to my parents in Dunsborough in the holidays; and then it was back to school.

We have survived another summer, God bless airconditioners! Autumn's on its way and I'm a happy camper. Autumn and winter are the seasons I love most. Jan and I have chain-sawed wood for the winter and I stacked my lot in the shed; I love a wood fire burning while it's raining outside.

Storm was off to Catholic Care for the weekend again, and this time he was happy to go now that he knew I wasn't abandoning him and that he'd won the ladies' hearts and would be totally fussed over. I dropped him off on Friday afternoon and stayed at Toni's house so I could have dinner with Rae and her husband. I had a great time. Doing what normal people do was fun, even if it was just for a weekend. I slept in the next morning—bliss—then indulged in a bit of retail therapy. I missed Storm, but this was fun; I didn't have to be responsible for anyone for a whole weekend. But of course I rang Catholic Care to check that all was well. Because he was going to the special school on Mondays, I could pick him up then from Catholic Care and drop him off at school. When I picked him up, he had his school uniform on and they had packed his lunch—magic, he was in a fine mood and all I had to do was get him to school.

Oh no! Seizures have started again. We are more accepting of them now, and shift instantly into the necessary routine. Storm doesn't struggle against falling asleep, as he used to and he knows I will be there if he needs me.

I was always prepared. I did a lot of the housework at night when Storm was asleep so that as soon as the seizures began I could sit with him and not feel that there was anything else I should be doing, Beds were made the instant we were out of them—house in order, laundry done. I could leave the house at a moment's notice, knowing that I wouldn't be coming back to a mess.

When he fell asleep after one attack, his body started shaking and a nerve on the left side of his head was pulsing. That had never happened before. I rang the Bindoon doctor but the surgery was closed. I rang the specialist in Perth but he wasn't in either, so I rang our GP in Perth. Finally, someone was in! He told me to take Storm to hospital. Me: "I don't think so." Finally I got through to the specialist on his mobile and he also told me to get Storm to hospital. I got the message, go to hospital. I raced to the hospital, more than an hour away and we were seen fairly quickly in emergency but by then Storm was fine. At least this time I wasn't treated like a neurotic single mother, always a bonus.

Storm was fine for the rest of the day. He had another attack the next day and then no more. I spent the day watching him and studying. I'd finished my course on iridology, even managed to pass and get a diploma!

Now I was doing a correspondence course on landscape gardening—
something completely different. The next morning turned into a beautiful
sunny day so we spent it outside in the garden. I had the joyful job of
climbing up large conifers which had grown up past the power lines and
needed to be pruned back by order of the power company. What a job that
was. I had to climb up and, while holding on to the tree, saw the tops off,
making sure they didn't fall towards the power lines. The things you do
when money is short! While I was up one of the trees, I saw a guy taking a
leisurely walk past the house. He obviously couldn't see me so I called out
hello and scared the daylights out of him. Oh, how I laughed . . . doesn't
take much to entertain me!

Another weekend at Catholic Care and this time Storm didn't seem
so happy about it. I was hesitant to leave him but was persuaded he would
be fine. When I got home, I rang to check. He had settled in and was fine, so
I had a chance to catch up on some sleep. I usually didn't get to sleep until
late at night and Storm would wake me early in the morning. During the
night I heard every movement he made, getting up sometimes during the
night to check on him. And if he didn't sleep, neither did I. He could go for
days not going to sleep until 2 or 3am, then waking up really early, so it was
unsurprising that I enjoyed sleeping when he went off to Catholic Care.

During the July school holidays we didn't go anywhere, just
enjoyed being at home. Something happened to Storm—he didn't have
any seizures, but for days he was unable to sit up independently. He also

seemed quite tired and was sleeping late in the mornings, which was most unlike him. He seemed happy enough, though. Because he couldn't sit up and play with his toys, I sat him in his stroller and we went into the garden where I knew he would be happy. Eventually he came good.

Back to school, and a couple of days later Storm had blood tests to see how his white blood-cell count was going. It was a little higher than at the last test and he had put on weight, which was great. The specialist didn't want to see him for at least six months. I didn't bother to tell him about the days Storm couldn't sit up; I knew nothing would be done and Storm seemed happy and fairly healthy. Life was running fairly smoothly—well, at least our version of smoothly, no seizures. Storm was sleeping well, he was loving school and hadn't missed much of it this term, and we had no doctor's appointments looming.

I am a bit tired though, what with getting Storm up, changing him into his school clothes, carrying him to the lounge room to feed him his breakfast and packing his lunch. After that, I strip his bed, put the sheets in to be washed, remake the bed, carry him to the car, then drive to school. I put him into his wheelchair, take him up to class and sit with him until his aide arrives. We discuss Storm's progress, then I head home, hang out the washing, vacuum and generally clean up, but really all I want to do is to just collapse on the couch.

No point bitching. I just don't like mess—and, let's face it, it wasn't as much as I had to do on the farm. I don't like to see the yard messy either, so I was always raking up leaves, weeding and pruning, I got my breaks when I went over to Jan's to share a coffee with her.

It seems the minute I thought Storm was doing well he got sick. He had two seizures an hour apart and they totally floored him. He had to stay home from school the next day because once again he couldn't sit up on his own. *How does he endure this life so well? I admire his guts.*

It was September and Storm's birthday was coming up. Nine years old, wow. Just before his birthday, I was in Perth on a Monday for school. In the afternoon, I decided to drop in on my friend Rae. Storm hadn't seen her for quite awhile and I'm positive he put the idea in my head. While we were visiting he had one of his attacks. Rae had never seen him have a seizure and said later she never wanted to see one again. Like me, she didn't believe they were epileptic seizures at all, she felt they were a pain in the back of his head, on the left side. Four days later she phoned to tell me she had watched a movie about a boy who suffered a serious head injury in an accident and wore a helmet because he only had part of his skull left. While he was lying in his hospital bed he had an attack just like one of Storm's and the doctor believed it was a migraine attack caused by the damage to his brain.

We were both amazed at this sequence of events: Rae, who has never before seen one of Storm's attacks, finally sees one and then, four days later, watches a movie (based on a true story) about a boy who has brain damage and suffers seizures exactly like Storm's! Neither of us believes in coincidence—we share a belief that things happen for a reason, and the reason isn't always clear at the time.

A couple of days after Storm's birthday, the attacks started again. He had seizures six days in a row, the first time that had happened in months. He had also started coughing and I had taken him to the doctor, who prescribed antibiotics. Neither of us was getting much sleep. When the attacks started, I put him in bed with me at night because sometimes it would take a while for him to start breathing again. During the day, I would sit him up on the couch with his toys, though he was too weak even to pick them up.

I bet he would cry if he could—I certainly cry for him. These are the days I find soul-destroying, I only endure them because Storm endures them. And then he is happy and playful again.

The seizures ended and his weekend at Catholic Care came round again, a chance for me to sleep! Storm went off happily to be pampered by the ladies. I know the weekend off was meant for me to have time to myself, but I actually think Storm got more out of it than I did. He didn't have any more seizures until December, so we had more than two months of good health. It was wonderful, and Storm didn't miss any more days of school, which he loved.

We had a visit or two from an occupational therapist and a speech therapist, but they only seemed to be checking up on Storm's progress, or lack of it, and then a physiotherapist turned up at the school to look at him. It was the first time in almost three years that any therapists had visited the Bindoon school. The principal, and Storm's teachers, had all tried to get help for Storm, always to no avail. But that all changed with one phone call I made.

In this world, it is not what you know but who you know! I have a family friend who was secretary to a politician, so I spoke to her about the problems we were having getting therapy for Storm, and was given the phone number for the Disability Services Ministry policy officer. I rang one morning before taking Storm to school. When a woman answered, I explained why I was calling—I told her how Storm had been going to the Bindoon school for almost three years without any therapy help from Disability Services and how I took him to a school in Perth once a week for help but didn't get any occupational, speech or physio therapy from them either. She asked a few questions, then rang off. I took Storm off to school and had just got back when I had a call from the local area co-ordinator for Disability Services. She had received a phone call from her boss and her words to me were: "So, what can we do for you?"

Well, lady, I want world peace, but most of all I want you to cure my son. No? Well, I want some therapists to come to his school and help him in any way they can. And so it was done, and we got the therapies. After three years, it just took that one phone call. I had thought I was speaking to the policy officer's secretary, turns out I had actually spoken to the minister. Coincidence? I don't think so; rather divine intervention and the universe providing. Mind you, if I'd known I was speaking to the minister, I probably wouldn't have said half the things I did.

I was worried that Storm's legs were getting worse; what I wanted most was physiotherapy for him and that is what we got. It was a good outcome to finish off the year and I was, would you believe, hopeful. They would employ a local physiotherapist to see Storm. I didn't know yet how often, because I guessed it would depend on finances, but nevertheless it was great news.

A vision impairment consultant also came to the school to assess Storm and set up a program to help him. She asked if she could take him to an animal farm with other children who were visually impaired. I agreed and we met at a designated place in Perth. While Storm went off to the farm, I shopped until it was time to pick him up. He was a happy chappie— apparently he had hugged a chook, rubbing his face in its feathers, and stuck his finger up a cow's nose. Go Stormy! I didn't even know there was assistance available from any vision impairment department. I'm so glad I made that phone call.

One morning in December I was woken by the sound of Storm coughing. I got up immediately and walked into his room and he was standing beside his bed, using the bed to hold him upright. He had "coughed" to get my attention—the bed was covered in vomit. My poor, poor Storm, he had been sick and I wasn't there. I picked him up, did what was needed and then put him in my bed where he fell asleep. Then I sorted out his bed. I don't know what caused him to vomit but it was very clever of him to get himself out of bed, it couldn't have been easy for him to get up and stand beside it because his legs had started stiffening. *He is always surprising me.*

The next day he had vomit around his mouth in the morning, Whatever he had, I got it too. I started dry-retching, and it progressed to vomiting along with diarrhoea. I had to get Jan to come over and carry Storm to bed because I was too ill to pick him up. Even after he recovered and I had stopped vomiting, I was still too weak to carry him, so I gave him his breakfast in bed and then Jan took him to school. I went to bed and slept the day away. When I woke in the afternoon I felt much better and was able to pick him up from school. That night, I put him in bed with me so I wouldn't have to get up during the night to check on him.

The school year was coming to an end and at the last assembly in Bindoon, Storm received a certificate for making a special and positive contribution to his class. I believe it had been a positive experience for him and also for the other kids in his class—he learned that certain behaviour was expected within the class environment, he was treated "normally" and I believe the other children learned from his disabilities. I had noticed that children came up to him and talked to him or helped him. It was heartwarming to see children who were neither afraid nor intimidated by his differences. And Storm simply loved people.

School has finished for the year and Storm seems a bit weary. I have found the last term of school is always the hardest for Storm, but I think that is so for most kids. He hasn't been eating much, especially his dinner; I think the hot weather affects him just like it does me.

One night, I was trying to feed him his dinner but after two mouthfuls I couldn't get him to eat any more. I told him I was worried about him, and he reached out, put his arms around my neck and kissed me on the lips. *Aah, what a cutie!* A few days later we visited Rae after school and he was sitting on my lap while I was chatting away. He started wriggling on my lap so Rae transferred him on to hers. He reached up and kissed her on the lips and while we talked, he kept kissing her on the cheek. *Womaniser!*

Chapter Ten

2002

Not a good start to the year. Storm had a seizure on New Year's Eve that floored him for days. I don't think the hot weather helped, he lay on the couch for days too exhausted to do anything. It was far too hot to go outside anyway and sitting with him was fine by me, especially since I was again ill with gastro. I vomited until there was nothing left to bring up and I had no energy to even stand upright, let alone lift Storm from his bed. I had to ask Jan to come over and help him out of bed and put him in the lounge room for me where I fed and changed him between running to the toilet to be sick. It was three days before I could pick him up.

The first day I felt better, I put Storm in the car to go grocery shopping in town but as I started to drive out, I realised I had a flat tyre. I could have cried, I was still feeling weak and would have loved to act like a "princess", and ask someone to change the tyre for me. But on the farm I was always getting flat tyres and changing them so I sucked it up, changed the wheel and drove to town. I was well aware I was going to have to learn to let people help me. Jan was already a great help, but I was still reluctant to seek help for anything I could do myself.

Storm had tonsillitis again, quite bad this time, and I hoped it was not an indication of how the rest of the year was going to be. I bought him some ice cream to soothe his throat and he thought that was pretty good. He recovered in time for his weekend at Catholic Care. After dropping him off, Toni and I went shopping for a stereo for me. I hadn't had one since I left the farm six years earlier, it just hadn't been on my need-to-have list. Most of the money was spent on Storm's therapies but now I had managed to save a bit for a small portable stereo.

After buying the stereo we visited Marteena who we hadn't seen for a long time and she gave us both a massage. I dropped Toni off and drove home, set up the stereo and played music for hours. I had a lovely weekend of music and was all relaxed when I collected Storm. He was glad to see me and clung to me, which was unusual, and I was worried that something had happened to make him that way. Before going home, I took him to Marteena's for a massage—he hadn't had one of her massages since she left Bindoon and, afterwards, he was all relaxed. I picked up a video on the way home and Jan's daughter, Emily, came over and watched it with us. *Yes, I know Storm can't see—I'm not in denial—but he can hear; you must not underestimate a child just because he doesn't express himself with words.* He loved the video and laughed during certain parts of it.

February arrived and so did my birthday. Rae, Toni and I usually had lunch together on each of our birthdays but this year I had to be persuaded to go to Perth because Storm had been having attacks a couple of days beforehand. Jan said she would look after him so I went to Perth. Just as I was leaving, two men arrived to put up a new fence along the front of my property. The previous post and rail fence did nothing to deter the kangaroos and I used to think the roos were laughing at me as they climbed through it. The new fence was my birthday present to myself and it was all up when I got back from Perth. I picked up Storm from Jan's and she told me he'd had three seizures while I was away. I felt so guilty for leaving him when he was ill.

The holidays were over and school had started again, yippee!! The Christmas holidays were far too long for Storm, and he got bored. This year he would be getting a Marteena massage every Monday after school in Perth—she had agreed to a price that suited us both. His legs were getting stiffer for reasons I couldn't fathom. I know the doctors said it was cerebral palsy, no matter how many times I told them the stiffness didn't begin to appear until after he turned six, about the time the seizures started. The doctors thought they knew, but they were wrong. Marteena's massages were so beneficial—she worked her magic on his legs and any other part of his body she thought needed attention. Afterwards, he was always relaxed and much more flexible.

It was best to give him his dinner straight after his massage. I would buy a frozen meal (he liked shepherd's pie), microwave it while he was having his massage and it would be ready by the end of the massage. After he ate, we would head off home and I'd give him his bath, which added to his relaxed state, then put him to bed. It was a good way to start the week.

Storm went off to Catholic Care just as I started vomiting again. Perhaps there was some connection between the vomiting and Storm going off—it was like I was sabotaging what would be an enjoyable break. Thankfully I was well enough to drive when it was time to pick him up again.

Then Storm came down with bronchitis. I was beginning to think it didn't look like a good year, health-wise, for either of us!

Change that thought! I don't want to put out to the universe that it's going to be a bad year, because that's what I will get. Thank you, universe, for the great year we are having and will continue to have!

People sometimes come into your life for a reason that might not be quite clear at the time. At the beginning of the year I'd struck up a friendship with the local hairdresser after going in to look at some clothes someone was selling at the front of her shop. When she invited me and Storm to her house for a get-together she and her partner were having with a few of their friends, I decided it would do me good to get out, mingle with people and brush up on my social skills. But I was as always concerned how they would take to Storm; that was always my concern, never Storm's, he charmed them as usual.

At the party, I met a couple, Kiwi and Peta. Kiwi is a Maori—what I'd expect a Maori elder to be—and I noticed that everyone seemed to pay him quite a bit of respect. We chatted and Storm sat happily on Kiwi's lap. A couple of days later, Kiwi and Peta turned up unexpectedly on my doorstep. They came in for coffee and Storm sat on Kiwi's lap again, totally in awe of him. You just don't know who is going to enter your life, why, or for how long; you just have to take the ride and see where it ends up.

Storm has tonsillitis again! It's the third time already this year and it's only April. He really should have his tonsils removed but it's too much of a risk; if he started bleeding we would have no way of knowing without constantly checking his mouth so he has been put on another course of antibiotics.

Six days later he started having seizures after a break of more than 10 weeks, the longest he had gone without an attack since they started. They floored him as usual and an infection in his nose just added to his misery. However, he recovered in a couple of days and by then the school holidays had arrived, just in the nick of time as we were both exhausted.

A new development: Stormy was to go to a new respite centre for five days. By now I knew he would be fine away from me for five days, but I wasn't sure how I would be with him out of my sight for so long. The new place, Landsdale Farm, had cottages surrounded by gardens and each cottage housed a couple of children with a carer. The set-up was on a much larger scale than Catholic Care, which made me feel unsure there were enough people to look after all the children, but they convinced me that Storm would be fine, so I gave in and off he went. As always, his absence left me with an ache in my stomach, and I rang every day to check on him. He had a great time, charmed all the ladies and when I picked him up at the end of the five days he was a very happy child.

I gardened to my heart's content while he was away; it soothed my soul even though I missed him the whole time. And he was only home five days before he was off again, this time to Catholic Care for the weekend. He didn't need to go, but I didn't get breaks all that often so when they were available I took them, and he was happy to go because he always got spoilt. I dropped him off, did some shopping them came home with the ache in my stomach to keep me company.

Next morning a friend visited and we were sitting on the verandah having a coffee when I got a phone call from the co-ordinator at Catholic Care. The ache in my stomach went into overdrive. Storm was tired and sleeping a lot, which was odd for him if he hadn't had a seizure. I told the co-ordinator I was on my way. It's an hour's drive to Perth, normally. This day I broke the record. When I arrived they took me into Storm's room. He was sound asleep so I tried to wake him up. He didn't respond. I rang the specialist but his secretary told me to take Storm straight to hospital. I carried him to the car—he was unconscious, and like a limp rag. I asked one of the carers for a rundown on what had happened so I could tell them at the hospital. She told me that at 5am Storm had a temperature of 37.5 so he was given Panadol, he had eaten his breakfast and then they had gone out on the bus. But Storm became tired so they brought him home, put him to bed and he went to sleep. They rang me at 11am. As I strapped Storm into his booster seat my heart was racing. *This is bad.*

I took off to the hospital, breaking more speed limits, even going the wrong way up a one-way street so that I could get to the hospital as fast as possible. I carried Storm into emergency and shouted to the triage nurse that he was unconscious. There was no waiting this time; we were whisked into the resuscitation room and it was an instant hive of activity while I related what I'd been told.

When the doctor lifted Storm's eyelids, his eyes were very bloodshot and when I commented on it, I was told it was conjunctivitis. What absolute bulls—t! Where did this guy get his medical degree—out of a Weetbix box?

They put a drip in Storm's arm, he was dehydrated, and they also gave him antibiotics. The doctor thought he might have a bacterial infection, so blood was taken for tests. We had to wait for hours before a bed became available and still Storm had a fever and hadn't woken up. I still can't believe how calm I was—panic left me the moment we arrived at the re-suss room. The nurses had moved around quickly but calmly and it calmed me. *I feel safe even though I don't know what is happening to Stormy.*

Finally, he was given a bed on a ward and was settled in, still unconscious. A doctor explained she wasn't sure what was wrong with him, but she didn't think it was a bacterial infection. Maybe the epilim had built up in his system, because it was as if he'd had an overdose, so they were going to withhold his epilim and run some tests to check his levels.

Later, I was just going to find a nurse to check his temperature and I saw Marteena and Rae. I must have phoned them at some stage but had forgotten about it. I was so glad to see them that I almost cried.

Storm was finally coming to, opening his eyes at long last, at least for a few minutes. Marteena tried to get him to smile but he just closed his eyes. Rae noticed they were bloodshot so I told her what the doctor in emergency had said. Rae was quite sure, like me, that it wasn't conjunctivitis but something that had happened inside his head.

We noticed that the left side of his body was hot and the right side cool. Marteena got his temperature down a bit with a cold flannel on his head and I tried to get him to drink when he opened his eyes but he only managed a few sips. He ate a few mouthfuls of ice cream before lapsing into a deep sleep.

Rae and Marteena left about 9pm and I sat up the rest of the night just watching him. I couldn't sleep anyway; I needed some quiet time to process the events of the day.

Storm slept peacefully all night and most of the next day but his temperature kept fluctuating, up and down. Test results showed that he hadn't overdosed on epilim. His white blood-cell count was really low and it did appear that he had a bacterial infection. I spent the day watching him sleep, even though I felt exhausted from my own lack of sleep.

Marteena came back with her daughter Sandra, who sat with Storm while we went off to the coffee shop for a pick-me-up and some fresh air. *Thank God for friends, and what amazing and caring friends I have!* Then the nurses set up a foldout bed for me next to Storm and promised me they would keep a close eye on him, so I climbed into bed and was out like a light.

Third day in hospital: Stormy was still sleeping most of the time and his temperature was still fairly high. The doctor told me he would be there for at least five days so I asked the nurse if I could race home and fetch some clothes and toiletries—I had been in the same clothes for three days and really needed to change. The nurse said she would keep a close eye on Storm while I was gone so off I raced—an hour each way but this time I kept to the speed limit. I showered quickly and packed a bag, watered and fed the chooks, then drove back to the hospital, walked into Storm's room and there he was, still sleeping—he had never slept so much in his life and it was all a bit freaky.

The stress must have finally taken its toll on my body. I was coming down with a cold, my body ached and my head was splitting, so I dosed myself up on Panadol. Storm opened his eyes only a couple of times during the day, so when he looked like he was settled for the night, I went to bed and was out like a light. I didn't even hear the nurses when they came to check on Storm.

Day 4: Storm was awake so I fed him his breakfast and he ate it all. Afterwards, I had to lie down because I was beginning to feel really ill. Luckily, Storm was still sleepy so I could have a quick nap. I woke when the doctor arrived. She said he was getting better. Apparently, the reason Storm was sleeping so much was because of the antibiotics which were quite strong—it would have been nice if they'd told me that earlier. It was actually a relief that Storm was sleeping so much because I seemed to be getting more and more ill and in the end, it was too much even sit up alongside him, so I lay on the bed and watched him while I dozed.

Day 5: I woke at 5am feeling worse and shivering with cold, so I got more Panadol from one of the nurses and went back to bed. I woke again when they brought in breakfast, and after feeding Storm I had a really hot shower to warm my bones. Nothing much had changed when the doctor did her rounds. His temperature would drop a bit, then go back up. *I'm going to need something pumped into me soon—I feel dreadful, never felt this bad in my life before.* A nurse organised for me to see a doctor in emergency who said my temperature was 38, not too bad, and I had a viral infection. "Take Panadol every four hours and drink plenty of water." I was already doing all that and now I had to use what little energy I had left to walk back to Storm's room. I felt so tearful and miserable when I got back to him that I climbed on to his bed and cuddled up to him while he slept.

Day 6: Storm's getting better and I'm getting worse. Again, I was sent back to emergency and this time I was told I had a bacterial infection. I was given a prescription and by the time I got back to Storm, I was exhausted. I took the antibiotics and collapsed on my bed. Thank God the nurses were there to look after Storm!

Day 7: Storm was finally recovering, lucky bugger. I was a different story—the antibiotics had done nothing and in the morning the nurses insisted I go back to emergency. By then I couldn't walk and even breathing was very hard to do, so one of the nurses wheeled me down to emergency. It was frightening not being able to breathe easily! I was given a bed and now they'd decided I had pneumonia so I was given oxygen and a drip was put into my arm for two hours, along with stronger antibiotics. After those two hours, I felt so much better that I was able to walk back to Storm's room.

The needle for the drip is disgustingly long and feels awful as it's put in and removed and my sympathy is with Stormy—he's had quite a few drips put in during his life.

I crashed on my bed; I don't ever want to feel that ill again. Storm was getting so much better; he was awake more often and his temperature was finally normal. He was eating well, such a relief, and we both dozed for most of the day.

Day 8: Storm was so much better and I was feeling a little better but still as weak as a kitten. The doctor said Storm was well enough to go home, so I packed up our stuff, dressed Storm, and finally we left. I didn't have his wheelchair so I had to carry him to the car and I was quite puffed by the time I got him strapped in. The life had been totally sucked out of me by the time we arrived home. I put Storm on the couch—I don't think he was feeling energetic himself—and he tried to pick up his toys, but in the end he went off to sleep. We both dozed most of the day away until I had to get up to feed and change him. That night we went to bed early and it was so good to sleep in our own beds.

Three days afterwards, in late afternoon, Storm was playing when he suddenly went very pale. I picked him up, put him on the couch and took his temperature which was a very low 34.5. A few minutes later he vomited, all over himself and the couch, everywhere! I changed his clothes, then put him on his beanbag while I cleaned up—I can handle many things but vomit is my weak point so I was dry-retching while I did it. Whatever was wrong with Storm passed after he vomited, he was better and even ate all his dinner. I had a sore stomach from the dry retching . . . perfect!

Though much better, Storm still wasn't well enough for school so we had some nice days together, just chilling out. I lit the fire in the mornings so it was warm and cosy and we spent the day in front of it. I cooked up some of our favourite meals—we both deserved a bit of pampering after our stint in hospital, so we hid out in the house together. I knew the moment he was ready to go back to school—he got very vocal and made a hell of a noise with his toys, banging them and throwing them around the room.

Sometimes, the noisy playing could get a bit annoying, especially in the long Christmas holidays, six weeks with only me to entertain him. So it was great that he could go off to Catholic Care, to a different environment with more stimulation and all those ladies to fuss over him. Even so, tempers occasionally flared between us and eventually, when I couldn't handle the endless vocalising and banging of toys, I would tell him to be quiet, which he was for a couple of minutes and then the noise was back in full swing. In the end, we'd get cranky with each other and when I told him to be quiet, he'd just raise his eyebrows as if to say: "Well, excuse me!" I'd end up making coffee and telling him that I was going to take a walk around the block and he couldn't come, ha ha . . .

I know he can't walk . . . that's why I say it! Storm isn't offended; we thrive on our black humour, which he has inherited from me. He rants at me and I'm straight out the back door. I feel a lot better after a walk and some fresh air—Storm is still making a racket but I'm now cool, calm and collected.

At last he was well enough to go back to school. His first day back wore him out so he was asleep by 7pm, which was very early for him.

Only 10 days out of hospital, barely recovered and moving back into the swing of life, he had three attacks in one day—which wasn't so much, he'd had more, but not just after recovering from a serious illness. Poor little bugger, they exhausted him and he was too tired even to eat. I was angry that this was happening and angry that I had to sit and watch him have seizures. He didn't have any the next day, but just sitting in his stroller in the garden exhausted him. On the third day I was getting him out of bed when all of a sudden he clutched at me and had a seizure. It tore my heart to see the fear in his face just before he had the attack.

God, I hate these attacks. It's as if someone is physically hurting my son and I'm just letting them do it. I had arranged for Lisa to cut his hair today, now I don't know whether to do it or not. Will it cause another seizure? Is his head hurting? It's all too hard. Could someone tell me what I should do? I hate having to make all the decisions. Take a breath, Mandy, you know all will be provided.

In the end, I did take Storm to get his hair cut—a drama with the clippers though, because he loved the vibrations and spent the whole time trying to get his hands on the machine. I had to grab his hands and hold them. We let him hold the clippers for a bit after his hair was cut, then I took him home. I gave him a bath to get the rest of the hair off him and he looked so handsome.

Finally he was back at school and I could have some down time. I went next door to have coffee with Jan, then came home and attacked the garden. I'd had enough of being cooped up inside the house—even if it poured with rain, I needed to be out in the garden with my plants, the birds and the fresh air.

After three days at school Stormy was off to respite for the weekend—a whole weekend all to myself. I slept in, had coffee in bed while I read, whipper-snipped the yard and fertilised the garden, then came inside and watched videos, it was just perfect. Storm must have had a good weekend too, because he was all smiles when I picked him up on Sunday afternoon.

On Monday, it was back to the Perth school for the first time in several weeks. Storm was happy about that, he was able to swim and he was mad keen on swimming. Me? I had to go for a tetanus shot—on my wonderful weekend I had been bitten by a rather large dog. He didn't draw blood but he'd had a good go at crushing the bones in my wrist and it hurt like hell. I had a bad bruise and the doctor said I must have a shot—what a bitch, I don't like needles.

Storm had his Monday afternoon Marteena massage and was suitably relaxed. He managed a whole week at school, but seemed less happy at the weekend. On Sunday night he had a temperature of 38.8, so I put him in a tepid bath and kept him there until the water went cold. It felt like a cruel thing to do in winter, when it was cold in any case, but finally his temperature came down and I was able to put him to bed. He slept in until 10am, so no school that day.

The next evening I was drying him after his bath when I noticed he didn't like me touching the right side of his head. I rang the doctor and managed to get a 6pm appointment. It turned out he had a fungal infection in his ear, so no school for the rest of the week. He was having a bad year.

He played in the lounge room the next day and in the afternoon he looked tired so I put him on the couch and he went off to sleep. He wasn't impressed when I woke him for his medicine, wouldn't eat his dinner and only had a few sips of water. His sleeping made me very nervous—he wasn't going to pull his unconscious trick again, was he?

He got better, and we managed a few good weeks of school, trips to Perth on Mondays and massages after school, then came the holidays. He hadn't been at school much this term but I was quite happy to have him home for two weeks, especially since it was winter, my favourite time of the year.

My friend Roma and her daughter Cherrie visited for a couple of days in the first week of the school holidays. They arrived on the Friday afternoon, and after putting Storm to bed, Roma and I sat chatting late into the night. The next day we drove to Perth, dropped Storm at Marteena's house for the day, then the three of us hit the shops as country folk do when they are in Perth. We picked Storm up about 5pm, bought Chinese takeaway for dinner, then drove home. Roma and I had another late night of chatting after Storm and Cherrie went to bed.

I planned to take Roma and Cherrie to the markets in Perth the next morning, but I had trouble rousing Storm—he seemed to be awake and ate his breakfast, but wouldn't open his eyes. I was all calm in front of Roma, acting as if nothing was wrong, but inside my head I was screaming:

"What the hell do I do?" He seemed perfectly fine except he wouldn't—or couldn't—open his eyes.

By this time, I was over doctors telling me he was fine when he wasn't, so I did nothing. He didn't have a temperature, so that at least was good. I dressed him, put him in the car seat (still he slept on) and we drove to Perth. When we arrived at the markets, I put him in his stroller and we had been walking around for a while when, finally, he opened his eyes. I'm sure Roma and Cherrie enjoyed the markets but my mind was racing the whole time, wondering what could possibly be going on with Storm.

I feel like I'm in a ship that is sinking but we don't know why the ship is sinking and there is no outward reason why it is sinking. So I'm going to carry on like everything is okay.

The next day, Roma and Cherrie left for the farm at 9am and it was 10 o'clock before I managed to get Storm to open his eyes. And this was the kid who always woke me early in the morning. I fed and changed him, then packed the car and headed to my parents' place in Dunsborough. I needed some moral support—family, people who believed what I told them, who didn't fob me off, who I could share these burdens with . . .

We arrived about 2pm. Next day, again, Storm didn't wake until 10am and he took a bit of rousing—but he was fine for the rest of the day. I dug up plants for my garden and he enjoyed being out in my parents' magnificent garden. He was eating well, too. We headed back to Bindoon that morning, after he'd slept again until 10. After yet another morning of being unable to rouse him, I decided to take him to his doctor in Perth—at least make the doctor aware of what was happening. Surprise, surprise, the doctor believed me and suggested that Storm could be having seizures in his sleep. Now we must fiddle with his medications, which meant more blood tests. Storm actually woke up on his own the next morning. What blissful relief.

Lisa was having a girls night out with her friend Peta, and Storm and I went along too—a bit of light hearted chitchat was just what I needed. Storm stayed awake the whole time listening to us and we didn't get home until 1am so we both slept in the next day. He woke of his own accord and I was jubilant. I thought things were back on track (well, our track at least) but in the afternoon he couldn't sit up. He lay on some pillows for most of the day and I lit the fire and sat with him, reading magazines to distract myself. *Will we both make it to the end of this year in one piece? Here's hoping!*

After much deliberation I decided I would take Storm to school in Perth on the first Monday of the new term. It took a bit to wake him up early enough, but he seemed fine after his breakfast, so we drove to Perth and I dropped him at school and went off to do some shopping and catch up with Toni. Storm had a good day at school and thoroughly enjoyed his massage with Marteena afterwards. He went to sleep early, which was unusual for him but not really surprising after all that had been going on.

He must be better, he has managed a whole week of school without one hiccup; he is even waking up at his normal early time in the morning. I'm exhausted, it must be emotional exhaustion and all I want to do is sleep. While Storm has been at school I have done stuff-all, just my basic house chores then I've lit the fire and dozed on the couch until it was time to pick him up.

Life was running smoothly for a change. Storm hadn't missed any school and I seemed to have got over my tiredness. I had begun stripping the wallpaper from the lounge room walls. I left that room until last because I knew it was going to be the hardest room and the most expensive—I'd been saving for a very long time for new curtains and a specialised paint. I could see through the wallpaper that the previous owners had taken a door out and filled it in very roughly with gyprock. It was going to need some disguising so I'd bought a paint called "French Distemper"—it goes on in two coats and the second coat has an additive that gives it a very rough-textured finish. Hopefully, it would cover any imperfections. But I was still pulling off seemingly endless wallpaper. I worked in the garden when it was fine and stripped wallpaper when it rained.

I had acquired another friend in Bindoon, Laurel, who shared my interest in gardening and I loved going to her home to chat and drink endless cups of coffee. I was also seeing quite a lot of Lisa and her friends. This was the most socialising I'd ever done and it helped to have some light-hearted moments to relieve the stress of caring for Storm.

I swear, if the heart could show scarring from the emotional pain that one has felt, mine would be covered all over in scars—it wouldn't be recognisable as a heart. Mine is the helpless heart that has to watch Stormy endure. And what would his precious heart look like? We can't wallow in the sadness of our lives, otherwise it would consume us and we would be a walking and talking misery, and that is not who Storm and I are. We endure, it passes and our humour prevails.

In the midst of all the wallpaper stripping and painting of dodgy walls, Storm began another bout of seizures. Again, I would like to slap the doctor who said the seizures didn't hurt. They did hurt him and they hurt my heart, too. So while he was having his seizures I held him and when he went to sleep I put him on a mattress in the hallway and went on painting the lounge room while he slept. He had two days of seizures and then they passed. This time he recovered quickly; he didn't lose his ability to sit up, so maybe they hadn't been so bad.

On Friday I took him to school and stayed for the assembly, at which Storm was to be presented with a certificate. I was sitting at the back when Fiona, one of Storm's aides, came up to me saying he had had a seizure. I held him in my arms until they called his name, then I carried him up to the stage so he could be presented with his certificate. I can't remember what it was for, but it should have been for bravery. Afterwards, I took him home and settled him on the couch to rest. The next morning, I woke up feeling like someone had beaten me to a pulp, my body ached and Storm didn't look too good, either.

We spent the whole weekend with me on the couch and Storm on a mattress next to me—I think we both had the flu or a really, really nasty cold. Jan brought over a wheelbarrow of wood for us to keep the fire going as we had run out of wood and I didn't have the energy to go looking for more on the block, God bless Jan.

We were no better by Monday so school in Perth was cancelled and there was more lying on couch and mattress. Storm was eating less—he must be feeling really crappy. By Tuesday I felt improved but Storm was no better, so again no school.

I had got a cash job weeding a neighbour's garden, so Jan offered to look after Storm while I worked for a couple of hours. When I picked him up Storm, Jan said he was running a fever. He certainly looked miserable. At home, I gave him some Panadol, undressed him down to just his nappy and took his temperature—it was 39, that's one hot little boy. Into a tepid bath for him (it was the middle of winter) and he didn't even mind because he likes his bath no matter what. I was freezing but I didn't light the fire and Storm was still burning up even though the house was so cold.

It took hours to get his temperature down and it was the wee hours before I felt I could safely go to bed and sleep. Storm was exhausted. Next morning, his temperature was high again so I dosed him up and rang the doctor as soon as it was a decent hour. It turned out he had tonsillitis again so that meant more antibiotics—he'd had so many already this year, it couldn't be good. But I felt relieved that the doctor had found out what was wrong. For Storm, there was no relief. We were back to inhabiting the lounge room with no fire because of his high temperature. Finally he was on the mend, the antibiotics kicked in and he was beginning to smile and play with his toys. Meanwhile I was feeling like hell so the following week it was back to the doctor to get the all-clear for Storm and be told I had infected sinuses. Well done, Mandy!

Storm was able to return to school and was booked to go to Catholic Care on the weekend. But on the Friday morning he didn't wake until 11am after being up most of the night. It was a toss-up whether I'd still send him off for the weekend and in the end I did because I was so exhausted, I knew I needed to get some sleep so I could cope. I dropped him off at the respite centre just after midday and was about to meet Toni for coffee when my phone rang. Storm's temperature had shot up to 40 and they'd put him in a cool bath.

He looked miserable and I'd had enough and I'm sure he felt the same. I drove him straight to the iridologist, carried him into the waiting room and asked if there was any chance I could see the iridologist today, preferably now. I was a woman on the edge and I think I looked like it. I didn't care how long I waited, we weren't leaving until I got some help. After just a few minutes, we were called in. The iridologist took one look at Storm's eyes and said his glands were blocked and his condition was worsening (I had kind of guessed that myself, just going by what we'd had to deal with so far this year). He also said Storm had a serious virus in his body. He told me I should grate up a red onion, a carrot and a green apple, strain it all through some muslin and give Storm the resultant juice twice a day. No tablets, just the juice. *Bizarre, but okay, that's what I'll do.*

I almost burst into tears at the supermarket when at first I couldn't find any red onions. But finally, I had them and we headed home. I made up the concoction and fed it to Storm with a syringe—it didn't smell too flash and Storm pulled a face but he didn't spit it out. I know I would have! He couldn't eat at dinner time, but at least his temperature was coming down.

The next day his temperature was fine but still he didn't eat much. I gave him more of the juice. The following day, he ate a big breakfast but not much else. But he was so much better! I don't know what the onion, carrot and apple do when they're combined but it worked a treat, such a simple thing!

Storm was back at the Perth school on Monday and loved his Marteena massage in the afternoon; he'd missed a few. In fact, he was well all week, went to school every day, ate well and even went to sleep early.

Catholic Care managed to fit him in for another weekend to replace the one he missed. It's usually every six weeks, so we were both overdue for a weekend of pampering. Storm got his pampering from the ladies at respite and I was able to have lunch with Toni and Rae, as well as sleep in and watch telly with the fire on while it poured with rain outside—it was perfect!

On September 19 everyone telephoned to wish Storm a happy tenth birthday. I made him a cake (chocolate, decorated with freckles, of course) which I took to the school for him to share with his classmates. He was in his element, the centre of attention, as every birthday boy should be.

Even though he was well, he still wasn't eating much and no amount of bribery with his favourite foods would entice him to eat more. I mentioned it the next time we visited Marteena. In the course of his massage, she found a crystal in his foot that coincided with the stomach area (Marteena also did reflexology) so she massaged it out and then massaged his stomach where she also found a lump, which she also managed to remove. I was amazed but, then again, Marteena is very talented. The next day he ate all his lunch, and the school told me he had been really hungry. I don't know what had been wrong, but it seemed Marteena had fixed whatever was causing the problem. *Storm is a mystery.*

The high temperatures came back, but this time I was armed with a concoction. I didn't know if it was the same type of virus, but I wasn't waiting to find out. I made up the juice and gave it to Storm and he had a rough night. Luckily it was now school holidays so he could sleep in. When he woke, he called out: "Mum, mum." It was music to my ears. His temperature was still high but he seemed happy to play with his toys in the lounge room. It had stopped raining so I did some whipper-snipping in the yard, stopping often to check on him. On one of the checks, I found him covered in sweat but his temperature was normal. *Maybe the fever has broken.* That was Saturday. On Sunday, he had a seizure while we were sitting together in the lounge room. He knew he was about to have the attack, because he reached out his arms to me, I grabbed him and held him close and then the seizure took over. I hugged him until it was over.

He couldn't sleep that night so I put him in bed with me and lay there wondering how our lives had come to this. *What purpose does it serve to suffer so much, how can we possibly retain our good humour . . . what a crappy year it's been for Storm!* And then he reached out to me again because he was about to have another attack. Again, I held him in my arms. *At least he knows I'm here for him.* He went to sleep afterwards with his foot touching my leg so he knew where I was. At 6am he had another attack and then his temperature went up. I wondered if the high temperatures and the seizures were connected. He was supposed to be going to respite for the weekend but I could see that wasn't going to happen. I gave him some Panadol, and a bath to get his temperature down. It was a quiet day, Storm just lay on the couch sleeping or playing with his toys.

The school holidays were great. We slept in, spent a couple of days in Dunsborough and visited friends around Bindoon, but that was it. Storm was officially better; he was noisy again after so many weeks of quiet, which I have to say were very eerie!

Lisa asked me to work in her hair salon on a now and then basis. Sometimes I had to take Storm along. I set him up in his stroller with a few toys and he listened to the conversations. I even caught him leaning towards the clients so he could hear what they were saying—definitely a people person. If it wasn't for Storm, I would have lived like a hermit, but he brought me out of my shell. That's just one of the good things he brought to my life.

Two weeks after the holidays ended he had another bout of seizures, same routine—when the seizures were over, back to school. School brightened his life and I'm sure his aides, as well as his schoolmates, can take credit for that. He loved his aides—and they treated him just like any other child. He particularly loved it when Carolyn sat him on a bean-bag in the library or under a tree and read to him. *If she stops reading, he pinches her.*

Something else was wrong; something different. He was very noisy and uncomfortable during his massage on Monday. Marteena said his back was out. She fixed it but he was overly noisy on the drive back to Bindoon. I gave him some Panadol when we got home, but the next day he was stiff and agitated. On Wednesday morning, he didn't appear to be breathing when I went into his room and he was floppy when I picked him up. I gave him a little shake and he took a breath. *Phew, that gave me a fright! I think I'm just going to hold him in my arms until my heartbeat slows down to normal again! What I love most in the world is not going to stay very long; my heart knows that he can't possibly stay.*

A couple of days later, he had me laughing. I'd picked him up from school and driven home. When I opened the car door, he reached over, grabbed the door handle and closed the door again. Maybe he was ticked off at me for some reason—he'd never done it before. I just stood there and cracked up laughing, it really lightened my heart. Storm had a way of lighting up my life and brushing away the seriousness of it all.

After days and weeks of Storm not sleeping until the early hours, I took him to the local doctor to see if he had any suggestions. He prescribed Valium. I gave it to Storm that night but he didn't sleep until 5am, then didn't wake up until lunchtime. Valium actually made him more alert, not tired at all. *It has the same effect on me so I think we'll pass on that particular drug.*

The rainy days passed and the number of hot days was increasing. It gets so hot it would suck the life out of the fittest person, let alone a child who has endured a year of illnesses. I was so over this year and it hadn't finished yet.

Storm was at school every day this week and I worked at the hair salon when asked besides my gardening job.

I usually went to the gardening job after dropping Storm at school and worked there until it got too hot. I was also busy looking for Christmas presents because it would be impossible to do any shopping once school finished for the year. Toni and I had Christmas lunch. I always enjoy my lunches with Toni and Rae, always lots of laughter. We exchanged presents and it was all good. Summer was definitely here. When Storm was in bed and it was still light outside, I pottered in the garden until it got dark. That was my time, at the end of the day, and I enjoyed it. It poured with rain for a couple of days before Christmas—very refreshing.

We spent Christmas with family, as usual, and it was very enjoyable. *Goodbye 2002, I'm over you; let's just finish it and hopefully next year will be better.*

Chapter Eleven

2003

I bought Storm a trampoline for Christmas—he sat on it while I gardened in the cool of evening; and now and then I would bounce with him. It was too hot to do much else.

We had a meeting at my house with Storm's physiotherapist and some people from Disability Services. He had a new wheelchair—the first one fitted to his measurements. The chair he had been using was a spare one from Disability Services and he'd long ago outgrown it. This one was fitted out especially for him and had a lot more padding.

February came, and with it my 40th birthday—where did the years go? I had to have a party, and one of the girls I invited was Tina, who I'd met through Lisa. She told me her mother was an artist and asked me if I'd like a sketch done of Storm. I agreed immediately. I gave Tina one of my favourite photos of him and her mum ended up doing two sketches—I gave one to my mum and the other is one of my prized possessions.

When school started again, Storm's routine was the same as the previous year—special school in Perth on Mondays, followed by a

Marteena massage, then school in Bindoon from Tuesday to Friday. His teacher this year was Ann Graham, who was his Education Support teacher when he first started school. And he had the same aides as last year, so no big changes at all. He was excited to be back at school. On the first day I had driven him to school and was putting him into his wheelchair when his aide, Carolyn, knelt down in front of him. As soon as she spoke, his face lit up and he leaned over and gave her a kiss. *What a little womaniser.*

I knew he'd be happy to be back at school. I'd done my best to entertain him; he loved to paint so I set him up with his paints and he had a ball. But I'm sure I didn't do enough to stimulate him and I bet I read him all the wrong books—he liked the books that Carolyn read to him. By now I was quite happy to share the caring around. The fact that Storm loved his other carers so much made it easier for me to leave him in their care, knowing they would never let anything happen to him.

When he had his first lot of seizures for the year, it was seven in one day, a lot for a small body to endure. The last of them struck just after 7pm. I was very concerned so I rang the Health Line and was told to take him straight to hospital. I was told that whenever I rang the Health Line, and usually it was a waste of both my time and the hospital's time because it was something I could cope with and had coped with in the past. But this time I decided, since it had been some time since he'd had so many attacks in one day, I'd feel better if he was checked out. I phoned Lisa and she offered to come with me, to keep an eye on Storm while I drove. We were at the hospital until midnight when they said Storm was fine to go home, so we grabbed some Maccas and headed back to Bindoon. At home,

I put Storm into bed with me because I was so tired and didn't want to have to get up through the night. He had one more attack and then he went off to sleep; I was asleep not long after.

Storm was like a wet rag the next day, exhausted and content to just lie on his mattress in the lounge room listening to the television. I rang Marteena to say we weren't coming to Perth and she told me her daughter Temily had said she was worried about Storm. This was at the same time as the attacks—these two usually spent time together on Monday afternoons when I took Storm there for his massage, and they certainly had a unique bond.

The next evening Storm was in bed and I walked into his room to check on him. The look on his face was the saddest I had ever seen and he had tears in the corners of his eyes. He hadn't shed a tear since he was two years old. It was gut-wrenching; I held him in my arms but I had no words that could comfort him and I was shedding my own tears. *There must be times when he hates his life—he must feel so frustrated at being trapped in a body that can't express what he feels.*

Storm had another hospital appointment, the beginning of many appointments about his legs. After taking careful measurements, they were going to put his legs in casts to make moulds for shoe inserts to "correct" his feet. I was not looking forward to it, and I was sure it would be uncomfortable for Storm, so I persuaded Marteena to come with us and was glad she brought Temily along to distract him with hugs and kisses. He behaved so well when they made the casts—he didn't move his feet or freak out at all with the strange sensations. It was all done quickly and efficiently and we were able to leave—and if it would help Stormy's legs, I was all for it.

Of course, these appointments are all because he has cerebral palsy. It doesn't matter how many times I explain to doctors that his legs weren't always like this, they've only been like this since the seizures started, they don't believe me. They know better and I'm lying because I don't want to face reality, blah blah blah. One day a doctor will realise I'm right, but it will be too late.

After dropping off Marteena and Temily, we headed back to Bindoon. We'd been invited to a barbecue for the birthday of Laurel's son, Mitchell. Storm had a great time with the other kids. He loved to pop balloons—don't ask me why, every time a balloon popped, he jumped. And then he wanted to pop another one, bit of a sick kid there, I think!

This year was looking a whole lot better than last year. Storm was generally happy and happy was all we aimed for in our lives. I had never socialised so much. I was working at Lisa's hair salon and in Vera Kay's garden and I felt useful. Laurel and I met up for coffee and to discuss gardening, which we both loved. But the main reason I was happy was that Storm was happy.

On Mondays, I spend the day in Perth where I can catch up with Toni or Rae. We might have lunch together and in the afternoons I always have my time with Marteena. I'm sure none of these ladies realise how important they are to me or the difference they've made to my life. They are light-hearted

people who never let me dwell on the sad side of Storm's life. I still have my
"poor me" days, and I give myself permission to have such days, but one day
only—more than that and my friends would kick my butt.

One day we went on a bus trip with a group of people from Bindoon to listen to a band playing in the park at Moore River. It was a big park with rolling green lawns and we set ourselves up under the trees with our picnic baskets. Storm lay on a blanket as we ate and drank and listened to the music. It was relaxing and so many people fussed over Storm. Good people, good music, good wine . . . good times!

Autumn arrived and I could start planting my bulbs and seedlings. Summers were too long and too hot and I hated watching my plants wilt and die in the heat. Also, Storm and I could spend more days in the garden—we'd been cooped up in the house all summer and were bursting to get out. Well, I know I was.

Another appointment at the hospital for Storm's legs—I sucked it up and took him all by myself. How brave am I! We had to wait for hours but at least it was cool. After school on Monday, Marteena had trouble massaging him—she said he was very tense. She could also tell that his head was really hurting him which I wouldn't have known. *I wonder how much more I miss?* At home I gave him some Painstop which I prayed would help.

Then he had an appointment with our local doctor to do blood tests to check his epilim levels. While we were there, I mentioned that Storm's head was hurting and I'd given him Painstop. I was totally shocked when he said he would do a blood workup to see if anything showed up. I hadn't really expected to be believed, let alone that anything would be done.

Storm's head stopped hurting, thankfully, and he seemed more relaxed. Next day, I stayed on at the school so I could catch up with his physio, Judy Dennis. Storm was being fitted with new splints. He did really well standing with them on, but absolutely refused to try to walk. Judy was another person who Storm really took to, even though her job was to get him to do more exercises. He didn't mind and some of the exercises made him laugh.

Even when he was only a year old and we were doing exercises twice a day, six days a week, he loved it. I'm sure he thought of it as a social gathering and he was pretty much the same when he went to Bullcreek for conductive education. Now, with Judy Dennis coming twice a week to the school, I think he knew she was trying to help him and for that he truly loved her.

His class was having a competition to see who could make the best outfits from plastic bags. After dropping him off, I raced over to the medical centre to get the results from his tests. His epilim levels were fine, but his white blood-cell count was still low—the drugs could do that. Nothing else showed up and since his headaches had stopped there was no reason for more tests.

After that, I raced back to the school to see how the plastic-bag competition was going. The kids had decorated Storm's wheelchair with plastic bags, and Storm was decorated in them as well. He looked very pleased with himself.

The next day was a Saturday. I was doing a first-aid course with St John Ambulance, Lisa's idea. I was worried about taking Storm, maybe he would get a bit noisy. I needn't have worried; everyone there was fine with him and he was quiet for most of the time. A couple of times I heard him laughing, so I relaxed.

We went shopping in Perth and that was a new experience because usually I didn't take Storm shopping. He was on his best behaviour, didn't make a sound and sat quietly in his wheelchair. But that didn't stop people staring at him.

Maybe I am over-reacting, but do they really need to stare? He doesn't have an extra head, in fact he's a good-looking kid. Well, at least he can't see them staring at him, so I stared back at the people who were staring at him, just to show them how it feels.

Now and then he showed me, just in case I forgot, that though he might not have been able to tell me what he wanted, or how he felt, he did know what I mean—that it was his body that was disabled, not his mind. It was Sunday morning and I wanted to lie in bed and doze; but I got up and went to Storm's room and saw he was awake. I asked him if he wanted to get up and he grabbed his quilt and pulled it over his head. This really made me giggle! It was a sure sign that he didn't want to get up, so I made him comfy and went back to bed. About an hour later, we had breakfast and it was a beautiful day all round, nice and cool.

The local doctor really did listen to me when I told him my concerns. Storm seemed a bit out of sorts so the doctor checked him over and it turned out his throat was a bit red so antibiotics were prescribed. How great was that? Not great that he had to take more antibiotics, but such a relief for me that I had found a doctor who listened to me. *This is big, folks!* I had struggled so long to be heard and this changed things so much. Now, Storm didn't have to get really ill before something was done and he didn't have to suffer for so long. There were times when the doctor found nothing wrong, but he didn't give me a hard time and I felt reassured. He never fobbed me off, he always checked Storm over—it was fantastic.

The weather turned cooler and we even had a few days of rain, so I ordered a load of wood delivered for winter. When it arrived, I carted it to the shed and stacked it, then started chopping it into smaller pieces. It came in big blocks and there was a lot of chopping to do which used to take me forever with an axe. But Dad bought me a wood splitter that did the job like cutting butter and took far less energy. *Oh, how I love the wet weather, the rainy days with the fire going—it's the best.*

Storm and I were invited to another birthday barbecue, this time for Jasmine, Laurel's eldest daughter. She asked Laurel if she could blow up some balloons for Storm to pop! Storm just loved it, popping balloons and laughing with the other children. He went to bed that night a happy boy.

Laurel had another daughter, Rachel, not long after moving to Bindoon. She and Storm got on really well; she would sit and play with him whenever we went around to their place, a bit like Temily when she was little. Laurel looked after Storm quite a few times, treating him just like any other member of her family. If he was exceptionally noisy, she would tell him to be quiet and then she'd get the eye-rolling treatment, the same as I got. Laurel always brought out a canvas chair for him to sit in, and it became known as "Storm's chair".

The first end-of-term holidays arrived, we could sleep in and not have to travel to Perth. Mum and Dad had sold their place in Dunsborough and built a house in Serpentine, which we visited for the first time. Toni was also there and we had a good couple of days before we had to come home. The block size is smaller than Dunsborough, just one acre, but it is only two hours drive from Bindoon—bonus!

The school holidays were so relaxing; the year so far had been the complete opposite of last year, but Storm was always ready to throw me a curve ball. We'd gone down the street to buy groceries and stopped in at Lisa's salon. One of Storm's aides, Julie Reynolds, was having her hair cut so I put him on the chair next to her. As we were chatting, I noticed he had gone very, very quiet and he seemed to be sitting stiffly, then his legs straightened out and suddenly his hands and legs went red and sweaty. I ran my hands down his legs and they came away dripping wet. I was fairly bulletproof by then, so I didn't over-react, just waited to see what would happen next. Later, he ate his lunch and seemed fine so what more could I do? On other occasions, he would be in bed and his legs would be sweaty enough to make the sheets wet. I'd mentioned it to the doctor and he thought it might be night sweats or something like that.

Storm's holiday weekend at Catholic Care. After dropping him off, I went to Toni's and we watched a movie, ate pizza and had a real girlie chat—a good night and I went home the next morning. Because Serpentine is not that far away, I visited my parents again for a couple of days. It's great having them closer and more accessible. Early on Monday, I fetched Storm and took him to Marteena's for a massage, and then we drove home.

During his first week back at the Bindoon school I got a phone call saying he'd had an attack—a bad one, his lips turned blue. But his breathing was okay. I used to think that when he stopped breathing during an attack and I got him started again, that I'd somehow saved him—that's not true, he might have started breathing again on his own, and it could happen when he was asleep in the night. What will be, will be and what is, just is. Our destiny is totally out of our control and nobody, but nobody, goes before their time. If they go, it's always their time. I believe in a greater power and I've found that accepting life and the cards we're dealt is a lot easier than trying to control our life or even understand it.

Laurel has got me addicted to a new hobby. She has been scrapbooking and making cards etc for a while. I went along to one of her craft parties and now I'm hooked. There's a large craft fair in Perth and she and I are going together. Jan is picking up Storm from school in case we're late getting back.

We spent hours at the fair, wandering around and looking at all the different accessories and embellishments, some of which we just had to buy, of course. I was soon a heavy scrapbooker (or a scrapper, perhaps?), on my third album of photos of Storm and starting a garden album. A group of us met every six weeks at one of our houses for a scrapbooking day, always great fun and we helped each other with our pages. Storm sat in his beanbag with his toys, listening and playing happily. There seemed to be so many more social gatherings this year, and Storm came with me wherever I went. We had a girls' night at Lisa's with her friend Peta and another lady, Jane, who I met through Lisa. It was great fun and again, Storm sat in his beanbag listening to our conversation. I am sure Lisa and Jane came into my life for a season and a reason.

I've always been independent but on some days I just wish there was someone else to help with my load. I don't mean just with Storm's care, I can do that with no worries, I mean with the running of the house and its maintenance.

The garden maintenance was no big deal. I did it when I was married and nothing had changed. But when things went wrong in the house, it was up to me to fix it and it wasn't always easy—not as if I had an endless supply of money to pay someone else to fix the problem. One day I kept getting this niggling thought that I should check the water meter, the thought kept popping into my head but I ignored it until I walked to the shed to put something away and on the way back I looked up at the roof to see the airconditioner dripping water—very strange, because it was the middle of winter and it was turned off. I checked the meter and the gauge was spinning round crazily, which meant quite a lot of water was running somewhere. There had to be a leak. I turned the water off at the meter because it was too late in the day to do much.

The next day, I asked Jan to look after Storm while I dug up the water pipe between the meter and the house—this is where I thought the leak must be. I started near the house. Laurel's mum, Pixie, and another of her daughters, Debbie, turned up to help. They'd heard about my problem and I didn't even have to ask, they just arrived. Thank you, God. We dug up as much of the pipe as we could that day and I turned on the water briefly for our bath and shower, then quickly turned it off again. After dropping Storm at school the next day, I came home and starting digging again. At one point the pipe ran under a huge rock that we couldn't shift so I'd have to wait two days for Laurel's husband, Reg, to come with his backhoe, remove the rock and dig up the rest of the pipe. What a drama!

We were still without water, I'd turn it on only for our baths at night and I managed to do a load of washing at Laurel's place.

In the middle of all that, Storm's aides at school reported he had been pinching them and trying to bite them. He tried it on me and got told off, but I guessed he was in pain so the next morning I took him to the doctor and it turned out he had tonsillitis again—more antibiotics but at least we found out the reason for the pinching and the biting.

Reg dug up the rest of the pipe and we finally found the leak. After having it attended to, all I had to do was shovel all the dirt back over the pipe. It turned out to be an expensive episode, the pipe had been leaking for a long time so the water bill was more than $1000, never mind the plumber's bill. The reason we didn't notice the leak earlier was because it's all gravel on my property so the water just sank downward and there was no moisture on the surface. After Storm's next massage, Marteena gave me one too. My back was out, no surprise after all that shovelling.

Storm went two months without an attack, so when he did have one it was a bit of a shock, even for him. He had it at school and I picked him up and brought him home. I set him up as usual on his mattress then he had another long attack which exhausted him. He fell asleep after that. I snuck out to the kitchen, made coffee and then sat with him, watching. He seemed listless when he woke, then had another attack about 6pm. This time it took him a while to start breathing again and he was miserable. I sponged him down and put on his pyjamas and cuddled him while I watched television, then I put him to bed. He had two more attacks the next day. They were longer than usual and I did my usual sitting and watching. But I needed to buy groceries so Jan's daughter Emily watched him while I raced down to the shops.

We took it easy for the next couple of days, with Storm sitting in his stroller on the verandah, listening to the sounds of the garden while I raked leaves. He looked more contented after a few hours in the fresh air. He recovered quickly, went back to school and was free of seizures for weeks. *I'm so pleased for him. He's always sad when he's ill but all smiles when he is well again.*

Often, there were light moments when Storm's aides told me what he'd been up to at school. Fiona was looking after him one day and was bending over when he reached across and pinched her on the bottom. I still laugh when I think about that. Another time, Carolyn was looking after him in class and another child was told off and sent out of the classroom. As the child walked past, Storm laughed out loud, and the whole class laughed with him. I'm sure he got away with a whole lot of things he shouldn't have got away with. But even I had trouble telling him off when he was being cheeky!

The doctors at the hospital want to inject botox into Storm's right leg, which is now tighter than his left leg making it harder for him to walk with his walking frame. It's getting worse as he grows. After years of being told that he has cerebral palsy, and never believing it, I sometimes doubt myself and question my beliefs. The answer is always the same. I believe he doesn't have it, there is definitely something going on because his legs are getting worse, but just his legs. His arms are fine. Now, they want to inject botox into his leg which will relax the muscle that is tightening and I feel it would be wrong of me not to do whatever I can to give him some relief. It's been a very hard decision to make, one that I hope I don't regret later on. I'm not totally convinced but I feel I've got to give it a try, at least once, to see what Storm gets out of it.

Storm was well, happy and cheeky and off to Catholic Care for the weekend. I usually told him when he'd be going to the respite home for the weekend, but this time I'd forgotten. On the way, I looked at him in the rear view mirror and he had a puzzled look on his face. When we got there, I carried him in and put him in "his" armchair and his expression changed. He'd figured out where he was! A carer asked him if he'd like a strawberry milk and he gave her the biggest smile ever—the charmer! I stayed overnight at Toni's then returned home after having a quick look at a scrapbooking shop in Subiaco which I'd never visited before. I had a do-nothing weekend—got into bed with my book, put the electric blanket on and just read and dozed, then read some more. I'd get up for a drink or something to eat, then leap back into bed—pure bliss on a cold wintry day!

It had been a reasonably smooth year for Storm so far. He'd had a lot of tonsillitis, to be sure, but thankfully hardly any attacks. I had a new job, cleaning a house one day a week for a couple of hours and there would be no problem if Storm was ill and I couldn't do it. This was all I was capable of doing. There was no way I could have a fulltime job, even during school hours, and in any case I also still had my gardening job.

The Bindoon school had its sports carnival, and this time Storm managed to make it. I sat with Laurel and her mum, Pixie. Storm was in a few of the relay races, the bigger kids pushing him in his wheelchair, and you could tell by the look on his face that he loved it. The kids knew they weren't going to win any race in which they were pushing Storm, but they wanted him to be in the race, which showed great sportsmanship and character. Storm was all smiles even though he was very tired by the end of the day.

A couple of days later, we were at Jane's having coffee and a chat when Storm had a bad attack. I took him home and put him on the couch. He couldn't manage to sit up afterwards. The next day was Monday but there was no way he'd be able to go to school so I rang Marteena and arranged to see her earlier in the day for his massage. I thought it would relax him to have a massage after such a bad attack, and it did. Marteena said his back was out and his head was still tender from the attack. She had remarked several times previously about his back being out, and I wondered whether it resulted from so much time in his wheelchair. It was why I liked to let him have time just lying on his mattress with his toys all around him. He went to school the next day and Laurel and I had a day scrapbooking at her house. We ended up staying for dinner.

A lady from some service or other to do with disabilities came to my house to look at the possibility of renovating the bathroom so it would be easier for me to bathe Storm. She suggested I use a special chair and shower him. *Over my dead body, lady. I'm not taking away the joy that Storm gets from his bath.* It took a lot of effort to get him into the bath and even more to get the slippery little sucker out of it, but there was no way I'd be stopping him from bathing. It was his great love and gave him a lot of relief. Even though the bath was by this time a bit small for him, he was still able to fit himself in so he could lie on his back and enjoy the comfort of the water. When his hair got a bit long between haircuts and he lay in the bath with his hair floating all around his head he reminded me of a sea anemone. If we couldn't have a bigger bath put in, I was not doing any renovations at all. *Something will turn up!*

September 19, Storm's 11th birthday. I sang Happy Birthday to him and gave him his noisy presents and got lots of smiles in return. When we arrived at the school, a girl from his class was waiting in the car park and she walked with us up to the classroom, while I wondered what was going on. The kids had blown up a whole heap of balloons and when we walked in, they all started to sing Happy Birthday. Storm got all embarrassed, I'd never seen that happen before. I had made my traditional chocolate cake with freckles for the kids to eat and I just couldn't get over what a great thing it was for the class to do. It was easy to see why Storm loved school, especially his teacher, Ann Graham, and his amazing aides. And of course, the great kids in his class.

Another time, I'd taken him into class and was waiting for his aide to arrive (I never left until I'd spoken to whoever would look after Stormy that day). Ann came over and was standing next to Storm while we chatted. I watched as Storm reached up and put his hand in Ann's hand. Talk about a heart-melting moment; how's that for a blind child?

On the day of the botox injections we were up at 5am. Storm had to fast and I kept him in his pyjamas. We drove to the hospital and filled in all the paperwork, then went up to Ward 6, Day Surgery, and had to wait for several hours until they took us up to the theatre waiting room. Then they put Storm on a gurney and, after checking the tags on his arms and legs, wheeled him into theatre with me alongside. They decided to give him gas because he was moving around too much; he didn't like them putting a mask on his face and he fought to get it off; but the gas soon took effect and he fell asleep. It was upsetting to see him trying to get the mask off, but I controlled myself. Then a nurse tapped me on the shoulder and said it was time to leave.

Outside theatre, there was a hospital volunteer helper who settled me into the waiting room to be plied with bikkies and coffee for what seemed like hours until the phone call came to go to the recovery room, where Storm was lying in a bed looking very drowsy. From there we were taken to another day ward where the other patients seemed to be alert, but Storm was still very drowsy. It was two hours before they said he was fine to go home and we left, though he still looked pretty sleepy to me. At home, I put him on the couch and gave him some toast and a drink. About 8pm, after I'd put him to bed, I heard a noise from his room and raced in. He was having an attack and his lips were blue, though his breathing was fine.

I didn't know whether he was having an adverse reaction the injections in his legs, so I rang the hospital. I tried to speak to the day surgery unit but they were all gone for the day. Eventually I was put through to emergency, and when I explained he'd had a procedure that day and was now having a seizure, they told me to bring him straight in. I called for an ambulance and followed in my car, fully expecting that we would end up coming home again that night, since it was only a seizure and he'd had countless of those before. It was only because of the botox injections that I'd even phoned for the ambulance.

Storm had another attack in the emergency room and they decided to admit him for the night. I was a bit taken aback—admitted just because he's had an attack, what's the big deal? Had I turned into a cold-hearted person, hardened by all the situations that I'd had to deal with?

Storm was allocated a bed in a ward where he'd been before and the nurses recognised him. He had one more attack, then slept through the night. I was pooped and a foldout bed was arranged for me alongside him. We spent the next day in hospital and Storm had more seizures throughout the day, just the normal everyday kind. He was fine the following day and we were able to go home. After one more attack he was back to normal by the end of the day and his legs seemed fine. I'd been very careful not to touch the area where he had the injections. He woke up so chirpy the next day that I took him to school and, when we got there, Carolyn was waiting for us. Storm was excited as soon as he heard her voice—*the kid's besotted with her!*

More school holidays—we slept in, we visited friends for coffee, and Stormy had a weekend at Catholic Care. I did nothing while he was away except go with Lisa to Jane's where we blitzed her garden by way of a birthday present. Lisa looked after Storm in the salon while I ducked out to clean Jackie's house and that's about all I did in those holidays.

All too soon, it seemed, we were getting up early on a Monday for school in Perth. After school, Marteena again said his neck was out and his head tender—I gave him some Painstop when we got home. It helped and he slept well—but without Marteena, I wouldn't have known that he was in pain.

The next day, Carolyn said he'd been agitated all day and had pinched her badly. I apologised for his behaviour and gave him some more Painstop—guessing that pinching was his way of communicating to us that he was in pain. He was still awake at 10pm so I put him in my bed and he went to sleep. He seemed exhausted the next day so I kept him home and he dozed until 2pm then slept in my bed again that night.

We returned to the hospital for the experts to check whether the botox injections had made a difference. It seemed not, but they reckoned I should consider doing it again in six months. *If it didn't work this time, what makes them think it will work next time?*

Later that week we were back at the hospital to see a dentist. Storm needed some work on his teeth, including a few extractions, so we were put on a waiting list.

We seem to be at the hospital quite often now and I must admit I'm getting better at dealing with all these doctors. I actually like one of them, Dr Anna Gubbay.

Storm had a couple of days with a sore head. I didn't touch his head at all, just dosed him up with Painstop and kept the house very quiet— for all I knew, it could have been migraine.

More appointments at the hospital, now they say the botox injections have worked and Storm just needed more time than other kids.

Then we had an appointment with orthotics, they've decided to make new splints for Storm's legs which meant putting his feet and legs in casts. The year was winding down, the beautiful cool weather was disappearing and the hot days are creeping in.

Storm woke up coughing, so we visited the local doctor. He had bronchitis, bang—just like that, and had to spend a couple of days at home. This was spoiling what had been a fairly good year for us.

At the end of November, when I was collecting Storm from the Perth special school, they told me that when they were drying Storm off after his swim, he said quite clearly: "Swim." Unfortunately, there was no time to put him back in the pool . . . but how amazing was that, people?

Rae's mother has died—she had a stroke and then passed away a few days later. It's a very sad time and my heart goes out to Rae and her family. I won't forget Mrs Chapman.

On our way to Perth the next Monday, I looked in the rear-view mirror and Storm had such a serious look on his face I wondered what he was thinking. I asked him would he like to visit Rae after school and he gave me a big smile, then his expression was all serious again. So I asked him if he'd like me to buy some flowers to take to Rae and I got a big smile. He seemed happy after that so we did just that. It was just after Rae's mother had died and she looked exhausted. Laurel watched Storm for me while I drove to Perth for Mrs Chapman's funeral. Rae's husband, Gary, gave a speech that was very moving.

School finished for the year, Christmas was close, and I'd done all the necessary shopping. My thoughts were still with Rae, her first Christmas without her mum. She told me her mother must have known she wouldn't be around for Christmas because she'd had everything and everyone organised very early. It's amazing what the soul knows.

Storm and I spent Christmas at Serpentine with my family.

Chapter Twelve

2004

I saw early on it was going to be a very interesting year. It was January 8, I'd dropped Storm at Laurel's so I could do my cleaning stint for Jackie. Afterwards, I popped in on Lisa at the salon and she told me ABC Radio had approached the local tourist bureau asking for any interesting community news. The tourist bureau told the radio people Lisa was planning to raise money to build a new bathroom for Storm. And tomorrow morning, Lisa was going to be interviewed on radio . . . wow!

Lisa was present at last year's meeting with the Disability Services people. The best they could offer was to renovate my bathroom and put in a bigger shower for Storm which we all knew he would hate. I must confess I hadn't given any more thought to raising money for a new bathroom—it seemed far too big a venture to me. But remember, whatever Storm ever needed in his life always turned up. *Sorry God, I'd forgotten this!*

While we were discussing the impending radio interview, Dawn Kay arrived at the salon. Dawn worked in the office at the school and she told us the Lions Club had approached the school to see if there was a child worthy of being nominated for its Child of Courage award. Storm's name came up straight away. How neat was that? I always thought of Storm as courageous but it meant a lot to me for other people to acknowledge his courage.

Lisa's interview went well and I taped it so she could listen to it later. I was just getting ready to drive over to give her the tape when she phoned to say that while she was opening the shop, two police-cars had rocked up. The officers asked to speak to the girl with the kiwi accent from the radio show, then proceeded to empty their pockets and raid the ashtray and glove box of each car and they gave her all the money they had. I was speechless—something that I thought was impossible was now looking very much possible. Yes, it was going to be an interesting year!

Storm had an appointment at the hospital to fit his new splints. He doesn't like them, they cover his feet and most of his legs up to his knees, and they're made of plastic so they'll be hot in summer. He has to wear long socks with them and they have to be worn every day for a couple of hours, even in the holidays.

I felt like such an evil person putting the splints on, all in the hope of straightening his legs. What mother wants to hurt her child even if it's going to help him? He often pinched me when I put them on. I knew they were uncomfortable and if there was any other way to help his legs, we'd do it, so forgive me, Storm. To make up for it, I set him up with his paints. Painting was one of his great relaxations and it helped him to forget the discomfort of the splints. He had a few attacks and they left him pale and sleepy. It didn't matter that I was supposed to put the splints on every single day—I wasn't doing it on the days he had an attack. That would be just plain mean.

January was bloody hot, as it always is. The new school year started on a Tuesday so Storm's first day was at the school in Bindoon. He was quiet when we arrived but then a few of the aides hugged him and when we got to his new class a few of the kids from last year came up and said hello. By the time I left, he was all smiles. I wasn't too happy though. His desk was next to the door and when the door was open, he was actually partly behind it. I didn't think he would be too happy about that but obviously the teacher was aware of how much he knew and was aware of. *We'll just have to see how it goes.*

I had a job interview with the Palmers, local sheep stud owners—a cleaning job with maybe some cooking. I got the interview through Peta Finch, who helps with their accounts work. It went well and I would be working two hours every Tuesday, on the same day as Peta so we'd be able to catch up—great! I could only take a job when the employer understood that if Storm was really ill, and that was bound to happen occasionally, I couldn't come to work.

Storm wouldn't be having massages with Marteena this year—a real shame because they really helped him a lot, but she had her own issues to deal with so she wouldn't be doing any massages. We were going to miss her.

I had my first day at the Palmer stud farm. No-one was home when I arrived except for two large, growling Dobermans and there was no way I was going to get out of the car. On my list of least-favourite dogs, the Doberman is right up there at the top. At last another employee, Kerry, turned up and let me into the house. I started on the housework and then Joan Palmer arrived. I hadn't done any gardening this year for Vera but I was still cleaning Jackie's house and now on a Tuesday I was working for Joan Palmer. As long as the work was in school hours, I was happy.

Storm wasn't that happy at school. I had even been called to pick him up because he'd had an attack and yet, when I got there, he was fine. It wasn't until he was moved from his spot near the door, into the middle of the room with a desk like the other children, that he turned back into the happy kid that he really was. He was all smiles the day they moved him and I realised he had been faking attacks because he didn't like sitting behind the door when it was open. The aides had figured this out and moved him. He couldn't stop smiling and he was still smiling later in the day when we visited Laurel. Never underestimate a child; the body might be disabled but the mind is still very bright. The next morning, I woke up to a chorus of "Mum, mum, mum" and he gave me the biggest smile ever. The world was perfect again for my Storm.

My parents are off to New Zealand for a holiday, and I'll be looking after their precious dog, Bud, while they're away. He'll be staying with us at our house.

Bud followed me everywhere outside of the house but wouldn't come inside no matter how much I coaxed him. However, as soon as Storm was home from school, Bud would come inside and sit with him. The trouble was, Bud was a large labrador and my house is quite small, so I was either stepping over him or tripping over him. A creature of habit, he didn't have late nights and when it was time for bed, he wanted to go to bed. My shed wasn't big enough for him so he was sleeping on the verandah.

Mum and Dad got Bud when he was a puppy. That was when we were staying with them just after I left my ex-husband, so he knew Storm since they were both very little and he was used to sitting with Storm. He's a very strange dog. I've only ever heard him bark once or twice in his whole life—he's such a well-behaved animal that it's scary!

Storm had tonsillitis again. A phone call from the school informed me he wasn't well and I'd just finished my cleaning job so I was able to pick him up straight away. He was hot and lethargic and the doctor's surgery was closed. It was Friday, so I dosed him up all weekend until I could get him to the doctor on Monday. But then I woke on Monday with such a sore throat that I couldn't even swallow my coffee—and I'm not happy if I don't have my morning coffee. The doctor confirmed that Storm had tonsillitis again (for what must be the hundredth time) and I had a throat infection—I can't get tonsillitis because I don't have any tonsils). We were both on antibiotics but couldn't go home and rest up because I had to drive to Serpentine—about a four-hour round trip—to water my parents' garden.

Storm rested in a rocker recliner (one of his favourites) while I watered the garden and then we headed back. It was way past Bud's dinnertime and he was beside himself with hunger, so he was top of the list of things to see to when we returned.

Busy times: I've got a bit more work, now it's three days a week for the Palmers. We have the day in Perth each week so that's when I have a whole day to myself while Storm is at the special school. I've been saving hard because I know I'll need to buy another car soon. This one has broken down a few times even though it's only six years old. Then again, we've done a fair bit of mileage in those six years. The jobs I have don't earn me much, but they help with the grocery bills so along with the pension we get I'm managing to save something. I won't be able to buy another car outright, but hopefully I'll only have to borrow half the amount needed. I've been looking around to see what sort I should get, it's going to have to be bigger than what we now have because Storm is growing. He'll soon be taller than me and that means he'll have a bigger wheelchair, so I need a car with a big boot. The universe usually provides, so I'm sure it will all work out.

In the last week of March Storm had a couple of days of seizures, which exhausted him. One night, after two attacks, he was sleeping when I walked into his room. He woke up suddenly, his arms reaching out, with dark pools of fear in his eyes. I grabbed him and his arms locked around my neck and his body tightened as the seizure took hold. How could I possibly not be affected? He was exhausted but slowly drifted off to sleep and I sat watching him for a long time. Eventually I went back to what I'd been doing. The attacks lasted four days but he recovered quickly and was eager to get back to school.

I always found March a hard month. After endless hot days and nights, we'd all had enough and just wanted the cool days to arrive. The gardens had wilted, the rain hadn't come and everything looked dry and miserable. All those hot days made me so tired. I know it affected Storm, too, and everything was just such an effort. We would veg out in the lounge room underneath the airconditioning vents and watch television, thinking: "Roll on winter, please . . .

Lisa formed a committee to raise money for Storm's bathroom and lots of ideas were put forward at the first meeting. I must give Lisa credit for getting the group together—some serious fundraisers there! I was seriously impressed with their determination and eagerness. After so many years of doing it on my own with not much help, how do you thank people who are so willing to give up their time to help a virtual stranger?

That was when I met Helen Mildwaters, who has become a great friend and shares my addiction to scrapbooking. Then there's Bob Blizard—he was with St John Ambulance for many years, as well as the Progress Society and the Seventh Day Adventist church. He's also involved in a local charity shop and many other things. Boy, does he know how to get people to donate money, and not just piddling donations—quite generous amounts! There's Wayne Beard, president of the local Lions Club. He works for a building company—how perfect is that? And Michele Rutherford, Jeannie Oliver, John Thompson and Tony Page, all of whom contribute a lot to the community and all of them no strangers to fundraising.

It really looks like this is going to happen! Storm is going to have his very own, specially-built bathroom situated next to his bedroom. The local co-ordinator for the disabled told me it would take years to raise enough money for this bathroom. Well, lady, stand back and watch. Storm doesn't have years. His needs are now and the universe knows this.

We need upbeat positive people to help uplift our lives and inspire us to go on in spite of difficulties—not people who seem to reinforce how hard it is, who are negative and stamp out hope. Thankfully, the positive ones make up for the others.

We acquired a dog. Jane rang to say someone she knew was moving and couldn't take their dog to the new place. Would I be interested in this dog? I said I'd have a look at it, but who would look after it if I had to rush Storm to hospital or if he was having an operation? I wasn't sure I wanted the responsibility. On the way over for a look-see, I spoke to the angels. If the dog liked Storm and Storm liked the dog, I would take it as a sign that the dog should come to live with us.

Jet was a cocker spaniel, black and fluffy. He came up to Storm straight away and Stormy reached out and played with his ears and collar. Just like that, it was decided—we were taking the dog! I was told he slept outside but Jet had different ideas—he slept in the house whenever he could and eventually had a bed inside as well as the one Dad built for him outside. I was totally conned by Storm—after that first day, he showed no interest in Jet and would push him away if the dog sat next to him.

This dog had some very unusual habits. We'd have to keep the door to the shed shut or he'd get at the dynamic lifter fertiliser (aka chook poo). If he could, he'd eat copious amounts of the stuff and it supposedly can kill dogs (he quickly acquired the nickname "Kill Bill"), but nothing could deter him, he spent hours trying to get into the chookyard to eat manure. He never bothered the chooks, but when he put a hole in the fence they all got out and destroyed my garden. He ate all the garlic chives right down to the ground. I didn't notice that until he came up for a pat, reeking of garlic. He also ate all the red chilis off the plants and in winter when I grew my broccoli and cauliflowers, he ate them too.

I distinctly remember going for a wander round the veggie patch one day and seeing that one of the cauliflowers that had been ready to be picked was gone. The outside leaves were still there but the whole cauli inside was just gone. It was a mystery until I thought to see what he'd do with a cauliflower, so I gave him one and watched in amazement as he carried it to the middle of the lawn and proceeded to eat the whole thing. Damn weird! I took a photo as proof.

I think Jet was meant to be company for me, which he was. He's a sweet-natured dog when he's not getting up to mischief. I still had Bud with me when I got him. I don't think Bud was impressed but Jet wanted to be friends. He wanted to lie next to Bud, but whenever he did, Bud would just get up and wander off. A few days later, my parents returned from their holiday and came over to fetch Bud. When they drove up, he saw the car and raced for the gate, he was ecstatic to see them. They'd had a great time in New Zealand and they brought me a load of wood. Dad chopped it into manageable lengths while Mum and I stacked it in the shed. All I needed now was for it to rain so I had an excuse to light the fire . . . mmm, that would be bliss! Storm had gone off to Catholic Care so he didn't get to see his grandparents this time.

The day after I brought Jet home, I had a little turn of my own. I was sitting outside early in the morning having coffee with Jet and something happened because when I looked at my watch, I'd lost an hour. I freaked out and rang Toni who told me to calm down—how could I possibly have lost an hour? The next day I saw the doctor and was sent for blood tests. But nothing showed up, just my cholesterol level was really bad. Maybe I was just stressed. In any case I didn't have any more of these strange turns.

The Easter holidays had arrived so I would have time to relax, maybe that's all I needed. Storm and I slept in on Good Friday and after lunch I put him in his stroller on the verandah and he played while I worked. After his bath, we played and laughed together. Maybe it was the chocolate consumed that day that made Storm so bubbly. While we were outside I washed Jet, because he was a mite smelly It was the first time I had ever seen a dog not roll in the dirt after a wash—he just ran around the yard and didn't try to roll in anything. Plain weird, he must be a city dog. Unfortunately, I noticed later that he still smelt.

We made the usual trip to see my parents during the school holidays and this time we had a smelly dog in the car with us. Jet insisted on sitting right next to Storm, who wasn't impressed. We only stayed a few days then it was time for home.

Storm didn't seem right so I took his temperature and it was up again. The only thing he wanted to eat was ice cream—a sure sign that he had tonsillitis. I don't know why, but it made him sleepy. I woke him for breakfast and he stayed awake just long enough to eat then went back to sleep and didn't wake up until 3pm. The doctor confirmed he did indeed have tonsillitis so more antibiotics were prescribed. *Those tonsils really need to come out but it's just too risky.* The next day, he actually coughed up blood. I needed to go to Jackie's house to work but I didn't think it was fair to ask anyone to look after a sick child, so I dosed him up and took him with me. He sat in his stroller with a few toys while I raced around, as quickly as I could, cleaning the house. He looked really tired so the sooner I could get him home, the better.

He hadn't fully recovered when we drove to Perth a couple of days later so he could accept his "Child of Courage" award. Lisa came with us and my parents were waiting at Toni's house. We all drove to the college where the ceremony was to take place. I don't know whether it was because we were in a strange, noisy place, but Storm really played up and I was getting cranky with him. In the end I took him outside and waited in the wings until we were called. Lots of children of all ages received awards that night and we heard some amazing stories.

Storm was still playing up, but when it was our turn he sat up in his wheelchair all nice and quiet and received his award. When the presenter spoke to him, he leaned forward listening as if butter wouldn't melt in his mouth. The little toad lapped up the applause and when we sat down he was on his best behaviour—he sure knows when to turn it on!

Storm is very proud of his award and deservedly so, he is a courageous child and what he has endured so far would certainly break a lesser person. I'm very proud of him and honoured to be his mum.

The school holidays were busy. We visited Laurel and Jane and Laurel looked after Storm while I worked—thank you, Laurel! I had a girls night out with friends and all this socialising made the holidays fly past quickly. Storm was a bit annoyed that he still had his physio in the holidays; I think he thought he would get a break.

Fundraising for the bathroom was going ahead (you could even say it was "storming" ahead). We'd put collection tins in all the stores in Bindoon, just for a start, and people were even giving us cheques. The Palmers donated and I know of one person who got back more than she expected at tax time so she gave us that money—the town's generosity was amazing.

Bob Blizard suggested that Storm have a spa bath; he was going to love that! I'd put him in a friend's spa and he really enjoyed it. They are bigger than a regular bath so he'd be able to stretch out. I was astonished that this was all really happening; I never could have done it all for Storm on my own.

I'm watching television and get up to check on Storm. Jet usually stays sleeping on his bed, but this time he insists on coming with me. In Storm's room, Jet puts his front paws on the bed. Normally this would wake Storm, but he just lies there and I realise he is looking bluish—and he's not breathing. I shake him and call his name—nothing. With my heart pounding, I shake him again, and he takes a big breath. At this, I burst into tears. After a bit, I pull myself together and sit for a long time just watching him breathe. Why didn't I call an ambulance? Calm down, he's breathing again and after six years of things like this I'm well aware he could leave me at any moment, but I just know today isn't the day. Experience has taught me that even if I do call an ambulance, there is every likelihood we'll be home in a couple of hours. Even though Storm didn't wake up during this episode, his breathing now seemed quite regular and there was nothing more I could do. I will confess that it took me a long time to get to sleep that night.

When Storm had a series of attacks, I would wake up in the morning wondering if he'd had an attack and died during the night. I'd lie in bed listening until I heard him move, then I could get up, knowing he was fine. *He hasn't had a seizure for 51 days, he's had tonsillitis and stopped breathing a couple of times but, really, he's having a pretty smooth time at the moment. He's loving school and I can see I made the right decision when I enrolled him into a normal school. I know he would be miserable if he was at the special school every day. But he's happy to go there one day of the week, mostly because of the swimming.*

As smooth as things were with no seizures—whew, it was busy! When Storm went off to weekend respite I used the time to catch up on my sleep. As well as he was, some nights he didn't go to sleep until the early hours and I didn't sleep unless he slept. I was always so tired, and so much in need of sleep . . .

On the bathroom front the Freemasons had chipped in with $5000, an extraordinarily generous gift. I was told we didn't need to raise much more before we could start building and it was only May. What was it the Disability Services lady said, that it would take years and years to raise the money? Yeah, right!

A boy who was raising money for a sports venture found he couldn't go after all, so he gave us the $2000 he'd raised; a man who was dying gave us $500; the government contributed $5000 in grants; and a guy with a bobcat agreed to donate his time to do some work with his machine.

More trips to hospital in connection with Storm's legs. He has had more X-rays and they'll be giving him more botox injections and they want me to consider an operation on his legs. This doctor walks in, very self-important, with his registrar following behind, and starts telling me what he thinks is wrong with Storm. He doesn't ask me what I think and I don't think he even knows Storm's full history. I'd like him to say: "Mandy, you tell me about Storm, tell me everything that's happened from the day he was born until now . . ." If he did that, I know he'd change his diagnosis. A medical degree has made him think he's God and the registrar tagging along behind him is

going to turn out just like him. Thankfully, not all doctors are like this one. I
have to decide whether to let them operate. I don't believe they've diagnosed
Storm properly and the decision is so hard. If I say no to the operation and his
legs get worse, I'll have to bear the responsibility for that. But I don't know if
going ahead with the operation will help Storm or even make him worse. I'm
damned either way. While I try to decide, Storm will be having more botox
injections in August.

Back into the swing of it, school for Stormy and work for me. I was
enjoying working for the Palmers. I remember the first time I took Storm
out to their place. He hadn't been well and they said I should bring him
with me so I put his beanbag in their lounge room and set him up with a
few of his toys. I was nervous about those two Dobermans taking a chunk
out of him but I needn't have worried. One of them, Milo, went and got
his own toy (a chop) from the lawn and gently put it into Storm's lap so he
could play with it. How's that! I thanked Milo but took the toy away from
Storm—I knew he'd put it in his mouth and that just didn't bear thinking
about. Both dogs were very careful around Storm—animals seem to have
an intuition about children.

Winter again so I was happy—the fire was burning and all was
right with the world. We'd had a long break from seizures but they had to
come, I suppose. The first of them gave Storm quite a fright, but at least
he had only one and after a day at home he was recovered and eager to get
back to school.

Another trip to the hospital to have his legs put in casts so they could fit him with new splints, again. He was growing so quickly he looked a bit like a daddy-long-legs spider, he just seemed to be all legs. When I picked him up, I'd tell him to put his legs around my hips or he'd have to walk and they were up in a second—he liked to be carried. Going on 12, he now weighed 24kg.

We visited a shop that sells hoists, wheelchairs and those sorts of things. Storm was getting a hoist for the bathroom so it would be easier to get him in and out of the bath. We were also getting an electric change table for the bathroom. The lady at the Independent Living Centre showed me all the different hoists and demonstrated how I could put Storm into the harness that connected to the hoist. Then we hoisted Storm right out of his wheelchair—and he loved it. I thought he might be frightened but no, he thought it was fun. So we chose a hoist.

A couple of days later, Storm had his first pony ride. Jane has two ponies and it was her idea to give him a go. At first he was nervous, then he relaxed and he really enjoyed himself, and by the end of it he was laughing. *It looks like he will be having a few more pony rides; it's great to hear him laughing.*

I discovered something else—if he heard coughing, Storm would instantly laugh. So when I wanted a photo of him laughing, I just had to start coughing. I'd love to know what it was that he found so funny. I also caught him laughing when I banged my foot on a door or something. *That boy has a sick sense of humour, for sure!*

The July school holidays came and passed, almost too quickly. Storm had his days with Catholic Care. I lit the fire and vegged out for at least one whole day. Storm had a couple of days of seizures but recovered very quickly.

We had a committee meeting at my house. We had raised an amazing $16,000 for the new bathroom. Now I just needed a building permit from the shire and we could start. *This is just so fantastic, thank you, thank you, thank you.*

Meanwhile, I'd been to the bank to apply for a personal loan to buy a car. I'd been scrimping and scraping, and had managed to save half the amount I'd need. Peta's sister knew a car dealer who was willing to help. I told him what car, year and model I'd like and he had started to look around. Everything was falling into place.

And perhaps just because things had been running too smoothly, Storm had a really bad bout of seizures. I was working at the Palmers' home when the school rang. I arrived to find Storm resting on a beanbag with an aide on either side, comforting him. I felt a bit mean taking him away from them. He had another attack in the car on the way home and I told him to hold on, we were nearly there. When I'd made him comfortable in the lounge room, I noticed his eyes were very bloodshot so they must have been fairly bad attacks. He drifted off to sleep, then proceeded to have another seven attacks, one after another. By the fifth one, I was worried that he wouldn't have the energy to breathe after any more, so I rang the local doctor. He told me to increase his epilim and how to do that. By the seventh attack, his body was just twitching and it was a terrible sight to watch. He was just so exhausted and he slept with me that night. I felt sure it would take him at least a couple of days to recover but, amazingly, he was quite chirpy the next day—though he was pretty tired.

The day after that he woke up really happy so I decided to send him back to school. He had a great day and even did a couple of stints of walking. I was amazed at how he'd recovered so well despite having all those attacks so close together. The next day was Saturday, a day I usually sleep in for as long as he would let me. When he called me, I went into his room and he was on the floor. He'd obviously fallen out of bed, unusual in itself, but he'd pulled down the quilt and pillow and made himself comfortable. I still felt bad that he'd fallen out of bed and I hadn't known . . .

Two weeks after those eight attacks in a row, he had a similar bout of seizures—seven in a row and so close together that he'd only just started breathing after one attack when he'd have another. By the last one, his body was twitching again and putting up his epilim made no difference. He slept with me again that night. The next day he had an attack early in the morning so I had to take him to work with me at the Palmers' house. I was also taking my sister because she would be doing some work there while the Palmers were in Mauritius, and we would be house-sitting for them. While Toni went off with their farmhand to see what needed to be done, I put Storm in Gordon Palmer's recliner and he was in heaven—I'd love to know why he liked recliners so much.

On Storm's twelfth birthday, September 19, we got the usual phone calls from the family wishing him happy birthday and I gave him his presents—more noisy toys. It was getting hard to find new toys that would amuse him. I made his traditional birthday cake and this year the day fell on a Sunday so we were able to sleep in. I took the cake with us when we went to Laurel's for morning tea and she had blown up a whole heap of balloons for Storm to pop. Laurel's parents were there also and we all sang Happy Birthday to Storm. He popped all the balloons and thoroughly enjoyed himself. Every time a balloon popped he'd jump, then he'd pop another one and jump again. After that we went to Jane's for afternoon tea and her neighbours Steve and Richard came over to wish Storm happy birthday and there was more cake with candles. *He's grown up so much and he sat at the table with us, so happy, laughing and chatting away.* Jane saddled one of the ponies and Storm had a ride. This was such a memorable day for him and I've often looked back on it as a really happy day for both of us.

Building of the new bathroom has started so there are often people working on the site. If I'm not working, I make sure they have morning tea with something to eat. It's not much, but I hope they know how grateful I am for all they're doing for Storm.

I bought another car. Peta's sister's car dealer friend knew someone at Toyota, so I got a good deal and the car I wanted. It was two years old but in great shape. For the first time in my life I had a personal loan—I'm really big on living within your means and personal loans don't quite fit in with that philosophy. At the bank, I'm sure they thought I was a bit odd. I hadn't borrowed much but it seemed huge to me. The loan was over four years but I paid it off in one, just couldn't handle that debt hanging over my head. I was pretty excited when I picked up the car and just to make things so much sweeter, my boss, Gordon Palmer, had spoken to his insurance company and I was offered a year's free insurance. All these great things happening to us—the universe is certainly looking after us!

Storm hadn't had many seizures lately and I was grateful for that. But he'd had a lot of high temperatures for no good reason, so much tonsillitis that I'd stopped counting, and those strange leg sweats. Even on the coldest nights, I'd gone into his room and his legs and the sheets were soaking wet. On the last day of September, he was quiet but otherwise fine; by 6pm he was burning up and his temperature was 40 degrees. I undressed him down to his nappy and gave him some Panadol. It was a cold night so I was hoping his temperature would drop without having to put him in a cool bath, but it stayed up. I rang Jane. She convinced me I should ring the doctor. And it was great that we had a doctor who you could call after hours, so I did. He told me to put Storm in a bath and give him Nurofen. I didn't have any so I rang Laurel, who brought some round. It was 3am before he cooled down and we were both exhausted.

The next day, the doctor checked him out and he seemed fine; there was something going on in his body that we couldn't see. He'd been booked into Catholic Care for the weekend and I decided he was well enough to go. Jane came with us and we stopped in at Maccas, ordered chicken nuggets and fries for him, and followed this with his new favourite—a chocolate sundae with extra chocolate. Can't tell you how much he loved them.

I spent the weekend helping on the bathroom project. The slab is down and the walls and roof rafters are already up. Mum and Dad are coming tomorrow to drop off the new bed that Dad has made for Storm—it's a day bed and Dad's design is just the best, I know Storm is going to love it.

When I picked him up the next day he had a cough and a runny nose and I felt guilty since I'd had a great weekend. He did love his new bed, but he was less happy a day later when we went to the hospital to try on his new splints. Dad had also made him an outside sun lounge and I set him up on the verandah on this because he was so unhappy about the new splints. He usually loved being outside but he was just sad. I could usually get him to smile, even if it was just a little smile, but not that day.

The Palmers were leaving for their holiday and although I didn't want to take Storm into a new environment when he was so unhappy, I had to because there was no-one else to look after their place and I'd said I would do it. Storm and I were staying in Joan's room with Storm on a foldout bed. We settled in—and I think it was all of five seconds before Jet settled in too. As if, finally, he'd been taken to a house that was more befitting of his status—mind you, he might have felt differently if the two big Dobermans hadn't been sent off to a kennel!

It was a huge house, not like we were accustomed to. Joan's ensuite had a large bath and I managed to get a smile out of Storm when he stretched out in it. And he got to sit in Gordon's rocker recliner, so it turned out the change of environment made him happy. We'd be there for three weeks and Toni was coming for a week to do some work for the Palmers.

Storm was not well, he was coughing and I tried lifting the bed head to help him sleep but he slid down again every time and started coughing again. I didn't like travelling when he wasn't well but we had an appointment with the orthopaedic surgeon about the operation on his legs. If I decided to go ahead, the operation would leave his legs weak for about six months. He had grown so much that the muscles in his legs were getting really stiff and it was getting harder for him to use his walking frame. The botox injections didn't seem to be doing as good a job as they should. I had six months to make up my mind about the operation and I didn't feel good about it—I just didn't know what to do. Storm was very tired after the drive to Perth and back.

Next day was my usual working day at the Palmers, and Peta would be working in the office. I made morning tea for all of us and Peta brought her girls with her because it was school holidays. Storm enjoyed having the girls there and he really cheered up, but by the end of the day he was exhausted so he went to sleep very early.

His coughing continued for too long so it was back to the doctor. It turned out his lungs were not completely clear and he had an ear infection. Happily, with a course of antibiotics he got better and was soon enjoying

Gordon's rocker again. We were toasty warm at night with the wood heater on and I felt we'd really settled in nicely.

Another appointment at the hospital, this time with Dr Anna Gubbay, who is involved with the botox injections. We both like her. Why? Because she listens to me—when I told her Storm's bones made a clunking sound when I pick him up, she didn't "poo-poo" me; she said she would organise a calcium test because children with Storm's problems were prone to osteoporosis. Storm and I are really warming to this lady!

Anna checked the range of movement in Storm's legs and it wasn't good. Finally, I had someone to discuss the operation with, and she was able to answer my questions. I could have hugged her for all this, but I didn't want to freak her out. I just needed someone to talk to about the pros and cons of the operation, someone who would give me honest answers. This I got from Anna.

As nice as it is staying at the Palmers, it is more work for me. They live about 20 minutes out of Bindoon town so a lot more driving is involved. I'd collect my mail and check on my place when I was taking Storm to school and I noticed my garden needed work. No time for that, it would have to wait until the Palmers got back.

I'm so glad I decided to put Storm in my bedroom, if I hadn't I wouldn't have heard the gurgling sound that woke me one night. I picked up his limp body and he didn't appear to be breathing—and what had caused the gurgling sound? I tickled his feet and eventually he started breathing again. He tried to sit up but didn't open his eyes and when his breathing was consistent, I put him back in his bed. I didn't feel any panic—I think I'm bombproof. I took him to the doctor in the morning and was surprised when he said I should have rung him at home. He lived not far from the Palmers and said he could have got there more quickly than an ambulance. Now I have two doctors who believe me, this is brilliant! His parting words were that if it happened again, I must phone him.

That night, as I was dressing Storm, I asked him casually if he'd wanted to leave last night and, instantly, he laughed. I have no idea what he meant by that. When I checked on him later, he'd gone off to that happy place where he smiled in his sleep. At such times, I could ask him questions and get an answer from the reaction on his face, so I said to him that if he had to go, then he must go. He seemed happy with that and smiled, so I left the room. *But I'm not happy . . . who am I to ask him to stay because I don't want to be without him? His soul is living in a body full of pain and discomfort and he can't speak because his body won't allow it and the older he gets, the more his legs hinder him. With all that, he still enjoys his life and he's not an unhappy child at all.*

The Palmers returned so we went home and the first thing I had to do was to spruce up the garden. While we were away the roof had been put up on the new bathroom and Wayne Beard had begun lining the inside of the walls. It was all going forward quite quickly.

Storm was still not happy. We hadn't had his usual laughs and chatter for a week or so and he hadn't been going to sleep until about 2am. The doctor told me to give him Valergen—I was willing to try anything, sure that he would feel happier if he got more sleep. It eventually worked; if I gave him the Valergen at 4pm, he'd be asleep by about 8.30—that's how long it took to kick in.

Storm was a real smartypants at school today. He's just making sure that people haven't pigeon-holed his abilities. A person from Disability Services had rocked up to his classroom to try out some different types of chairs—so that Storm could sit at his desk without being in a wheelchair all day. They put him in an office chair and while they were distracted, he stood up and took a few steps to his desk. I would love to have been there, just to see it happen and see the looks on all their faces. Just when you think you've figured out what he can and can't do, he does something to remind us we should never take him for granted.

Storm might have be sleeping better with the Valergen but he seemed very agitated, and some mornings he was so tired that I let him sleep until 11am. If he was in pain, the Painstop wasn't helping, so I decided to take him to the doctor. I explained that I had noticed he got more agitated if I lay him down. The doctor checked him all over, even his teeth, and suggested I take him to the dental clinic. He also gave me a script for a stronger painkiller, which helped—he certainly wasn't so agitated. *The dental clinic at PMH will look at his teeth on Monday, six days away.*

Monday was an early start, because we had to be at the clinic by 8.30am. Then we waited until 10.30, to be told the dentist was ill and could we please come back after 3pm. Storm had been sitting in his wheelchair all that time and now we must go away and come back at 3 o'clock—sure thing, we've got nothing better to do with our lives! So I took him to special school for a couple of hours then returned to the hospital. It seemed he needed a few teeth pulled—some of his baby teeth were still there and needed to come out so he was put on an emergency list. *I hope we won't have to wait too long and that this is the reason he's so unhappy—although it certainly hasn't affected his appetite.*

The new bathroom was almost ready. The internal walls and ceiling were done and it was time to choose the tiles and taps—the first time in my life I'd been able to choose tiles for anything at all and it was great fun. The tiler arrived a couple of days later and the spa bath was installed—a two-person spa, rather large, but it was a big bathroom, actually the biggest room in the house. It was the beginning of December and only a month or so before we could start using it—in less than a year we'd raised the money and built a bathroom—great going!

Storm hadn't had an attack for a month and then he had six seizures in a row on the very day he was due to receive a certificate at the school assembly. I took him just so he could get his certificate and he was very proud to accept it—he was very much aware of its significance. It cheered him up on an otherwise crappy day. He had 10 attacks over three days but recovered quickly, probably because there were long breaks between them.

He has had his baby teeth taken out and because he doesn't seem to recover well from the anaesthetic we stayed in the hospital overnight. But he was fine to come home the next day, no drama at all.

I was just getting Storm out of the car at school one Thursday morning when Carolyn, one of his wonderful aides, rocked up, saying she would help. But instead of taking Storm to his classroom, she wheeled him into the staff room and all seven of his aides were there, with Dawn Kay, the receptionist, holding a camera. *Okay, what's going on?* I was presented with an amazing canvas painting that Storm had done. Everyone had been involved and it would have taken quite a while to do, because it was at least a metre square. They also gave me a framed collage of photos of Storm doing all this, with help from all these women. I just loved it. And I loved that they did it for me, it's my favourite thing. I hung both the painting and the collage on my office wall and they've been there ever since. Not a day goes past that I don't look at it and I am so grateful for everyone's thoughtfulness.

A couple of days later, school finished for the year. We spent Christmas with the family, same as last year. We loved 2004!

Chapter Thirteen

2005

This is the year that nearly destroyed me. I thought I was fairly bombproof, but I wasn't. It started off with no hint of what terrible things were to come. It was too hot to do much more than laze around—there was nowhere we had to be, so lazing around was easy to do. Carolyn offered to look after Storm so I could have a day shopping all by myself. I took her up on her offer and had a great day in Perth—but I think her daughter, Paige, could have done without Storm's presence. Apparently, he was really noisy and she would ask him to be quiet because she was watching television but it wasn't long before the loud babbling noises took over again. I loved that Paige felt comfortable enough to tell him off as she would tell any child off for being too noisy. Storm loved it, too.

Storm's legs continued to drip with sweat and the doctor didn't have an answer for it. But he did say it was the healthiest and most cheerful he'd ever seen Storm. He seemed to be in fine form, all smiles and cuddles and cheerful sounds. I still had my jobs to do in the school holidays so I took Storm with me; to him it was more of a social outing.

We had physio appointments with Judy Dennis during the holidays, at the Silver Chain office. Storm even walked from the car to the office and back again. He couldn't stand upright on his own but I held his hands. It must be such an awful feeling to walk with tight muscles. He enjoyed the physio, particularly some of the exercises, but he was tired by the time we got home.

We stayed with my parents for a few days, as we did every year, and Mum cooked all of Storm's favourite foods, as usual. More work was done on the new bathroom, and the plumber and electrician finished their bits so it wouldn't be long before Stormy could try out his new bath. Very exciting!

The school holidays flew by and Storm was itching to get back to school. He was even eager to get back to the special school in Perth. After another shopping day in Perth (and another chocolate sundae fix) he was so happy to know that the next day was the first day of school. His teacher was one he'd had before, so he recognised her voice as soon as she spoke to him. Then Carolyn came up to him and he got even more excited when she told him that she would be looking after him in the afternoons. He'd been at school only three days when the seizures started again. He had three of them, none of them too bad, and although he did seem a bit jumpy afterwards he was fine within a couple of days. It was a bit sad that it had happened in the first week of school, especially since he was so happy to be back there.

We tried out his new bath! The hoist certainly made it easy to lower him in and Storm was in heaven, stretching himself out and trying to find the end of the tub with his toes. He couldn't stretch out in the old bathtub because he'd grown so much; now he was flipping over on to his tummy and shoving his head under the water, blowing bubbles and splashing the water everywhere while he laughed and chattered. I could tell it was going to be hard to get him out of the bath. I sat on the change table enjoying his total happiness and it was the equivalent of someone winning lotto, this was Storm's lotto.

Then he was off to respite for the weekend and as I drove off I looked back to see two ladies fussing over him and he was lapping it up. *How blessed are we that there are people who dedicate their lives to people like Storm. They have beautiful hearts and they give their love so freely. I cannot praise them enough for their compassion and I don't see any pity in the way they treat Storm. I wouldn't be able to tolerate pity.*

I reckon we've got it so wrong in this world. The highest-paid people are the film stars, the CEOs of big businesses, the sportsmen, etc, when the people who should be earning the most are the teachers, nurses, ambulance offices, firemen, aides—people who dedicate their lives to the welfare of other human beings. They're the ones who are worthy of the really high salaries.

I love Storm so much but I'd be lying if I said he hasn't been challenging and extremely hard for me to cope with, both emotionally and physically. His time at Catholic Care gives me time for me—a couple of days away from being totally focussed on his needs.

Now that the bathroom was finished, I decided to hold a barbecue so I could personally thank everyone for all their help. Bob Blizard had done more than just help to build the bathroom; he had organised someone to remove a dead tree and have it chainsawed up so that I'd have firewood for winter. I came home from work one day and there he was, carting leftover sand from the building and using it to fill in where we'd done all the digging for the water leak. He and his wife are both amazing, giving people, always raising money for something or someone. I met some truly decent people during the building of the new bathroom and this barbecue gave me an opportunity to thank them all, as well as having an enjoyable get-together.

The frequency of Storm's attacks seemed to be diminishing. It didn't matter whether it was the drugs controlling them or something else happening—when he did have an attack it still affected him in the same way as before, but at least it was not as often as it had been.

I had organised to go to Peta's house for a scrapbooking day and had just got all my gear into the car when Storm had an attack. Bugger! I had so looked forward to this day out, I decided we should go anyway. Storm was sleeping between attacks so I laid him on the back seat of the car and drove to Perth. Everyone was fine about him not being well (it happened occasionally that some people got upset seeing the attacks). I made him comfy and started with my scrapbooking. He looked happy to be there as he listened to us chattering away. At one point, I looked around the room and thought: I love all these people, they mean so much to me.

There's Peta, who I initially met through Lisa. She's calm and matter-of-fact and she just enjoys life. And Helen—I met her when she joined the committee to raise money for Storm's bathroom. She is a registered nurse and works at the medical centre. She has a great heart and the simple pleasures of her family and her friends are the most important thing to her. Her sister, Gail, is very much the same and they have a close relationship which is heart-warming. Then there's Sophie, how can I describe such a lovely friend? She is a single mother, like me, totally devoted to her daughter, also named Storm, would you believe it? She is also a volunteer ambulance office and you couldn't find a more dedicated one. A couple of times when I've called an ambulance, it's been Sophie on duty and when I see her, I sigh with relief. I know she will look after us and she's just so professional. I love her humour and she will have me in fits of laughter when she describes an event; even the antics of her beloved horses will set me off giggling.

All these women took Storm on board without batting an eyelid—he was just another child and they all had children. I sometimes get tearful when I think how blessed I am to have such strong friendships. I'm sure they don't realise how much they lifted me up on the dark days.

This was to be Storm's last year of primary school and I faced the daunting decision about where he would go for high school. Bindoon doesn't have a high school. Gingin is about a 20-minute drive from Bindoon and quite a few of the kids in Storm's class would be going to the high school there. Or there's another one in Bullsbrook, a little closer towards

Perth. I was not looking forward to the adjustments Storm would need to make and the thought of it all made me sick to my stomach.

I have this feeling that Storm won't like high school. But no matter how I feel, I'll have to find a school for him. I couldn't possibly send him to the special school every day; I know he'd be unhappy if he was going there fulltime.

So I bit the bullet and made appointments with the two schools. First I went to the school in Bullsbrook. They already had one disabled child but, unlike Storm, his disability was just physical. I was shown around and it soon became clear how different and difficult high school was going to be. I came away from the appointment with a heavy heart and not feeling confident that the principal would encourage me to enrol Storm. So I wasn't feeling very hopeful when I visited the school in Gingin, but I was nicely surprised. The principal was quite amenable about Storm coming to the school and asked what adjustments could be made to help him. The big issue was transport; if I was driving Storm to and from school it would cut into the hours I could work. But if that was what needed to be done, I'd adjust to it. I felt a lot better after the meeting and the decision was an easy one—Storm would go to the high school in Gingin next year. In hindsight, I should have known it would all work out. I've learnt to have faith that the universe will always provide, but sometimes this gets forgotten. This fear that Storm would be unhappy was my fear, not his.

The doctors at the hospital decided Storm must wear the splints on his feet and legs at night; it just felt cruel and I hated having to put them on after he'd had his bath. He was so happy in the bath and then I must put these poxy splints on to stretch the muscles in his legs. How could he sleep with his feet pulled flat? I felt miserable when I put them on, it seemed like a form of punishment and he didn't look happy.

Storm enjoys going to bed at night. After a day of sitting upright in his wheelchair and doing his walking exercises, he is usually very content to lie in his comfy bed until he drifts off to sleep—but now it's uncomfortable. On the nights when I can see he's too uncomfortable with the splints on, I take them off after a couple of hours and I don't care if it's the wrong thing to do. If I hear him moaning in the night, the relief is obvious when I take them off. This is making the decision to have the operation an easier one.

It was the end of April and Storm's health had been good, no tonsillitis, very few seizures and the doctor was right—it was the healthiest he'd ever been. But not long after the appointment to discuss the splints, he was in pain when I picked him up from school and his urine was brown and smelly. I thought maybe it was an infection or maybe he was dehydrated—sometimes it was hard to get him to drink enough. Looking back, I see now that this was when Storm's bodily functions were beginning to break down. I had to race over to the school again a couple of days later—he was doubled up in pain. I changed his nappy and when we got home I treated him for constipation, thinking this might be the problem. Sometimes, sitting him on his toilet could help. He ended up passing wind (I'm being polite) and he felt better and slept well that night.

I took him to the doctor the next day, because he'd never suffered with constipation. The doctor thought he had a virus, one that looked like a cold but made the glands swell so that when Storm tried to have a bowel movement it really hurt him. He decided I should give him Panadol every four hours. Once that kicked in, Storm was back to his happy self. But a few days later he developed stomach cramps and I could see there was something wrong. Cramps, smelly urine and constipation—all things he'd never had before. I was worried and uneasy and felt like I was in the eye of a storm; calm now, but something bad was coming. What?

Another appointment at the hospital and the doctor has convinced me, so the operation on Storm's legs is scheduled for August and they will put pins in his knees to stop them from growing (I think that's the reason), and cut his hamstrings. It all sounds bloody gruesome but they say he'll be able to sit up more easily after it's done.

In this uneasy calm, I tried to distract myself from the feeling of impending doom that was creeping up on me. I visited Laurel often and probably drove her nuts. I also visited Jane who regularly had a girls night at her place so there were lots of people to distract me. I took Storm to the iridologist to see whether he could tell what was going on. He said it was hormones—Storm's pituitary gland was growing and affecting his pancreas, but the pancreas wasn't working properly and I needed to give him lollies because he was short on sugar. He also said the thing in Storm's head hadn't grown during the past two years, which perhaps explained why he hadn't had so many attacks lately. He said this thing in his head would never be found . . . and it never was. I couldn't see how more sugar would make a difference, but it did. I'd never given Storm many lollies (his favourite was snakes) so he was happy to be allowed to have more than usual. After that he didn't have any more trouble with bowel movements and the stomach cramps were gone. He was happy again.

Storm's teacher has found a way to improve his fine motor skills. She showed me how—by giving Storm a jar with jelly beans in it. The motivator is he gets to eat what he can get out of the jar. This teacher, Robin Revill, is very good at pushing Storm forward and, since Storm loves to please, he tries damn hard.

At the beginning of June Storm had another bout of seizures for two days, but recovered quickly. It was cold—June 12 was the coldest day in Bindoon for 39 years! We spent the whole day in front of the fire and I loved it. Winter revives me.

The weirdest thing has happened to me, twice now. I've had panic attacks. God, they're embarrassing. Luckily, I was at home both times. I put it down to this feeling I can't shake, the feeling that something bad is coming.

It was a busy time at the Palmers'—they'd sold the farm and would be moving in August to a house in Denmark, on the WA south coast. But the distraction of it all was good for me.

Storm's weekend at Catholic Care. I was carrying him in and one of the carers was sitting in his usual rocker recliner. She was quickly told to move because that was HIS chair. I had to laugh when she leapt out of it. When I left, Storm was chomping happily on a chocolate frog. He looked so happy and healthy. *Maybe there's nothing bad coming, after all. Maybe I'm just a drama queen. Boy I hope so!*

We had a meeting at the Bindoon school to try out new walking frames for Storm, and a new kind of standing frame. And since he's grown out of his wheelchair, he was measured up for a new one. They set him up in this flash new walking frame and it had lots more wheels so it was easier for him to push. We walked him out of the library and on to the verandah and he just took off! We had to race in front of him to move mats and bins out of his way—it was unbelievable.

One classroom of kids saw what he was doing and raced to the door to cheer him on. I'd never seen him walk so confidently, he obviously felt very secure and safe in the new frame. It was the most expensive one, of course, but Judy Dennis said it was definitely the one he needed and they'd make a plan about the cost. Storm was so happy and the feeling I had of impending doom seemed silly—but I still couldn't shake it.

In the July holidays (*wow—half the year has gone already*), Storm had one day with a really high temperature but I managed to get it down with Panadol and a cool bath. Once again I wondered what was causing these fevers. I took him to the doctor and he gave Storm some antibiotics in case it was a virus. Whatever it was, he'd shaken it by the next day. It was really important that he was in the best of health when it came time for the operation.

It obviously was a bigger deal than I'd realised. We had to go to a meeting to discuss what would happen after the surgery. Storm would be in hospital for at least eight days and there were exercises I'd have to do with him. I was bombarded with all this information and it was all bit much to take in. I was told I'd need extra help, and they organised for Silver Chain in Bindoon to send someone out. *I'm still not happy about putting Storm through this operation—it's going to be very painful for him.*

At the beginning of the new term Storm wasn't happy about going to school, quite unlike him. He was doubling over with pain and even his aide, Julie Reynolds, couldn't get a smile out of him. He didn't even want to get out of bed. One morning he looked so sad that I just couldn't take him to school and he lay on the couch for the whole day. I dosed him up with Panadol—not good for him to be having so much but it did seem to give him some relief from the pain, wherever it was. I didn't know what else to do to help him and when it got too hard I snuck out into the garden and cried my eyes out.

On another day I took him to school hoping it would distract him from the pain but I soon got a phone call saying he was in bad shape so I raced over, picked him up and took him straight to the medical centre. The doctor's locum thought it might be his appendix playing up, so I rushed home and packed a bag while he wrote up a referral. Then I drove like a maniac to Perth and handed the letter to the triage nurse at PMH. An X-ray showed his bowel was seriously backed-up. This had never been a problem before and now it was a big problem. And they weighed him and he'd lost two kilos, which he couldn't afford to lose. I was given laxatives and suppositories for him—isn't it just lovely some of the things us mothers have to do?

After five days, there was hardly any improvement and he was so miserable that I took him back to our local doctor. He gave me some Picalax, which is what people take when they're going to have a colonoscopy—it's supposed to clean the bowels out in three hours. Well, it took 11 hours and poor Storm had terrible stomach cramps and then, well, he just exploded! I got him to the toilet just in time. He certainly felt better afterwards. By then he hadn't been to school for two weeks so, in his misery, I took him along to work with me.

I'd told the Palmers I'd take two trailer-loads of stuff down to Denmark for them. I felt very torn about this, but didn't want to let them down. The trip was scheduled for the same weekend as Storm's respite, and just before his surgery. I gave him another dose of Picalax and warned everyone at Catholic Care what I'd done; I was worried his surgery would be postponed if his bowels weren't sorted out. He was angry with me when I dropped him off and he had every right to be. I hated myself for having to do it but I'd made a commitment to the Palmers. It was a long drive to Denmark and back again, but Toni was with me and helped me load up and unload. I phoned every day to see how Storm was going—but it didn't appease my guilt much. Apparently the Picalax worked a treat—Storm's bottom had exploded (again); and he was feeling much, much happier. I can just imagine what blissful relief it was for him.

On the Monday I took him to school in Perth. It was going to be a week or so before he was well enough to go again and I wanted him to have a swim. And I needed to do some shopping. That night I took something to help me sleep because I knew that otherwise I would lie awake all night worrying about the operation the next day. *I still don't feel good about the surgery, but I must trust what I've been told—that it will be a great help to Storm.*

In the morning he had his breakfast early, since he had to fast after that. Jane came for coffee and picked up the dog and we left for Perth. It was pouring with rain but we still arrived at the hospital in plenty of time.

A volunteer "Apricot Lady" took us up to Ward 6 and I put Storm in a rocker recliner next to his bed, with his much-loved squishy pillow that Joan Palmer had given him. That rocker recliner would be my bed for the next few days because there wasn't room for one of those folding beds. Storm had stomach cramps and I didn't know whether he was just hungry or his bowels were still giving him trouble. He went into theatre at 3pm and he'd been fasting since seven o'clock in the morning so he must have felt rotten. The anaesthetic injection put him out straight away but his eyes remained wide open, which really freaked me out. Then the Apricot Lady took me to the waiting room. About 6pm, the surgeon came out and said the operation had gone well and that it would be about another 45 minutes. Time went by and then the anaesthetist came and said it would be another 15 minutes. I was very impressed that they'd come to speak to me—far too often, nobody told me anything. Finally, I was taken up to recovery and Storm was there, still sleeping soundly. I was just pleased to see him!

Later, when he was settled in his bed back in Ward 6 and almost asleep again, I snuck out and rang everyone to say the operation had gone well, then got some dinner from the cafeteria before it closed for the evening.

I couldn't look when the nurses came to check on Storm; his legs had those drains coming out of them and I didn't even want to think about it. He was woken up every 30 minutes for a check and then every hour, poor mite.

It was a bad night. We were in a ward with three other beds, all with crying babies, and one of the mothers was snoring. How she could sleep in one of those poxy rocker recliners was beyond me! And in the morning when a physiotherapist turned up to exercise poor Stormy's legs, he didn't like it one bit. I didn't realise until later that he still had an epidural in his spine. The fact that it was still in there showed the seriousness of the operation and it was all a bit overwhelming for me so I was pleased we were in a hospital where the nurses were doing most of the looking after.

Storm dozed for most of the day but was woken for exercises and a bath, both of which must have been painful, to judge by the look on his face. When he slept, I walked up and down the stairs for something to do—I couldn't go outside because it was raining cats and dogs. After two nights without sleep, I was getting a tad grumpy and I wanted to take that rocker recliner from hell and set it alight. I would rather lie on the hard floor than try to stretch myself out in one of those poxy chairs. Finally, they took the epidural out—luckily after they did his leg exercises. The day had dragged, but Storm was okay.

The night nurse is super-efficient, but bloody noisy! I swear, if she shines that light in my eyes again, bad things are going to happen. And she was a bit rough when she turned Storm—he didn't like it at all.

Day Four in hospital and I'd had hardly had any sleep and Storm was miserable. He hadn't had a bowel movement since the operation and he wasn't eating. The physios exercise his legs twice and he did really well, brave little man. But he was very quiet and his temperature was creeping up all day. He had two seizures when his temperature peaked.

The doctor decided to do blood tests and give him something (finally) for his bowels; I was sure he'd feel so much better after another clear-out. Odd that he was suddenly having all these bowel problems. And the nurses found a flat for me—not a whole flat, just one of a number of small rooms created on a big enclosed verandah. I was happy for the opportunity to lie horizontal, and the room had an intercom so they could call me if something happened.

Storm was given antibiotics in case his lungs became infected—this can happen from lying down over long periods. He hadn't been able to sit up since the surgery. While I was sitting with him one day, I felt someone close by and I could smell a perfume that reminded me of my late grandmother.

Hey, Gran! If that very efficient nurse comes on tonight—you know, the one who loves to shine that light in my eyes—how about scaring the crap

out of her? That'd make my day, it would, because I'm sleeping in the "flat"
tonight.

I sat with Storm until about 10pm then had a shower and changed into my pyjamas. It felt really weird to be walking around a hospital in pyjamas—all sorts of people walking past and I have to go down a floor to the showers, it was very strange. I'd had the best night's sleep for a long while and felt human again. I was annoyed when I heard that Storm had had a seizure at 11pm and they didn't call me. What part of "call me if something happens" didn't they understand? But at least he had had his breakfast.

The nurses gave him a sponge bath, since his legs were in splints. But they took the splints off to wash his legs and found a pressure sore (a blister). They carried on about how bad it was and I couldn't look—a big drama was made so I thought it must be really bad and I'm no good at really yukky stuff. The head nurse dressed it and she told me she'd nursed a lot of children who had had that same operation and she's never seen one as good as Storm. *Of course he's the best—that's why he got a bravery award!* Storm was enjoying the praise.

I was shown how to exercise his legs, can't say I enjoyed making him bend his legs and I gave the leg with the pressure sore a break. He was feeling better but then he went and had a seizure and his temperature went up again. Still no bowel movement and it was Day Five.

Day 6: I slept in the flat again, bliss. Storm was asleep when I left him at 11pm and still asleep when I checked on him at 7am. I quickly showered and changed. The nurse changed the dressing on his pressure sore and I decided to look at it no matter how gruesome it was. After all, I'd have to dress it when we got home. When I looked, I was amazed at all the fuss over something that just looked like a couple of layers of skin had come off. *What drama queens they are, and they made me look like a pathetic mother because I wouldn't look at it before.* Storm was able to sit up for a while now but it must have pulled on his legs. He had another seizure, too, and would have gone off to sleep afterwards but it was visiting hours and rather noisy.

At last they gave him an enema and we had lift-off! Life has to be sad when a mother is happy just because her child is pooing. He was much more comfortable after that and even ate all his dinner. I went off to my bed about midnight and was quite shocked that I didn't wake up until 8am. I raced to Storm's bed; he was still dozing, with his breakfast on a tray next to his bed. When I asked the nurse how he went after I left last night, she said they'd had trouble getting him to put his head on the pillow, and I felt guilty that I'd left him. The physios put a board on his wheelchair so he could sit in it with the splints on and his legs straight out. *That's going to hurt! I'll have to manage all this on my own when we get home but I know I will, somehow.*

Time for the leg exercises and Storm didn't like it much. Not much fun for me either, with Stormy grimacing and wincing. I wanted to stop but couldn't—we were committed to this.

I rang Mum and she was really ill with flu. Then I rang Toni and she told me Rae's sister, Ownie, had just been diagnosed with throat cancer.

I was tearful and upset for Ownie and Rae for the rest of that day; wanted to ring Rae but thought it best to wait until I could trust myself not to cry.

Day 8 in hospital and again I slept in the flat, so fortunate to be able to do that. At 7am Storm was still sleeping so I had breakfast and then sat with him. The doctor said we could go home, so I rang Jane to tell her the good news. But when the nurses changed the dressing on Storm's legs, they said he wouldn't be going anywhere that day. I had a bit of a giggle—the nurses are sometimes the boss, the doctor hadn't seen Storm's legs without the splints. So then I had to ring Jane back and say we weren't going home that day after all. I confess I was relieved—I was nervous about looking after those dressings at home, and all the exercises, and trying to get him in and out of the wheelchair on my own. *I don't even know how I will get him into the car, he'll be so difficult to carry with his legs in splints.*

Day 9 and we really could go home. The drip was taken out of Storm's arm and I was given instructions on how to look after the wounds on his legs. A nurse helped me to put him in his wheelchair and came with me to the car park to help me put him in the front seat of the car. We hadn't been home long when Laurel's mother, Pixie, turned up and I was glad to see her. I knew I could call on her or Laurel if I had a problem. Then Bob Blizard arrived—the carport would be going up at the weekend. I was so thankful for that, because I'd just had to get Storm out of the car in the rain and having a carport would be fantastic.

Everything about Storm's management was taking much longer now so it was taking a while for me to get organised in the mornings. He was still having sponge baths and I had the exercises to do with him twice a day, not to mention getting him in and out of his wheelchair. A lady from Silver Chain came the first morning to help me, and later Jane came and watched Storm so I could buy groceries.

Julie Reynolds, Storm's aide from school, came for a visit and he loved that. I felt quite spoilt with all the help I was getting, but I had to learn to do it all myself and I knew I could. By the time I went to bed I was practically passed out with exhaustion.

After four days at home, I had to take Storm back to the hospital to have the dressings removed. He still wasn't having bowel movements and I had no idea what to do about it. I felt sick at the thought of how it must be for him, so I put aside my tiredness and simply tried to make him as comfortable as possible.

He was happier with the dressings off and the pressure sore was healing well. He sat up a lot, the most since the operation, and he was exhausted when I put him into bed that night. The next day would be his first back at school—only for a couple of hours because the amount of time he spends sitting up had to be increased gradually. The only good thing I could see was that it was still cold, so at least his legs wouldn't get too hot in those splints. The only time they came off was during the exercises and that wasn't an enjoyable time either.

Janette (another of Storm's wonderful aides) met me in the school car park and helped me with Storm at home time. I'd managed by myself that morning but it wasn't easy. I think Storm enjoyed the distraction of school, but he still had stomach cramps so he was miserable. The next day was better and he enjoyed being fussed over. Then he had a day off school and could lie on the couch for a while with his favourite toys—in between the exercises and having to sit in his wheelchair. I was finding it all very hard emotionally. I hated seeing him so sad and in pain and felt I'd done a terrible thing.

When Storm is asleep, I have a cry but I've got to suck it up, crying doesn't help him. I've got to find my inner strength—it's wandered off when I wasn't looking. It's just a moment of weakness, I've had a long talk to myself and I will be fine tomorrow.

A lady from the bathroom committee told me her son had offered to do some Bowen therapy on Storm. If it would give him any relief, I was all for it. It did, and we set up another session for the following week.

Back to the hospital for a follow-up, and the surgeon said Storm's splints could come off during the day and he should do some weight-bearing. *He is going to be so happy!* I couldn't believe it was already three weeks since the operation—we were so tired when we got home from the hospital that we both just lay in the lounge room like lizards sunning themselves.

The next day I was able to send Storm to school without his splints, but I hadn't been home long before the phone rang: Storm was vomiting. *Unbelievable.* When I got there I saw he wasn't just vomiting, he was vomiting up old blood, so I put him in the car and raced over to the doctor's surgery. Luckily my friend Helen was on duty and she grabbed the locum doctor and he saw Storm straight away. He took one look at the vomit (I'd taken some with me to the surgery) and said I must get him straight to hospital because he could be bleeding internally. Jeez . . . thanks for giving it to me straight!

Right about now would be a good time to freak out, but then I remembered I'd found my inner strength again. Helen rang for an ambulance and I sat very calmly with Storm waiting. It was Sophie and Rose who arrived in the ambulance and I was so happy to see them. I felt calm as they loaded Storm on to a gurney and put him in the ambulance. I followed in my car and Sophie gave me her mobile phone so she could contact me if things got worse and they needed to take off with sirens flashing. When everything goes pear-shaped, Sophie and Rose are the people you want with you.

We had no more drama on the way and the doctor in emergency thought it best to admit him. *They think he might have a stomach ulcer—unbelievable. His life has just turned to shit, not even 13 yet and look at all he's had to endure!* He was in Ward 7, with chairs that folded out into beds with sheets and a pillow, not a poxy rocker recliner in sight. If I could just get a bit of sleep, I could deal with anything. *Bring it on!*

Storm was fasting and had a drip in his arm, but he was just so quiet. Luckily he was given some toys to play with. I sat by his side and the doctor didn't show up until 4pm the next afternoon so Storm had had a whole day of fasting. They said they would do a procedure to look into his stomach and see whether there was an ulcer. That would be on Friday; it was Wednesday now. Finally, Storm was allowed some toast and something to drink. To be honest, I was glad to be at the hospital, it relieved me of some of the responsibility of caring for him. The feeling of being in the quiet before the storm had gone and now I felt we were in the storm. The storm was raging in my son's body and I felt there would be mass destruction and loss for both of us. *I have to hold on to my strength to get us through this. Storm won't see my fear, I am going to be so strong and I will do whatever is necessary.*

Next day, he had to fast again until 5pm when he was allowed some toast. I was determined to be cheerful for him, and did the exercises on his legs, that distracted him even if it was a painful distraction.

On Friday he had the procedure. It showed nothing much more than a tiny erosion in his small intestine, but he was given tablets for ulcers and we were allowed to go home. I wasn't sure I believed this was the reason he vomited up so much old blood and I felt very uneasy. He was still having stomach cramps. *I can't sit here and do nothing.* On Monday I managed to get an appointment with the iridologist in Perth. He said Storm's body was full of mucus and that was stopping it from functioning. I was to take him off all dairy products and I was given some tablets to help him. *God, I hope this works.* I also went back to the local doctor to see if there was anything else I could do. He said I must keep going back to the hospital until something was done. So I came straight home and began packing in case we had to stay over in the hospital. Jane turned up in the midst of all this and that was when we noticed that Storm's stomach was quite distended. *Oh God, what now?*

Jane took Jet home with her and I put Storm in the car and raced to the hospital. It seemed to take forever to get from the emergency waiting room into one of their beds and the whole time Storm was sitting up in his wheelchair with a distended stomach, it must have been so uncomfortable. Finally, a doctor did an ultrasound and it looked like his bladder was the problem. They put in a catheter and extracted almost 450ml of urine. The poor boy was much more relaxed afterwards, but what did it mean, was there something wrong with his bladder now? *What is going on? I just can't process all of this in my head and all I want to do is sob my heart out. But this is not the time to weaken, he has to know that the confident, happy mum he is used to is there for him.*

We were admitted to Ward 5 and Storm slept comfortably that night. The next morning, Dr Anna Gubbay came in and I was so happy to see her. She thought the bladder problem had just happened and was not connected to anything else going on. But there was still a problem with his bowel and I thought that, somehow, it was all connected. The day passed quickly but I felt uneasy and my stomach was churning with fear.

The catheter was taken out the next day but had to be put back when he hadn't urinated in nine hours. Something had definitely gone wrong. Storm's health was just getting worse, first his bowel, now his bladder. And then he had two seizures in the night. *Is there no peace?*

Dr Gubbay came in the next morning, and said she would speak to the urologist about Storm. At least it was all being taken seriously. It appeared we'd be in hospital for the weekend and it was Storm's birthday, what a way to spend it. All we could do was wait, so I kept doing his exercises and a physio got him to do some standing with his splints on. He didn't like that at all.

The urologist decided to remove the catheter and just do intermittent catheterising during the day. Storm actually passed urine on his own that night and I felt hopeful. How sad it is to get excited when your child does a wee.

The next day was quiet and Storm needed to have a catheter several times as he couldn't go on his own. And the day after that was his birthday. It would have to be his most miserable birthday ever; I'd had no time to get him anything and I felt awful. I just sat with him and loved him.

Somehow, the lady who organised activities for the children got wind that it was Storm's birthday so she arrived with presents. She gave him a battery-run piano and the ugliest stuffed gorilla you've ever seen and Storm loved it. He played happily and I was ecstatic just to see him smile.

The urologist decided to give him a catheter with a bag for a week, to give his bladder time to recover. Then we were to come back and have it removed and see what's what. *I can't express how frightened and awful I feel.*

The nurses came to put the catheter in and I wouldn't let them. I told them I needed to speak to Dr Gubbay before they did it. I didn't care what the nurses thought, I wanted Anna Gubbay's opinion first. I really valued her opinion—she seemed to be the only one who realised there was something really wrong and she'd treated him before with his leg problems. I'm not a deeply religious person but I believe in a greater power, be that

God or something or someone else. I believe in life after death—that we go on after our physical death—and I believed God or whoever it was had sent Dr Gubbay to me to get me through this. So I dug in my heels and wouldn't let anything be done until I saw her. This wasn't going to be until the next day so Storm had intermittent catheters until then.

When Anna came the next morning we discussed everything and she thought the catheter and bag was the right way to go. But she recommended a test first in which they put dye through the bladder to see what shows up. This was all done and we were home by about 5pm. *I'm hoping the bag isn't too uncomfortable for Stormy.*

It had been two weeks since Storm had been to school so I asked if I could bring him in for just a couple of hours because I knew it would cheer him up—I really needed to do something which would give him some joy. When I took him up to his class, the children had rearranged their desks so that his desk was right in the centre with all the others around it. I could have cried, they all cared so much for Storm and he must have sensed their empathy. It was such a lovely thing to do and it cheered him up immensely.

I was asked to bring him in for the school assembly the next day to receive another certificate. It was quite an effort to get organised and get there in time but so worth it. They called out Storm's name and Julie Reynolds took him up to collect an award for having the courage to overcome obstacles with a smile. And he was full of smiles when he accepted it. But that wasn't all—his class gave him a belated birthday party and there were chips and lollies and nibbles to go with a cake I'd made. This cheered us both up and Storm just loved the fuss that Julie made of him. What more caring group of people could ever be found? He had another birthday party on the weekend, organised by Jane. Mum, Dad and Toni all drove up for it and we all did our best to be cheerful and upbeat. I know he just loved that everyone, especially Jane, had put in so much effort.

After a week, it was time to go back to the hospital to have the catheter removed and see if Storm's bladder had recovered. I was really on edge. The hospital rang to say a bed would be available at 2pm and, while I was getting ready, Anna Gubbay phoned to say the tests done last week had shown there was a thickening of the bladder wall and that the urethra seemed small. I can't remember what all that meant, but I was upset. I thought things would be all right and I'd been giving Storm the tablets from the iridologist but they obviously hadn't helped. I rang the iridologist and he said I should keep up with the tablets for another week.

By the time we got to the hospital, I was tearful and upset. Dr Gubbay came in just after the catheter was taken out, and asked me to walk her through Storm's life from birth up to now. It was the first time in Storm's whole life of 13 years that a doctor had said that. After I finished, she said she wanted to do more research into Storm's condition. I said it really started to slide from 1999 and he'd been deteriorating ever since.

Anna left and I settled in with Storm; he managed a few wees on his own but I was too scared to be hopeful. *I know that is wrong, I should be putting positive thoughts out to the universe but I know, I just know this is not good and where it's all leading is going to be even worse.* Those poxy recliners were back to haunt me and I got about an hour's sleep that night.

The urologist turned up with the registrar the next morning and proceeded to tell me Storm would have to be catheterised intermittently forever and if that became a problem he would have a bag put on. Then he waltzed off out of the room. The shock on my face must have registered with the registrar because a couple of minutes later he came back and said that maybe the urologist might have been a bit drastic—that it was early days and Storm most probably wouldn't need a bag. He was so lovely. I didn't know it at the time but I would see that registrar once more.

A lady was organised to show me how to catheterise Storm— whoopee, I get to learn a new skill and I must learn even if I don't want to. *Permission to cry?* The lady was great, she showed me what to do and I managed without a problem. Everything had to be sterile so Storm didn't get an infection and for the rest of the day, it was left for me to do. *Bang, just like that!*

In the afternoon Storm was having bad cramps so I catheterised him and he seemed better afterwards. This made me think that it wasn't his bowels that had been causing the cramps all along. I had to test the urine every time he was catheterised, to guard against infection, and it didn't look good. It appeared he might be getting an infection already. *I don't think we will be going home soon.*

Actually, I thought we'd be going home that day, but Storm had a temperature and his urine was sent off for tests. A female neurologist came to see him and asked a lot of questions. I'm getting used to doctors who

I've never seen before just rocking up and starting in with their questions. She asked me if I was sure Storm was deteriorating. *Are you mocking me, woman? Anyone who knows Storm can see he is getting worse, and worse.* I suppose she had to ask. But I'd spent 13 years of my life watching Storm deteriorate. How could she question that?

By lunchtime the next day the test results were in and Storm did have a nasty infection. He was sleeping a lot and eating little. So we would not be going anywhere for a few more days, at least. I noticed that I felt a lot better when Storm was asleep. At least then he was removed from what was going on in his body and I could relax.

The next day (Day 5 of this hospital episode) he was very washed-out but he'd been urinating on his own without the catheter. I'd been giving him the tablets from the iridologist when the nurses weren't looking, maybe they were helping. Because of renovations to the ward we were in, on this day we were moved up to Ward 7, into a room with four other boys but no television (we'd been spoilt before in a single room with a telly).

I slipped down the stairs on my way to have a shower and hurt my leg. *Boy, do I want to go home.* Storm wasn't sleeping at all and he looked terrible. The infection wasn't getting better and now he had a drip in his arm and they were putting stronger antibiotics through the drip. I was back to trying to sleep on the recliner from hell—I asked if we could be moved so at least I could have a foldout bed, but no such luck.

The antibiotics were fairly strong and Storm was sleeping a lot, which was okay by me. After his breakfast I went for a walk and when I got back I saw they'd moved his bed while he slept. *It is now against the far wall and I'll be able to sleep on a foldout bed tonight. Thank you universe, so much.*

It was the best night's sleep I'd had since we checked in seven days earlier. And Storm did two big wees on his own—exciting stuff, folks! However, I still had to catheterise him during the day. Mum and Dad said they would drive up to Bindoon to whipper-snip my yard beause it was so overgrown with weeds. I was so grateful—we might be going home the next day and the last thing I wanted to deal with was a messy garden.

As it turned out, we did get to pack up and go home the next day. I felt devastated. Storm's life was only going to get worse and I didn't know how much more suffering I could watch him endure. It was the first time I ever felt I could take my own life, and not just my own. I wanted Storm's pain to stop and I just knew it was going to get really bad.

On the drive back to Bindoon I considered the best way to end our lives together. I was very matter-of-fact about it—this was the only decent thing I could do for Storm. I had ideas—we could take an overdose of sleeping tablets and then I could set up the car to gas us both. By the time we were home, I had it all very clear in my mind that this was what I needed to do. I couldn't end Storm's life and stay here by myself—I wanted to go with him.

But the universe intervened. We hadn't been home long and I'd just set Storm up on the couch when Jane arrived. I don't remember if I rang her, but there she was. She said: "You're thinking of taking your life, aren't you?" Oh shit, it sounded awful when someone else said it! I confessed that was exactly what I was thinking. I wanted to end Storm's pain but I couldn't just take his life, I must go with him. Of course, she talked me out of it and made me promise not to do anything silly. I thought it was selfish of me to let him go on in so much pain but the urge passed, after much talking by Jane. I couldn't go back on my word so we'd just have to ride this out to the end.

I was glad to be home but now I had to adjust to catheterising Storm on a daily basis. Luckily, my job with the Palmers had finished since they moved, and I wasn't going to be able to clean for Jackie anymore. If and when Storm went back to school, I'd have to go there at least once during the day to catheterise him.

I set him up in the lounge with a tray on his wheelchair. I sprayed shaving cream all over the toys on the tray and he was having a fat old time playing in the shaving cream while I raced around doing the housework. I'd adjusted to the catheterising and it didn't bother Storm at all. *It gives him relief, so he thinks it's A Good Thing.*

Storm went back to school after a few days and I'd go up there about 11am to catheterise him, then come home and go back when it was home time. Helen offered to help out with the catheterising, which was just so great. Stormy seemed okay at school; he was back to having physio twice a week and I'd do the exercises twice a day at home. We plodded on like this for 11 days, then it all turned to shit again.

He had been awake all night and nothing would make him go off to sleep. About 4am, I found he had old blood around his mouth—obviously he was vomiting it up and swallowing it again. I rang my local doctor who said I must call an ambulance. Then I had to ring Jane to ask her to pick up the dog, since I didn't know how long we'd be at the hospital. When the ambulance arrived, I was relieved to see Sophie was one of the officers!

At the hospital, I'm sure they didn't believe my story that Storm was vomiting up old blood, but when a nurse saw a bit dribbling out of his mouth, things started to move pretty quickly. They'd been about to send us back home and next thing we knew he had a drip in his arm and had been admitted to Ward 8—a private room with its own bathroom.

The doctor who attended Storm last time he vomited blood didn't bother to come and see him, she simply sent her registrar and the only decision made was to increase his ulcer medications because they found ulcers in his stomach. The only thing I could do to give him any pleasure was to bathe him, so that's what I did. I could do no more except give him all my love.

Dr Gubbay checked Storm over, which was more than the doctor who was supposed to be looking after him did. We were there for three days and went home on the fourth. It was a Friday, and I rang the iridologist to make an appointment for Monday. Whatever was going on with all this vomiting, it had left Storm too weak to sit up on his own—on the drive to Perth on Monday I had to put his beanbag in the car so he could lean on it, otherwise he just toppled over.

The iridologist examined Storm and said his pituitary gland was the cause of the problem. It was the reason his bladder had failed and the cause of the vomiting. He thought he might be able to fix it but he couldn't say for sure whether the medication would help. *I'll try anything at the moment.*

The next day I sent Storm to school because he seemed well enough to go and it would be a lot better than being at home with just me to entertain him—he enjoyed the noise of school. I was back there at 11am to catheterise him, back home; then back to the school at 3pm to take him home. He was very tired and asleep before 8pm. I still had to catheterise him and he slept through the whole procedure. Over the next few days, he'd fall asleep at school and they'd leave him to sleep for a bit. And there were several times I had to catheterise him while he slept.

It's all getting too much for him, and the year had started out so well. The new bath has been the best thing ever for Storm. He wouldn't have been able to use the old bath with his leg problems and it is a great relief for him to have a bath at night.

One night he was sitting on the change table while I dried him off and he reached up with his arms and pulled me to him and kissed me on the lips. This just melted my heart! He knew I would do anything I possibly could to change the current circumstances and the way he had to live.

Two Mondays in a row, Storm was trembling and quite upset when I fetched him from the school in Perth. Then I had a call from the

Bindoon school to say he was in pain. I took him straight to the doctor, who recommended I keep him out of school on Mondays for a while and give him Panadol every four hours to see if it helped.

Soon after that, I'd brought Storm home from school in Bindoon school and his legs seemed very stiff yet his right foot was floppy and I could get no reaction when I ran my nail along the sole. I decided to wait until Judy Dennis did his physio and discuss it with her. I explained my concerns and she checked his legs and could see something was definitely wrong. I had Anna Gubbay's mobile phone number so I rang her, explained the situation and gave the phone to Judy so she could speak to the doctor.

Anna said she wanted me to bring Storm in straight away. Five minutes later she rang back to say there was a bed for him in the teen ward, Ward 7, and I should take him straight there. I knew it was serious, but I didn't panic. *I'm a calm chick in a crisis and I haven't fallen apart—yet.*

With Storm in the car, the wheelchair in the boot and our other luggage, I calmly drove to the hospital. But I knew this was it. When I arrived I settled him in his bed before filling out the admission forms, then went back to sit with him.

Anna arrived after lunch. She had scheduled an MRI and after seeing Storm she decided to move him up the list. His foot was still floppy and by now his legs had become so rigid that I could hardly straighten them. Something really bad was happening. I knew in my heart that this time Storm wouldn't leave the hospital alive. It was November 10.

A neurologist examined Storm and kept mentioning Parkinson's disease. She wanted to try a drug to see if it would relax his legs. It was administered before I realise that it contained valium, which as I already knew didn't relax him at all. It kept him (and me) awake until 3am and we were like zombies the next day.

I tried to do his leg exercises after breakfast but I could hardly bend his legs. So I gave him a bath, which he loved.

We'd progressed from blocked bowels to runny bowel movements—wonderful! It was Friday November 11, Remembrance Day, and they were hoping to do the MRI on Tuesday, along with a lumbar puncture. *Here we are at the end and they are finally going to do an MRI.* They also decided to try another drug to see if it would ease the stiffness. I really didn't think they knew what they were dealing with.

A physiotherapist did exercises on his legs and showed me how to place pillows between his legs to stop them from turning in. He managed to sit up in his wheelchair for dinner—sat up really well and I thought it was bloody amazing. I put his legs in the splints for an hour even though I couldn't get them completely straight. *It's weird how they became so twisted and stiff so quickly.* He drifted off to sleep and I lay on my foldout bed full of worry. *I know he won't be going home ever again. I know with calm certainty that he's dying.*

It might be weeks, or months, but I know it is the end and there isn't a tear in me to shed. Death is the only decent thing that can come for Storm, to bring relief from his pain. It would be selfish of me to want to prolong his life just because I can't bear to part with him, and I know he doesn't want to leave me, either. I will have to be strong so he knows he can go.

Dr Gubbay took me into a private room to discuss Storm. I know she also realised this was the end for him, even though she didn't say it to me directly. I valued her honesty. I was going to need her on my side to get through this and we agreed the main objective was to make it as pain-free as we possibly could.

Maybe you will judge me for not telling my ex-husband that Storm was dying. It's okay if you do. I know in my heart that I did what was best for Storm, and his father had had no contact with him for eight years. The need to protect Storm was very strong in me and I bore no ill will towards my ex-husband. But I was the one who'd been there the whole time and I knew that only I could make the right decisions for Storm, no matter how painful it would be. *We still don't know what is really going on in Storm's body and I don't think we're ever going to know now.*

I rang Mum to let her know and I think she and Dad also knew this day was coming. An eerie calm came over me, as if someone or something was lifting me up so I could do this.

I will have the rest of my life to mend from the pain of this experience, now I need to be strong. I intend to give Stormy all the love I have—to make this as peaceful as I can for him.

I've written the rest of this as a diary; I know no other way to do it.

The Final Chapter

NOVEMBER 12, 2005

It's our third day in hospital and already we've slipped into a routine. After catheterising Storm and feeding him breakfast, I made sure the nurses would watch over him while I drove quickly back to Bindoon to fetch a few things from home and find some photos of Storm from his babyhood until now. Anna Gubbay has asked for them so she can get a clearer picture of how his body has deteriorated.

I hadn't been home long when Jane arrived to see which plants would need hand watering. I am so grateful for her help. I scanned photos on to the computer then printed them. I think I've chosen the best of them. Then I said goodbye to my house and left, I was in a rush to get back to Storm. I feel bad that I haven't dropped in to see Laurel but I rang her and explained what was happening.

Finally, I cried. Finally, as I drove back to the hospital, I was sobbing my heart out. I had only been away for the five hours it took to drive to Bindoon and back and I felt awful. How am I going to bear my life without him in it? I was all out of tears by the time I got back to the hospital.

Storm looked uncomfortable and in pain. His stomach was swollen and he couldn't sleep until he was given something to ease the pain. Nobody seems to know why his abdomen is distended and I'm past wanting them to find the problem. All I ask is that he be free of pain. *Just take the bloody pain away.*

NOVEMBER 13

His legs were even more rigid this morning. I hope they're not too painful. Anna came in and I showed her the photos. Of course she thought he was a real cutie and she could see how different he had been. The neurologist also saw the photos when she arrived and she said she couldn't understand what had happened to him.

Should I be happy that, finally, they all realise that something terrible has been happening to Storm as he grew older? Whatever it is, it's never going to get better. Storm has been miserable and in pain today. His abdomen is still swollen, he has a temperature and his blood pressure is up. He has never had a blood pressure problem.

The day dragged, and in the evening a nurse sat with Storm while I walked around a park near the hospital. I needed to feel some fresh air and see some trees after being stuck inside. Storm would also love to be outside but he's never again going to feel the wind on his face or listen to the birds singing—unless it's in the next life he goes to. *This is insane.*

NOVEMBER 14

Storm had a rough night, he called out to me in the night, and my heart is no longer breaking—it's broken, shattered into tiny pieces. All I want is for them to give him something for the pain that is raging through his body. Why are they hesitating to give him strong painkillers? Do they really believe he can survive this? His temperature is still up, his stomach is still swollen and he is scratching it all the time. Anna has asked for some X-rays to be taken this afternoon.

His legs are worse, they can't be straightened at all now and the left one has turned in even more. I've put a pillow between his knees so they don't rub, but still he is getting pressure sores and he is miserable. I'm amused that some of the doctors believe that Storm is going to get better when they don't even know what they are fighting. He's been scheduled to see a dietician and a skin specialist—he's getting acne which I was trying to clear up (and lost the battle). If they want to clear his skin up, go for it, I say.

Jane has organised for me to leave the hospital for a meal. I know it's to get me away from everything I'm dealing with and it probably would be good for me. But I'm going to have many, many days on my own in the future—days when I can go anywhere I want to go and do whatever I want to do. Right now I just want to be with Storm. In the end I do leave for an hour's break but I felt guilty that I left him while he's in such pain. While I was gone, he had the X-rays and they showed his bowel was again extremely blocked.

His temperature is high, he is moaning in pain and he has vomited. Someone decided to put a gastro tube in his nose so that liquid can be introduced, which would help to empty his bowel. His hands have been bandaged because he has pulled the tube out, and now he has a drip in his arm for the antibiotics. He's vomiting again.

In all of Storm's life, I have never seen him in so much pain and I want to scream at them to please give him some painkillers. He's not going to survive, they must know that! Finally, at 2am they gave him Phenergan and he drifted off to sleep.

They say God lifts us up through troubling times and there must be some truth in that as I find I can deal with everything that is happening. I don't feel hysterical or even emotional. I just deal with each thing that happens and move on to the next. A calmness has come over me and an acceptance that what will be, will be. And my black humour has risen to the challenge. I will endure with strength and humour and screw the rest. It's so awful to see Storm's hands bandaged, it's the worst thing ever. He can't use his hands and he can't even play with his adored Elmo.

NOVEMBER 15

I'm exhausted today. I had hardly any sleep last night, but at least Storm doesn't seem to be in as much pain today, though his temperature is still high and his breathing is really bad. Rae and Toni came to visit us. They didn't put it into words but they both know this is the end. We left for a little while to have coffee. I know they're concerned for me and I love them for that but one thing I will do, and do well, is this thing for

Stormy—to help him through this. Rae's life is not so great at the moment either. Her much-loved sister, Ownie, is having treatment for cancer and I know Rae is doing everything she can to help her.

They're giving Storm a stronger antibiotic because the other one wasn't helping. His breathing has become a little better and at last he slept. I'm still doing the catheterising. I know the nurses would do it if I asked, but I want to do this one thing for him.

NOVEMBER 16

Anna Gubbay came in just after Storm's breakfast. She is concerned about the way he is breathing (big breaths through his mouth) and has asked for more blood tests. She admits they have no idea what is happening to Storm and I really appreciate that she is so honest with me. He hasn't had the MRI because of the infection.

My parents and Toni arrived while he was having more blood tests and I was making coffee. I can't watch certain things any more. We chatted a bit over coffee then went back to see how Storm was doing. He was awake so we all sat around the bed talking. He enjoyed that. We didn't talk about what's happening, we know what's happening. I needed and got some light-hearted banter from my family—just like I get from the nurses. God has sent me the best nurses to help us through this difficult time. I am blessed to have them. Then Leanne and Sue, two of Storm's aides, visited. Storm enjoyed every one of his visitors. At 6pm I climbed on to his bed and cuddled him to me. He became quite animated; he was babbling and saying "Mum, mum". He actually seemed happy. It's been a full-on day!

NOVEMBER 17

Still more blood tests after breakfast. One of the nurses from the night staff told me Storm stopped breathing briefly about 4am. I think she expected me to be shocked, but he's done this to me before, it's nothing new.

NOVEMBER 18

What a day—for some reason I woke up really upset. Storm's temperature is really high and more blood tests are needed to see why. I spoke to Toni, Rae and Jane this morning and, because I was so upset, they all dropped everything they were doing and came to me. I appreciate this and by talking it over with them I was able to figure out why I'm so upset. I am worried that maybe I have made the wrong decision—not to prolong Storm's life. What if it's possible that he'll get better? It was a moment of fear that passed. It's a very hard decision to make—to let a life go, and it's even harder when it's your only child.

Anna Gubbay visited and spoke to Jane, I don't know where I was at the time. She told Jane they think Storm has an autogenic condition of the brain that is causing the problems with his legs, bladder and bowel, as well as the high temperatures.

Rae's visit was extra special to me. Her sister Ownie is having chemotherapy so there's a lot of coming and going to the hospital and Rae has a lot of stress in her life at the moment. I went for a walk in the park after she left and while I was away Storm had more X-rays on his bowel. I bought him some lollies while I was out and he enjoyed chewing on them, but it never got to stay in his stomach as he's got a bag draining his tummy. Then I took the bandages off his hands so he could play with his toys for a bit. I had to watch him closely in case he tried to pull the gastro tube out, but he was really good. After a while I re-bandaged his hands. His temperature is still high. Mum rings me every day to see how he is doing and just to have a chat with me.

NOVEMBER 19

I couldn't wake up this morning, I was so exhausted. I finally dragged myself out of bed at 8am and catheterised Storm. He was sleepy too. After that I made myself some coffee then went back to bed for a while. My bed is a foldout one right next to Stormy.

Later, while Storm was still dozing, I snuck up to the Starlight Megazone which is where people can use the internet for emails etc. I researched the autonomic nervous system. It appears the autonomic nervous system is responsible for the function of the lungs, heart, bladder and bowel, as well as the sweat glands and tears. Makes sense too as it would explain why he lost the ability to cry when he was two years old. That must be when it all started—if that's what it is.

The gastro specialist examined Storm today. She said they'll put in a different type of drip that will feed him nutrients—he hasn't eaten for the seven days he's been in hospital. I suppose the drip will prolong his life but I'll be damned if I will let him starve to death. He's had some medicine today for the constipation and then he'll have a Fleet enema tonight. Don't ask me what that is—if it helps, that's what is important.

Julie Reynolds telephoned to see how Storm was. And when I told him she'd phoned to ask after him, he smiled. The nurses put patches on his feet to numb where they plan to put a line in for the new drip. When the doctor came to put the line in, I asked one of the nurses to sit with Stormy because I just couldn't do it. She understood and I went for a walk in the park for a bit. The doctor was still putting the line in when I returned so I sucked it up and cuddled Storm until it was all finished. His veins are collapsing which is why they've had so much trouble getting the line in.

I remember reading somewhere that Mother Teresa said: "Life is an achievement and death is part of that achievement. The dying need tender loving care, nothing more." This is so true. Giving Storm all the love I have is the most I can do for him.

NOVEMBER 20

Had a rough night—Storm was in pain and restless all night, and slept very little. I woke up late and the nurses were already giving him his saline enema and he didn't look happy. I hope they didn't wake him up to do it. I was upset that they hadn't woken me. I know they think letting me sleep is the right thing to do, but I can sleep forever when this is over. I had a cry in the shower and felt better for it.

When I got back Jane's neighbour Richard was sitting with Storm. He persuaded me to go downstairs for coffee and as we caught the lift back up afterwards, Carolyn jumped in. Storm was so happy to hear her voice, as soon as she said hello he reached out to give her a hug and he even smiled a little. It's been so long since he smiled.

After Richard left, Carolyn and I sat with Storm for a bit, then she left. Storm seems better for the visit, though. It brightened his day and mine too. He just adores Carolyn and I'm so grateful that she visited him.

One of the nurses suggested I give Storm a lolly so I raced downstairs to the hospital shop for some. He likes jelly-babies and chewed happily on a couple of them. But later on we saw they'd given him cramps, so his stomach still isn't coping with any kind of food.

NOVEMBER 21

Rough night again, but his temperature is fine. Toni is coming this morning to sit with Storm while I go to Bindoon and check the garden and pick up the mail. Jane is also coming in for a visit. I changed and showered and was ready when Toni arrived. As usual, I cried all the way home—it got all the sadness out and done with. I stopped at a shopping centre and bought myself a jigsaw puzzle. I'd been given one at the hospital and enjoyed the distraction it provided. That one was finished so now I wanted another one to do.

It's very peaceful at home. I watered the plants and checked on the chooks, then collected the mail and headed back to the hospital. While I was away, Anna Gubbay had come and spoken to Jane again. They will hold off on feeding Storm orally or giving him any drinks by mouth and hopefully he'll be stable enough to have the MRI. And then we might have an idea what's going on with him and where to go from there. After Toni and Jane left I set up my new jigsaw puzzle. Storm's stomach and bowels are causing him some pain tonight and I'm hoping the pain eases and he can get some sleep tonight. *Some strong painkillers would be better.*

NOVEMBER 22

I'm so damn tired in the mornings, but a few coffees get me going. Storm had a rough night again. He was wriggling in pain so I catheterised him at 4am to see if that gave him any relief. There was 550ml of urine—no wonder he was wriggling in pain, it must have been excruciating! It's because he now has this drip in his leg. I should have realised that he'll need to be catheterised more often now.

Rod rang to say they would be coming in to the hospital to visit us, he's obviously on his two weeks off—I'm losing track of time.

The doctor visited this morning. Storm slept most of the day. I love it when he is asleep; then I know he is pain-free and comfortable. Sleeping takes him away from what is happening to his body.

The gastro specialist also came to examine Storm. He said the line in his foot can't stay in for much longer and maybe they would need to put a more permanent line in. I said no—we would need to discuss it with Anna Gubbay before any decisions are made. Anna arrived about an hour later—the gastro lady has obviously spoken to her and that's fine. Anna said they would put a gastro tube back into Storm's stomach to see if he could tolerate small doses of glucose.

There is a boy in the bed across from us who has had part of his leg amputated. I introduced myself to his mother and we chat whenever she's there. We have both had similar experiences with the medical profession.

Today she brought in a cross-stitch for me to do and showed me how to get started with it, very thoughtful of her.

Rae rang to see how we're going but I'm more concerned with how she is going with her sister. Then Rod, Jacqui and Chevy arrived with food and drinks. We laughed and chatted while Storm slept through it all. Then Toni turned up, it ended up being quite a nice family gathering! Mum phoned, just as she phones every day. Sad news—they had to put Bud down. I can't believe it—he got really ill really quickly! I remember the day my parents brought him home, because we were living there at the time. He knew both of us all his life and whenever we visited, he'd always sit close to Storm. It's very sad.

NOVEMBER 23

Another rough night. Storm called out for me during the night, he does that a lot now. I catheterised him at 8am, made coffee and went back to bed. I thought I'd dozed for just a couple of minutes but it was 10am when I woke up.

A lady arrived with some flowers for me from Roma. There was a note attached: "A morale booster: You're really something, do you know that? In spite of whatever may happen in your day, you are going to stay that way—trying and giving and living life in the best way you know. So keep your spirits up and keep things in perspective. It's going to be okay. Love, Roma." It really was a morale booster for me. I must have rung her to tell her about Stormy, but I can't remember.

I went off to shower and change and by the time I got back, Storm had a gastro tube and his hands were bandaged again. I'm going to have to watch these nurses. The minute I leave the room, they sneak in and do stuff to Storm.

This afternoon Julie, Carolyn, Janette and his teacher Robin Revill rocked up—this kid is loved by so many people. His classmates had made a card and all signed it. And they made a tape for him with all the kids wishing him well. Storm and I both enjoyed this visit and were sorry to see them leave. Storm's stomach has started to hurt so they've cut back on the amount of glucose he's getting.

NOVEMBER 24

Storm had a horrendous night. He moaned in pain for most of it and Panadol didn't help one bit—he obviously needs something a whole lot stronger. In the morning Anna Gubbay came. She said that because his stomach is so swollen they will stop giving him glucose and tonight they will try a different drug that, hopefully, will help him sleep. The line in his foot was taken out because his foot was turning red. About 5pm, a registrar came in to put a line in his other foot, so I went off for a walk in the park. When I came back, Storm was fine. Thankfully, they didn't have any trouble putting the line in this time.

NOVEMBER 25

Another rough night. Storm is still moaning in pain. I catheterised him at 2.30am and again at 5am, hoping it would give him some relief but it didn't help at all. I don't understand any of what is happening to him. And I don't understand why they won't give him something stronger to ease the pain. I just can't bear watching him in so much pain.

I was still in my pyjamas, with about an hour's sleep under my belt, when Toni arrived at 10am. She is coming in every day now. I showered and changed, then she and I went for coffee while they gave Storm another saline enema. Hopefully it will give him some relief. When Toni left, I napped on my bed, since Storm was sleeping for most of the day. But he must be feeling a little bit better—I managed to get a smile and even a hug out of him. In the evening I went for my usual walk around the park—my little bit of country.

NOVEMBER 26

I slept a little more last night. Storm still had cramps so he didn't get much sleep, but he spent the day dozing while I did my jigsaw and a bit of cross-stitch. The nurses gave him another bowel treatment, which he tolerated, but it ended up giving him cramps and he had a bad night—no bowel movement, just cramps and pain.

NOVEMBER 27

Yet another bad night—no sleep and Storm is very unhappy and unresponsive.

NOVEMBER 28

Storm woke up this morning with a tremor in his left arm and in both legs. *What the hell!* When Anna Gubbay arrived, I showed her. She decided that while Storm was "under" for the MRI and lumbar puncture, she would also give him botox injections in his legs to see if it helped. His legs are totally screwed now, they can't be straightened at all. Heaps of pillows have to be used to stop them from turning further inward, and he has one between his knees so that they don't rub together. Eventually he was sleeping peacefully so I decided to drive home to check the house and get the mail. Of course, I cried all the way again. I seem to cry only when I get in the car and drive away from my son.

There must have been a storm in Bindoon, because there were fallen tree branches all around the property. I picked them up and carried them down to the back of the block. I'd told Jane I was coming and she arrived with Ruby, her dog. Ruby has known Storm since she was a puppy and always fussed over him. She raced into the house looking for Storm and when she couldn't find him, she jumped on his bed. Jane and I had lunch and then I locked up and dropped in to see Laurel and collect the mail. I know Laurel feels bad that she can't bring herself to visit Storm in the hospital. I reassured her that I understand—maybe it's for the best that she remembers Storm the way he was, not as he is now, all wasted and in pain.

When I got back to the hospital, Storm looked half asleep so I quietly leaned over and whispered that I was back. He reached out, pulled me into a headlock and wouldn't let go. He was upset for some reason—did he think I'd left him and was not coming back? Never, Storm. Never! I carefully climbed on to his bed, cradled him as best I could and we drifted off to sleep.

NOVEMBER 29

Hard to wake up this morning. I took a sleeping tablet last night but now I'm groggy. Storm didn't sleep well either. He called out "mum" in the night so I sat with him for a while.

Finally, it's the day for the MRI and everything else. Just after 2pm, they wheeled him into the theatre and I hugged him until the anaesthetic took hold and he went off to sleep. Then, tearfully, I left. There were so many doctors that I couldn't stay even if they'd allowed it. I waited for him in his room. *Please God, let them find something so we can do something, anything to relieve him of the pain.* About 6pm, they took me to the recovery room, then later back to his room. Another rough night and his stomach is distended again. Catheterising doesn't help.

NOVEMBER 30

Anna visited this morning. No word yet, radiology must look at the test results first. Toni arrived and I know she will distract me and make me laugh. Poor Storm seems very uncomfortable and has dozed for most of the day. Anna's registrar has the neatest Irish accent. I chatter away, making conversation just so I can listen to him. He took more blood to make sure Storm isn't getting an infection. We've made it through another day.

DECEMBER 1

Both Storm and I slept well, yippee! I feel so much better after a good night's sleep. Richard was visiting us when Anna Gubbay arrived. *They have actually found something!* There's a problem in his spine at the T6, it's showing inflammation. They don't know what it is or what's caused it, and surgery won't help. They also don't know whether it is treatable, or if it will get worse. *My guess is it's going to get worse, because it has been getting worse.* They found other abnormalities, too, but these could have been there since birth. They're asking for assistance from doctors at other hospitals and the radiologist has scheduled a meeting for tomorrow to go over the MRI imaging. Thank God they actually found something. It may all come to nothing, but something showed up and better they find something than nothing.

They've stopped the glucose and now they're giving Storm a food supplement through the gastro tube. He slept all day while I pondered all the new information Anna gave me this morning. While I was pondering, Jane turned up for a visit.

About 7pm, Storm was suddenly gripped with pain and he hugged me tightly through the spasms. I don't know if the pain is in his spine, his stomach or his legs. Frankly, I don't care—I just want them to give him something to make the pain go away. *Please.*

DECEMBER 2

Storm had a painful night; nothing gave him relief because nothing was strong enough. I still don't understand why they won't give him stronger painkillers.

Anna Gubbay arrived to say the spinal cord is inflamed at the T6 (I thought we already knew that) and they are going to do a spinal lumbar puncture where the infection is. They took him off for that and he came back sound asleep. Then they said they were moving him to intensive care.

There they'll put a line in his arm that will go all the way to his heart. This will mean they'll be able to increase his pain medication. Finally! Anything else they want to do which will ease the pain—bring it on. We can take it and I can wait until later to fall apart.

Intensive care is a sad, sad place. I'm glad we're not there permanently. The doctor started explaining what was going to be done to Storm, but I stopped him. If they could promise me it wouldn't hurt him, they must just go ahead—but please don't tell me all the details—enough is enough. They did the procedure and we were back in the ward by 5pm.

Another doctor arrived. He wanted to run some tests that involve putting electrodes on Storm's foot to see how his muscles react, and he wanted to do it RIGHT NOW. I was a bit hesitant; not sure why he wanted to do it. But I relented and agreed it could be done. Afterwards, the doctor said the tests showed nerve damage in his legs which would have resulted from the spinal cord being inflamed. The tests had made Storm's legs very uncomfortable—they were trembling. *Bloody mean man, he hurt my Stormy.* And he thought he was telling me some new big news! I had already figured out that the damage must have been caused by the spinal cord, it was obvious, really. There was nothing profound in what he told me. It's been a full-on day and we're both exhausted. But I have noticed Storm isn't having seizures any longer. Ponder that, doctors!

DECEMBER 3

I didn't wake up until 11am, can't believe I slept through all the noise. The nurses were catheterising Storm and said I could go back to sleep but I didn't, I felt guilty. I had breakfast and then turned on my mobile phone—there were angry text messages from Jane and Toni wanting to know why my phone was switched off. Oops. I wouldn't have slept in if it was switched on. But still, I feel rather refreshed for it.

Peta rang to say she would be coming in with Paula and Sophie. I know Peta dislikes hospitals and avoids them at all costs, so I appreciate the effort it will take for her to visit us. They all turned up at lunchtime with Chinese food and the most beautiful bunch of flowers. We talked and we ate, then we talked some more. Sophie soon had me in fits of laughter and we all know that laughter is the best medicine! Mum rang as usual to see how Storm is travelling. I have nothing new to report and Mum says they will visit tomorrow. Storm did a really runny poo and stunk out the room.

DECEMBER 4

Storm didn't sleep until 3am so the nurses let me sleep in until nine. My parents and Toni arrived a while later and managed to get a few smiles out of Stormy. He didn't sleep the whole day—the first time he's been awake all day for a long while and it's not good, since he didn't sleep much last night.

Laurel rang to ask how Storm was doing. I didn't have anything new to tell her. I'm surprised I haven't put on heaps of weight because all my meals are from the cafeteria and I'm sure they fry everything. It's been a very quiet day. I went for my usual evening walk, I really look forward to that.

Storm has been wriggling around in pain tonight. He's had all the painkillers he's allowed, so there's nothing more that can be done for him. They took the bag off the gastro tube when they gave him the pain medication so it wouldn't drain back into the bag, and that was 45 minutes ago. I asked a nurse to put the bag back on, and as soon as they did stuff began draining out of his stomach and he stopped wriggling. Then he was able to sleep. It's amazing the things you learn in hospital!

One of Storm's nurses is a lot older than the others and I really didn't give her enough credit for her ability to do her job. I'm sorry about that. When I spoke to her, I learnt she usually worked in intensive care, with dying babies. It was she who used a syringe to get some air out of Storm's stomach when he began wriggling in pain again. I'm so grateful she was there.

DECEMBER 5

Life goes on, no matter what. My car needed servicing so I left early to drop it off at the Toyota place. Rae lives nearby so I called in to see her, but she was just leaving for a meeting. She suggested we meet in Subiaco for lunch—a good idea and it's within walking distance of the hospital. I made sure the nurses would keep a close eye on Storm, and left to meet up with Rae. While I was walking, it occurred to me that the line in Storm's foot, feeding him nutrients, was keeping him alive and all he was getting out of it was pain. How had I missed this? I didn't want to prolong his life when it was so painful for him. I wasn't in denial that he was dying—why was I delaying it when all it meant for Storm was more pain? I was so upset by the time I met up with Rae and Toni, I told them my thoughts and said maybe it's time to ask for the line to be removed. What a dreadful decision to have to make.

After lunch Toni and Rae sat with Storm while I went off to collect the car. The service people proceeded to tell me about all the things that were wrong with it, all needing to be fixed, all going to cost a lot of money. What a lot of bull it all is—I can't deal with it now!

Back at the hospital, Toni, Rae, Leanne, Julie and Carolyn were all crowded around Storm's bed talking to him. Carolyn had even brought an alcoholic drink for me. Little did I know that I was really going to need it by the end of this day.

The doctor who'd hurt Stormy with the tests on his legs turned up and I made the mistake of telling him I didn't want Storm's life prolonged; I wanted the line supplying the nutrients removed. He then proceeded to tell me that if this was done, Storm's body would turn on itself, like cannibalism, it would take 10 days for him to die and he would suffer terribly. When he left, I broke down completely. I just sobbed and sobbed and couldn't stop.

One of the nurses hugged me and tried to comfort me. I told her I want to let Storm go; I don't want him to go on suffering. And while I don't want him to leave me, I know he can't stay. The nurse had heard everything the doctor had said, and she told me it was possible to make sure Storm didn't suffer. Devastated doesn't describe how I'm feeling. I feel broken. I don't know how to do right by Storm. I've put aside my desire to have him with me and I just want his suffering to end.

After my shower, I took a tablet to help me sleep and the nurses checked on me several times, asking if I was okay. It's the first time I've cried in front of them.

DECEMBER 6

I'm going to see Jane today. She and her husband have moved to another town, quite far from Bindoon. I don't want to leave Stormy, but I've said I will visit her so I must.

I was dressed and ready to leave when Anna Gubbay arrived. I told her I wanted the line taken out of Storm's foot, and she understood that I didn't want to prolong Storm's suffering. She said there is an ethical dilemma because they don't know what is wrong with him, there is no definite diagnosis. But she would discuss it with her colleagues and get back to me. I have done all I can. I told Storm I had to go out for a while but I'd be back as soon as I possibly could.

I picked up Toni and we drove to Jane's new home. The house is nice and so was the visit, but really, all I wanted was to be back with Storm. It was very late when we got back and I felt terrible that I'd been away for so long. Storm wouldn't smile at me but eventually I got a hug out of him. I don't blame him for being cross with me; I shouldn't have left him for the whole day, I don't even understand why I agreed to go. While I was away, they X-rayed his stomach. I don't want to be away from him for so long ever again.

DECEMBER 7

Some darling nurse turned on all the lights in our room at 7.30am. She's going on my hit list!

I was sitting with Storm after breakfast when Marteena and one of her twins, Sandra, arrived. I thought Storm would be all smiles to hear their voices but he was very solemn. Later, Toni visited and she sat with Storm while I bought lunch in the cafeteria. I was still waiting to be served when Toni rang, a doctor wanted to see me. This doctor told me they can take the line out of Storm's arm and foot and just keep one in his arm for fluids so he doesn't get dehydrated. And they'll put in one for the painkillers. We have come to the point where Stormy is going to be allowed to die. Toni and I were tearful after the doctor left. We distracted ourselves from the grief in our hearts by doing some of the jigsaw together. This is so bloody awful!

Late this afternoon, the lines were taken out, along with the gastro tube. Storm is happier. He knows he is leaving.

DECEMBER 8

Didn't get much sleep last night—Storm was in a lot of pain. Today they are going to review his pain management. We're not trying to keep him alive; we're letting him go. It's all surreal to me. I can't understand this detachment I'm feeling. I should be grief-stricken, I should be an emotional wreck. But I feel calm, sad but calm. I feel like a damn hard bitch. I should be falling apart because my child is dying. There's time for that later, I guess.

I'm not going to fall apart sobbing, making it hard for Storm to leave me. He needs to think I'm going to be okay when he goes, even if it's a lie.

Everyone has been told there is no hope for Storm and that he is going to die. *I knew this. I knew years ago that this was going to happen one day.*

Rod rang from the Argyle mine to say I could call him on his mobile if I needed him. Normally, they're not allowed to carry a mobile phone on the minesite; but after telling his boss about the situation, he's been allowed to have it on him.

Jacqui and Kyra visited. Kyra's just finished a painting of a beach scene for me. The paint is still wet—I'm so moved by this gesture. More visitors—Storm's teacher, the principal and another teacher from the Perth school. They gave me the portfolio they'd made up of Storm's time at the school.

Toni arrived before lunch and we sat by Storm's bed for hours, just talking and doing the jigsaw puzzle. Storm listened to us, all smiles, and held Toni's hand. When Toni had to leave, he wouldn't let go of her hand and she sat down again and talked with him until he let go. How hard this must be for her, coming in here every day, then home to her empty house and the real world outside—I feel cocooned here in the hospital.

When the nurses bathed him tonight, he hugged them. He's trying, in the only way he knows, to thank everyone—he knows he's leaving soon.

Rae phoned. Ownie isn't good and they will operate on her throat tomorrow. *God this is awful.* We have been moved to a private room with two beds in it. I'm allowed to sleep in the other bed rather than a foldout bed. It's nice to be in our own room.

DECEMBER 9

Storm had a better night than he's had in a long time. When Toni arrived, we set up the jigsaw close to his bed. Then the nurses set up a machine to give him morphine through the line in his arm, along with fluids to prevent dehydration. Surely this will ease his pain. He holds tight to his Elmo toy and listens to us talking.

I was catheterising him when Richard arrived for a visit at the same time as a social worker. Toni and Richard went off for coffee while the social worker asked me how I'm feeling. I don't know how I feel—it's all too surreal. I do know this is the end and I feel terribly sad. I don't know if it's because I've had so many sad moments to deal with, but this just isn't affecting me in the way it should. The fact is, he's not dead yet. I feel I have been grieving for many years and yet I know it's not going to be real until he leaves.

Anna Gubbay came in twice today to check on Storm, and I very much appreciate her concern for him. When the nurses were moving Storm in his bed, he hugged them—he's making sure he thanks all those who have looked after him so tenderly. They have put an air-mattress on his bed now so he won't get pressure sores. He seems comfortable with the morphine; it is sweet relief to know that the pain can be eased so quickly. I gave him a lolly to chew on, he liked that.

Rae visited, too. This is such an awful time for her—a child she loves dearly is dying and her sister who means the world to her is struggling to survive.

DECEMBER 10

This ward has never had a dying child, Storm really should be in the cancer ward but I've asked if we can stay here. I'm used to the nurses and many of them, male and female, have been there since the beginning so I didn't think I had it in me to go somewhere new where we'd have to get to know new nursing staff. But it was up to the nurses and, luckily for us, they are happy to nurse Storm through to the end.

Everyone knows now there's no hope of him surviving, so I guess people are coming to say their goodbyes. Today it was his physio, Judy Dennis. Then Carolyn—she brought a photo of Storm playing the piano at school in Bindoon. He was pulling a face for the camera, I just love it. Then Jane arrived. While Storm was sleeping, she and I walked to the Subiaco markets. I love going for a walk after hours of sitting by Storm's bed. Toni was there too, of course. She brought Mum and Dad in—this has to be awful for them too, losing their grandchild.

A new doctor came this morning. She is going to take Anna's place when Anna is not available. I really like her too. I summoned up the nerve to ask how long they thought Storm had left—a couple of days, they said. (*It took a month. Storm was never a child to be told what to do, and this was no different.*) Anna sat with us for a long time in the afternoon, just talking in general—it was very pleasant. And Storm's morphine was increased this evening. Hopefully it will be a pain-free night for him.

DECEMBER 12

Anna Gubbay was here early, I was still in my pyjamas. I want Storm free of pain but it's just not happening. Now it seems he is allergic to morphine and has to have a different painkiller.

Toni came in, as she does every day. And Jane visited too. Storm has slept most of the day and, as usual, I feel better when he is asleep. The pain can come on quickly. Suddenly, he grabbed the rail of his bed and I quickly asked the nurse to give him a shot of the painkiller, which relaxed him. His breathing was shallow, so shallow I could hardly see that he really was breathing. So I sang "You are my sunshine" to him until he drifted off to sleep—he could be going. However, his breathing improved after a bit and again, there is a calmness about me.

I washed an outfit that I'd brought with me which we could dress him in when he dies, how morbid is that? I even asked Jane to bring in the hair clippers so I could cut his hair. It's grown so much and he looks gorgeous when it's clipped short; and I want him to look his best. I don't understand why I'm doing what I'm doing. He hasn't worn clothes for weeks now, and in any case we wouldn't have been able to dress him with those crippled legs.

DECEMBER 13

Though I slept well, I was agitated all day for reasons I couldn't fathom. I bathed Storm and thought he might go to sleep afterwards but he was in such pain that I asked the nurses to give him a bolus (a large dose of painkiller). Then he did sleep. I rang Laurel to tell her how Storm was and I rang Helen to ask if she could water my plants. Toni and Richard visited and soon after they left, Julie Reynolds arrived. I can't be bothered going to the cafeteria to buy something fried for my dinner, so I found a vending machine and bought some crisps. I stretched out on the bed next to Storm while I ate my exciting dinner. Storm woke in pain so I immediately asked a nurse for more painkiller.

DECEMBER 14

Storm had a settled night, and so did I. It's so much quieter in a room of our own. A nurse brought me a coffee and muffin, which was just what I needed. When Toni arrived, it looked like Storm would be sleeping for most of the day, so we walked into the city to do some Christmas shopping. I don't really want to shop for Christmas, but life goes on no matter how much you want it to stop. Storm gave me a hug and a kiss today. It's really hard for him to raise his arms so I appreciate the effort it's taken for him to do this.

DECEMBER 15

I'm getting slower as the days pass. Today, I was still in my pyjamas when Carolyn and Fiona arrived. They sat with Storm while I showered and changed and afterwards we were sitting around chatting when a lady from vision impairment arrived. It's been a good day for visitors today— just as Fiona and Carolyn were leaving, Rae arrived. She and I sat beside Storm's bed talking, and then Toni turned up. The nurses adjusted Storm's medication while all this was going on—up to 4ml an hour now. We all believe he is close to the end of his journey.

Anna Gubbay was the next one to visit. She told me the subject of an autopsy had come up during a meeting at the hospital. She thought I wouldn't agree to it—see, she really does know me well. It's my greatest fear that the hospital would insist on an autopsy, but Anna says I don't have to agree to it. I am very relieved. I believe Storm's life has been a mystery and he should take that mystery with him when he leaves.

DECEMBER 16

I woke at 3am, very agitated—Storm was awake too and not at all comfortable. I catheterised him and got more than 200ml of fluid and he soon settled down and went to sleep. He and I are still so very connected. I know what he's feeling and I know what he wants. I know it sounds silly but it's like our souls are connected. What will it be like when the connection is broken? Or will it be broken?

It was another full-on day of visitors. Toni brought Mum and Dad in about 11am, then Jane arrived. Then Rod, Jacqui and Brandi and it was a real family gathering. We had to go to the park, of course, so the smokers could have a puff. I'll say this about my family: We have had our moments, but all of what is happening now has really brought us together.

Eventually, everyone left except for Jane. She came to the chapel with me to see the minister. Silly things prey on my mind. I want Storm to have some sort of blessing or some kind of last rites. I'm not Catholic so we thought the minister at the hospital chapel might not be able to help. She was lovely. I was tearful as I spoke to her and she said to me it didn't matter what religion we were—she would bless Storm. She came back with us and did it right then and there.

The social worker was the next visitor. I don't know what to say to her—sometimes I worry about what I do say, I might sound unbalanced.

Storm is in pain now every time he is moved. So before they turn him they give him a bolus of drugs. He weighed about 30kg when he was admitted and he's only about 18kg now, all skin and bones. I've brought his blue bear in for him, the one that Marteena gave him years ago. He loves playing with the ribbon on its neck, but his hands are shaking too much.

Once again they have increased his drugs for pain. He has a bolus when they turn him but within 15 minutes he is in pain again and has to have another.

DECEMBER 17

Storm had a fairly pain-free night which is all I pray for. He's slept for most of the day and I've done nothing much—watched some television, did a crossword, nothing much at all.

Peta turned up with her kids about 5pm. I'm impressed that she's come to a place she finds it so hard to cope with. Later, a nurse asked if I would like her to do some Reiki on Storm—you bet I would! I went for a walk while she did it and she told me afterwards that Storm held her hands. I've noticed he wants to touch people more and more lately. I think that's lovely!

DECEMBER 18

I woke up tearful again, but a shower made me feel better. Toni arrived early and since Storm seemed settled, we walked up to Kings Park and sat on the lawn enjoying the view of the river and city. Later, back at the hospital, we played Scrabble. After she left, I was tearful again. I'm embarrassed by this.

Storm was in such pain today he had to have several big doses of drugs. Even though the painkillers are dripping continuously into his arm, it's not enough. I think it's time to increase the dosage again.

DECEMBER 19

I haven't been home for a while so when Toni arrived, she looked after Storm for me while I went to Bindoon. Usually I cry while I drive but today, I don't have a tear in me. I even tried thinking of really sad things to make myself cry but nothing happened. I had coffee with Laurel, checked on the house and garden and picked up my mail. By then I felt I'd been away from Storm for too long. Driving back, I felt ill and had the shakes, and had to stop to buy a drink. It must be stress. The nurse offered me a sleeping pill tonight and I didn't refuse.

DECEMBER 20

Storm slept well, but I didn't. Despite the sleeping pill I was awake all night, feeling ill and tearful. I got up in the middle of the night and showered. I cried in the shower—well, that's good, at least I can still cry.

They're changing Storm's painkiller again, putting him on fentanyl, which should stop him from feeling itchy—he's been itching and scratching a lot recently.

Toni phoned to say she didn't know whether she could visit today. I understand—Storm's not leaving yet, and she really needs a break. I bought some Christmas paper to wrap presents. Here I am, in a hospital, my son is in bed next to me, dying, and I'm wrapping Christmas presents.

Toni did come, after all. When she left I felt really tired and cold so I had a hot shower and then climbed into bed and watched television while Storm slept.

DECEMBER 21

Woke at 3am. Storm was in pain so I quickly found a nurse to give him a bolus of fentanyl and he dropped off to sleep fairly quickly. As I've said, we have a connection thing going on.

I decided to walk to Subiaco. I phoned Toni and she said she'd come with me and while I waited for her, I rang Helen and Jane. The pain-management team came in and after seeing how many boluses of fentanyl he is having they are going to put a fentanyl patch on him—this will release the drug into his system a bit like nicotine patches do. They're hoping it will stop the need for boluses.

Later, at the markets, I looked for socks for Stormy. I didn't have any with me and when he is dressed after he passes, I don't want his feet to be bare. The only socks I could find were black ones with a spider on each foot. Storm was awake when we got back. I would have preferred him to be sleeping because at least then I know he is not in pain. But he gave me a hug, so all is good. When Toni left, I got into bed and watched television.

I've been offering Storm little sips of water, because he seems thirsty, but I must only give him a little bit, every half hour or so. The nurses gave him a saline enema and catheterised him but his sheets got a bit messy so I held him in my arms while they remade the bed. It's been a long time since I held him like that and I became quite tearful. Miraculously, even he had a tear in his eye—and when I wiped it away, he shed another. *Oh God, this is so painful.*

That night I explained to Storm that all I could find for his feet were socks with spiders on them. I said only the three of us—he, Toni and I—knew about them. I told him I would go to a psychic after he had passed away to see if I could contact him. If he said something about the socks, I'd know it was him and that he was there, on the other side. You can think I'm crazy or stricken with grief and you would be wrong. *I know what I'm doing.*

DECEMBER 22

What a bad, bad day. Storm was okay, but he woke very early—5am. Jane sent me a text saying she would visit, but at 11am I received another message saying her car had broken down on the way and asking could I come and get her I didn't want to leave Storm but I couldn't just leave Jane stranded, either. I phoned Toni to see if she could sit with Storm, but she was at the dentist. I explained my dilemma to the nurses and they said they would sit with him as much as they could. I raced to the scene of the breakdown and waited with Jane for the tow truck, then we followed the truck to her sister-in-law's house. After a quick cuppa we drove back to the hospital and when we got back to Storm's room, Toni was there. Toni went off with Jane, she's going to drive her back home and stay the night.

Then Storm vomited up old blood again—it seems his stomach can't even tolerate the water I have been giving him. I held him in my arms while the nurse changed the bedding. Next, he had a massive runny bowel motion, with blood in it. His body is giving up. Again I held him while clean sheets were put on the bed, but they had to give him a bolus before I could pick him up. He dozed and seemed settled but by 8pm he was in pain again and needed another bolus. The patch isn't working any more.

DECEMBER 23

Storm had a really rough night, and is vomiting up old blood up again. I'm sure it's because I gave him the water. Anna Gubbay came in really early. She is up-to-date with what's happening and wants to see what changes are needed. I remember, very early in the piece when they didn't know what was what, Anna said we needed Dr House (from the TV series) to come in and put it all together—for sure, a woman with my sense of humour.

I rang Toni, who was still at Jane's house, to say I didn't think she should come today because Storm is worse and vomiting blood. I just know it's going to be too much for her to deal with, even if she thinks she can. Why should she have to watch it? I know today is not the day.

The pain team say they will increase Storm's fentanyl patch up to 100mg and double the dosage going into his arm, as well as giving him drugs to stop the nausea. I'm all for it. If doubling the drugs allows him to be free of pain but shortens his time, then so be it.

He had a few bowel movements on his own and vomited old blood a few more times, but he does seem more comfortable since the fentanyl dosage has been increased.

The Reiki nurse gave me a book called *Life on the Other Side* and I'm eager to read it because I firmly believe the soul goes on. Another of the nurses brought me lollies and the social worker gave me a present. I'd forgotten that it's Christmas in a couple of days; I've been cocooned in this hospital for weeks now.

DECEMBER 24

Storm woke me about 3am. I thought at first he was gasping for air; in fact, he was snoring. It was so cute, and I went back to sleep. Today I visited Toni at her home and we talked for ages. Yvonne, one of the angels who had looked after Stormy at Bindoon school, was with him when I got back. She came with her daughter and she'd brought some wildflowers from her property.

I even got a phone call today from my cousin Eleanor in New Zealand. Mum must have rung her to let them know about Storm. Eleanor's dad is also very ill in hospital. She is a nurse so she asked about Storm's drugs. I told her about all of them and she was satisfied that he was getting enough to cover the pain. I thought that was lovely. I also spoke to her father, my Uncle Geoff.

Storm's having quite a lot of fentanyl because he is in so much pain, so the doctor who is relieving Anna Gubbay was called. While I waited for her to arrive, I was hugging Storm and he put his hand up for a high five—he's trying to play a game with me, how amazing is that? Finally, after the doctor made some adjustments, he went into a deep sleep, tightly hugging his Elmo toy.

DECEMBER 25

Storm had a peaceful night. I showered and dressed before the doctor came. I rang Jane to wish her a Merry Christmas—what a joke! It was decided that Christmas would be celebrated at Rod and Jacqui's this year because of the circumstances. I didn't want to leave Storm, not on Christmas Day, but one of the nurses reassured me that she'd send text messages to say how he was while I was out, so I relented. My parents, and Toni, were already there when I arrived. I had a really good time with lots of laughs—there's always plenty of laughter when we all get together, and the text messages kept coming to say Storm was fine. Nevertheless, I didn't stay too long.

Back at the hospital, a nurse came in to say goodbye to Storm. She has two weeks off and didn't know if he would still be around when she got back. He put his arms out and gave her a big hug. Then another nurse gave Storm a present—some cooked spaghetti and a can of shaving cream. Gee, I wish I'd thought of that! I'd mentioned ages ago that Storm loved to play with shaving cream and spaghetti. We covered the bedding with a sheet and put the spaghetti on a tray and as soon as I started spraying the foam on to the spaghetti, Storm's arms were reaching out to play in it. A few nurses were watching this and in the end we all had shaving cream on our hands. Storm was massaging hands left, right and centre and having a great time. Toni turned up and joined in the fun too.

We'd just cleaned up after all that when Leigh Anderson and her partner came for a visit. I haven't seen Leigh for years and it was so nice of her to visit on Christmas Day.

Presents had been put by the doors of each room earlier in the day and Santa Claus arrived and handed them out to all the children. Storm received a beautiful lime-green rug with a zebra sown on it. *(That rug covered him until he died—he just loved the soft feel of it.)* It's been a really lovely day.

DECEMBER 26

My parents and Toni visited today, but otherwise it was very quiet. Storm dozed for most of the day. I noticed a tear rolling out of his eye while he dozed—he's obviously very sad. He has lived longer than the doctors ever thought he would. I know he doesn't want to leave me and I don't want him to leave—but he can't stay, either. I sat next to him and spoke quietly. I told him I love him so much and that he's going to a wonderful place where he will never, ever feel pain again, He'll be whole and he'll be able to run and skip and see; and one day we'll be together again. It seemed to settle him, and he slept.

DECEMBER 27

I woke up feeling dreadful—my body feels like lead. I spoke to Toni and Jane and said they needn't come in today. I just wanted to be by myself. Storm is sleeping, so I walked into town and back again. Then I lay on my bed, facing Storm, and dozed off. He called out to me in his sleep once and I touched him and said I was right here. He must be sleeping very lightly because he hears everything. When a nurse said she would put some drops in his eyes, I saw him grimace. In the evening I got a few hugs and while I was holding his hand, he pulled my hand up to his lips and kissed it. He takes my breath away.

DECEMBER 28

This morning I woke up determined to get my finances in order. How bizarre is that? I phoned Centrelink, explained the situation and asked what I had to do when Storm passes away. They were very helpful and told me what to do. Then I went to my bank and paid off the car from my meagre savings.

Storm seems to be having a few days of relative comfort. I got hugs and kisses again today; he had a bit of pain in the evening but he has gone the whole day without needing any extra fentanyl.

DECEMBER 29

When I woke this morning I was really upset to see that Storm was lying on his side, facing away from me. I know he doesn't like lying on that side. Then I read his chart and it showed he'd been turned but didn't have a bolus before he was turned. Now he was breathing quickly and obviously in pain. I became very tearful—I shouldn't have taken that sleeping tablet. If I hadn't gone to sleep I would have been awake when they moved him. I called for a nurse to give him a bolus and, finally, he settled and was able to sleep.

Toni turned up and we went for a walk to town. As we were leaving, Carolyn arrived and said she would sit with Storm. I felt reassured because I knew she would tell the nurses if Storm was in pain—no doubt about it. Later on, Storm was playing with a toy dog that a nurse had given him for Christmas. This nurse suggested I get the shaving cream out for Storm to play with—my mind has gone to mush, fancy having to be told how to entertain my own child. I did get out the shaving cream and Storm loved it. I put the foam all over my hands and he played with my hands.

I haven't taken a sleeping tablet tonight, not after what happened last night, and I lie in bed, watching Storm. At one point, he looked like he wasn't breathing and I thought: "This is it." But I was wrong. He moaned and groaned in his sleep for most of the night. The little girl in the room next door kicked up a ruckus most of the night, but luckily it didn't disturb Storm.

DECEMBER 30

Not much sleep last night and I look like hell this morning. Toni brought mum and dad for a visit. She's made a picnic lunch for us to have in the park. Storm has been quite uncomfortable and needed several boluses of fentanyl. He's been wide awake all day and very thirsty but I'm not allowed to give him water. I put cotton swabs in the water and he's allowed to suck on it. It worries me that he is so thirsty.

DECEMBER 31

The last day of 2005. We've been in hospital for seven and a half weeks and I have no idea how much longer this is going to go on. I feel like I could do it forever, if I can still be with Storm.

I must confess something: I've been a bit of a bitch. This is a teenage ward and we have a few anorexic girls on the ward. The disease turns them into girls who behave very badly. I know it's the condition that causes their behaviour but today I'm in no mood to put up with them. My son is dying, he loves food and would love to be able to eat something but he can't. Meanwhile, these girls are dying because they won't eat. You see my dilemma? Anorexia turns their behaviour into ugly behaviour. Or I suppose it could just be normal selfish teenage behaviour—I don't know. There is a washing machine and dryer on the ward for everyone to use, but these girls think it's totally for them. They would sometimes take my clothes out of the washing machine or dryer halfway through the cycle and put in a blouse of their own to wash or dry. I'd come back and find my clothes on the floor, wet and half-washed. I'm a woman who is dealing with a lot. I don't need this. I'd made a complaint to the nurses but to no avail. So today, when I go to get my clothes out of the dryer, it's all lying on the floor half dry. And floating around in the dryer is one solitary lovely white top. I took the lovely white top out of the dryer, threw it to the floor and proceeded to jump on it and rub it on the floor. Then I folded it nicely and left it there and put my clothes back in the dryer. End of confession.

I had the rest of the day to myself. Storm had been awake all night, not good, his body has become tolerant to the drugs so the pain team increased his fentanyl again. It took a while to kick in but eventually he went to sleep.

Peta visited after lunch and we walked to a liquor store to buy some drinks and nibblies to see in the new year. After she left, Anna Gubbay came in and checked on us. Storm is asleep, he in his happy place and that makes me happy.

I set myself up in bed with a can of cider and my nibblies and watched the Edinburgh Military Tattoo at midnight. Storm slept through it all, it means nothing to him that it's a new year—he's going to a new life without me.

JANUARY 1, 2006

Storm slept all night. I dozed on and off—haven't taken a sleeping tablet for a while now. I woke feeling like I'm getting a cold. Storm's painkillers have been increased so now he sleeps most of the time. He is turned every couple of hours because of a pressure sore. By the end of the day I was cranky. There were nurses coming and going and I just want to be left alone with my boy.

JANUARY 2

It was about 3am before I got to sleep, then woke about 6am and couldn't get back to sleep because of all the comings and goings in the ward.

Storm slept right through, for which I'm thankful. When he is awake I worry that he's thirsty or in pain. I tried to give him some water on a large cotton bud. He wanted it but he didn't have the strength to suck on it.

The nurse who is looking after him is wonderful. She has done palliative care before and I find her a great support. Today she was concerned that he was awake and aware, and she also thought he was feeling thirsty. This is my fear, too; I want him to sleep. The nurse rang Anna Gubbay and Anna was glad of the call. She has really stuck her neck out for us, and decided to give Storm other drugs to sedate him. I told the nurse I was shocked at Storm's strength to go on and she said she wasn't surprised, because he has a strong heart. Later on, another nurse came in and we discussed how he is still awake, so Anna will be contacted again. He can only have three boluses of the new drug—after that, there is nothing they can do to help him sleep. He was awake enough to give me a hug.

JANUARY 3

I took a sleeping tablet last night on the condition that the nurses promise that if anything happens, and I mean anything at all, they would wake me. The pain team came in this morning. They say they will give him a stronger dose of fentanyl. I told them I don't want him awake anymore. I want him to sleep because if he's awake, I can't bear the thought that he is thirsty or in pain.

Every time he wakes, I tell the nurses he needs another bolus. I can't bear this, I'm going to lie to get him the drugs he needs to sleep. I have to do this for him. He has started making gurgling sounds while he sleeps. They say they'll give him a drug to stop it. I don't understand what it means and I'm not going to ask.

The time is near. I can feel it.

JANUARY 4

The nurse woke me at 5am. Storm's breathing was erratic, his fingers were blue and he looked opaque. I sat by him and touched his hair. I sang to him—*Amazing Grace*. I've always sung that to him. I rang Jane about 9am to let her know it's almost time. She will ring Toni, who is with my parents in Serpentine. I sat by Storm's bed for hours and fell asleep a couple of times. A nurse sat with him while I went for a walk in the park or when I needed to get something to eat. By 2pm, I was exhausted so I lay on the bed facing Storm and had a nap.

Anna Gubbay sat with us for a while later on, but eventually she had to leave. This is hard for everyone. A nurse who has been with Storm since the beginning is leaving to do a stint elsewhere in the hospital, so she said her goodbyes.

Storm was gasping for hours, then his breathing quietened and his colour improved to a nice pink. I don't think he's going anywhere today. I didn't want to take a sleeping tablet when it was time for bed, but the nurse—the one with the gorgeous Irish accent, persuaded me to take one. Storm knows I am close by. He's having boluses of fentanyl every 15 minutes, so there were comings and goings all night long.

JANUARY 5

I woke at 4am and checked on Storm. His breathing seemed fine. I sat with him, saying it was time for him to let go. I am going to be okay, I said. I have all these people around me to care for me and watch over me. *I had to make it convincing—who am I kidding?* After breakfast, I went for a walk. Anna came by later in the morning. She said she'd been phoning the hospital during the night because she thought Storm would go last night. But he didn't.

The pain team came again and increased Storm's fentanyl to 12ml an hour so he might not need a bolus every 15 minutes. Once it kicked in, he went into a deep sleep and looked very peaceful. His face is clear of pimples, his skin is glowing and his face looks beautiful. He really does look gorgeous. I sat with him all day. Nobody visited, and I didn't want anyone to visit. I think everybody knows the time is close and they're giving me space to be with Storm for the last moments of his life. He doesn't look like he's dying, just sleeping.

JANUARY 6

Today was just like yesterday. I was alone with Storm and by his side all day, leaving only for meals or to go for a quick walk to the park—but never gone for long. I sat with him all day, looking back over our lives, wondering how I'm going to go on without him but knowing I will, I have to. Tonight I lay watching him while he slept. He looks so much smaller—like he did when he was eight years old. He's been asleep the whole day. I fell asleep.

JANUARY 7

At 1am the nurse woke me. She told me the time has come, Storm is dying.

I sit close to him, brushing his hair and speaking to him quietly. I tell him how much I love him. His hands are cold and he looks peaceful. I tuck his Elmo further under his arm and his breathing stops. He is gone, gone from me forever.

Today my world as I've known it is finished, gone, never to be the same again. I am all alone in this world without him. I can't cry, and I don't know why. Everything is silent. The nurses quickly take the line out of Storm's body and the machine is taken away. They ask me if I want to help dress him, but I just can't. I make coffee and come back and sit with them while they dress my son. I feel alone and empty. The registrar pronounces Storm deceased. He says the whole hospital knows about my Stormy.

I've rung everyone and told them. Toni is in Serpentine with my parents, they are driving in; Jane is also on her way.

While the nurses were dressing Storm, his head rolled away from me and that's when it hit me—he is not just sleeping, he really is dead. But still, I didn't cry. I just wanted to run. I couldn't get out of the hospital fast enough. So I packed everything and sat with the shell of my precious son, Storm, who has gone and left me all alone in the world. I am waiting for Jane to arrive. I've put some rosary beads in his hands and his beloved Elmo is tucked under his arms.

Jane arrived to pick me up. I didn't know why I was going with her, but I did, missing my parents and Toni. They said goodbye to Stormy and then went on to Toni's house. We got there first and waited for them. Then we all sat around the table drinking coffee. It was still early in the morning. Afterwards I went home with Jane. I wasn't thinking straight—I really should have been with my family. I curled up on Jane's spare bed and cried and cried. Finally, I cried. Storm is gone; it really doesn't seem real.

Mum, always one to do the right thing, rang my ex-husband and told him Stormy had died.

I had to make all the arrangements for the funeral and most of my family turned up to be with me while I did it. It was a really nice gesture. The days between Stormy dying and his funeral are all a bit of a blur. I stayed with Jane, I don't know if this was the right thing to do or not. *It's too hard to think about why I'm staying here. Maybe I'm here so I can be away from all the pain my family is feeling. I don't know if I could handle seeing their sadness.* I seemed to have forgotten how to breathe. At first I didn't understand why I kept feeling so dizzy. It wasn't until Jane told me I wasn't breathing that I understood. I had to remind myself: Breathe.

Rae drove all the way to Jane's house with flowers for me and a leather box for all of Stormy's photos. I am so grateful. I have asked Rae to do the eulogy as I know she will do a wonderful job of it and Stormy would want it.

The funeral was on January 13. It poured with rain at first, then cleared up just before the service. I wore pink. My parents, Toni and Rod carried Stormy into the chapel and I walked in front of them. I felt no tears. God was carrying me.

Kyra read a poem and Rae did the eulogy—it was amazing. She wasn't sure she'd be able to do it so she looked at me the whole time she was speaking. She also wrote a poem about Storm. We sang *Amazing Grace*, the last time I would ever to be able to sing it to my son. Then the time came for the coffin to be lowered away. It's so very final. I need someone to tell me how I'm going to get through this.

Everyone was there. Storm's teachers and his aides, Anna Gubbay and even some of the nurses were there. So many people from the country had come. I felt very touched that so many came to say goodbye to my son. Jacqui had put white gardenias around the coffin, and she organised the wake at her home. Her sister made all the food. Everyone was being so wonderful.

To the world he was one, but to me he was the whole world! I don't have any insightful words which will express what I'm feeling. I know that I will move on. Life does. But right now, I feel a part of me is missing. Breathe, Mandy! Just breathe.

STORM'S STORY

(RAE'S TRIBUTE POEM)

Why do I have eyes if I cannot see?

Why do I have legs if I cannot walk?

I have a throat. and it seems a voice,

But somehow I cannot talk.

My life must seem so strange

To those of you who can use all these,

But I don't need my eyes;

I use my ears and hands to see

And in my dreams I walk so free

And talk with so much ease.

So though I'm not the same as you

I was always very pleased

That you allowed me to get to know you,

And that you taught me how to see

That though we have our differences

We can accept this and just be

Learning from each other.

I do not wonder how it might have been;

I love the way I see the world

And the way the world sees me.

You are you and I am me,

And thank you for accepting me,

'Cause though I may look different

I'm as cheeky as can be,

I'm just the same as any young boy

As I'm sure you've come to see.

So you be you and I'll be me,

And together we'll be free.

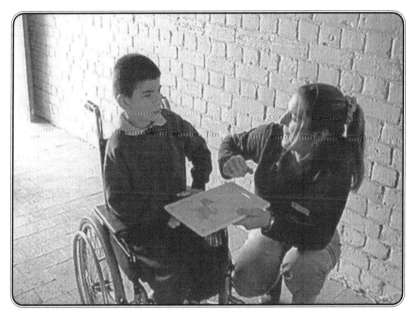

Storm with Aid Carolyn

Storm with painting and his Aides

Storm 2005

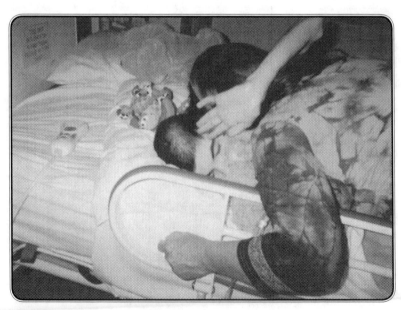

Taken a couple of days before he passed.